EXTRA-SENSORY PERCEPTION

May Frances Turner   June Bailey
            A. J. Linzmayer
T. Coleman Cooper   C. E. Stuart

EXTRA-SENSORY PERCEPTION

by

J. B. Rhine, Ph.D.
Associate Professor of Psychology
Duke University

with a foreword by

William McDougall
D.Sc., M.B., F.R.S.

and an introduction by

Walter Franklin Prince, Ph.D.
Research Officer of the
Boston Society for Psychic Research

Branden Press Inc.
21 Station St Box 843
Brookline Village MA 02147

© Copyright, 1964, by Bruce Humphries
Library of Congress Catalog Card Number 64-21051

Printed in the United States

New Edition, 1973

Second Printing 1983

ISBN 0-8283-1464-0

CONTENTS

39303

ILLUSTRATIONS

LIST OF ABBREVIATIONS

E.S.P. Extra-Sensory Perception. Perception without the function of the recognized senses.

P.T. Pure telepathy; that is, extra-sensory perception of the mental processes of another person. 'Pure' refers to the absence of objective representation of the mental act or image, which might permit of clairvoyance by the percipient.

P.C. Pure clairvoyance; extra-sensory perception of objective facts. 'Pure' refers to the elimination of telepathy from the experimental situation.

B.T. Clairvoyant card calling, with shuffled and cut pack of 25 cards placed face down before the percipient. He calls the top card and the call is recorded and the card removed. After 5 calls, or after the entire 25, the calls are checked against the inverted pile of called cards. B.T.-5 represents the condition of checking after every 5 calls; B.T.-25, after the whole pack.

D.T. Clairvoyant card calling, with the cut pack of cards remaining unopened until after the 25 calls are made. Calling 'down through', without removing the card called until the end of the run of 25.

D or Dev.[1] Deviation from mean chance expectation (np).

np Number of trials multiplied by the probability of succeeding on each trial, which gives the mean chance expectation.

[1] This and the following abbreviations are more fully explained in the Appendix to Chapter II, page 40

p.e.   Probable Error of np. This is the deviation from np at which the odds are even that it was or was not due to mere chance.

X This is the value of the deviation divided by the p.e. When the deviation is 4 times the p.e. ($X=4$) or more, the deviation is regarded as 'significant', *i.e.* reliably showing a principle beyond 'chance' activity.

FOREWORD

By Professor William McDougall

The work reported in this volume is the first fruit of the policy of naturalization of 'psychical research' within the universities. It goes far to justify that policy; to show, first, that a university may provide conditions that will greatly facilitate and promote this most difficult branch of science; secondly, that the university may benefit from such liberal extension of its field of studies. On the former head I will say nothing; it is for the instructed public to judge of the value of this work. On the second head I may properly testify here that, to the best of my judgment, the group of students who have taken part in this work have reaped in a high degree the chief benefits which scientific research has to offer, namely, discipline in careful experiment and observation, and in logical thinking, practice in faithful co-operation, and the gratification of pushing back the bounds of knowledge, in this case in a field of peculiar difficulty and significance. There has been no hysteria, no undue excitement, among this group of students, nor has this work unduly preoccupied their minds to the detriment of other activities.

Though it would be unseemly for me to pronounce upon the value of this work, I may properly say a few words to help the reader to form his estimate of it. On reading any report of observations in the field of psychic research, invariably there rises in my mind the question—What manner of man is this who so reports? And I find that my estimate of the validity and value of the report depends very largely upon the answer to that question. A report may appear to be above serious criticism; and yet a brief acquaintance with its author may suffice to deprive it (for me, at least) of all claim to serious consideration or, on the other hand, may convince me that its statements must (provisionally at least) be accepted at their full face value. I do not stop to explain or to justify this attitude of mine. I believe it is well justified and to be very general among all who are interested in this field. Therefore I may assume that readers of this report who have no personal acquaintance with the author will welcome a few words from me about him and some of his collaborators, while the author, recognizing the purity of my motive, will pardon my intrusion on his privacy.

In introducing Dr Joseph Banks Rhine to the reader, I must premise that almost all I have to say of him is true also of Dr Louisa E. Rhine, his wife. Both have taken their doctorates in biology at the University of Chicago, both had begun promising careers as university teachers of biology, and both have resigned these. When Dr J. B. Rhine burnt his boats, gave up his career in biology and came over to psychology and psychical research, it was with the full consent, endorsement, and parallel action of his wife—a unique and remarkable event in the history of this subject. For the Rhines are no monied amateurs. They are working scientists without worldly resources other than their earnings. When the facts became known to me I was filled with admiration and misgiving. Their action seemed to me magnificently rash. I had always plumed myself on indifference to worldly considerations; but here was a young couple who made me seem small, made me seem to myself a cautious, nay, a timid worldling. Nor was this action prompted by some overwhelming emotional and personal interest, such as the desire to make contact with some lost loved one. The motivation was, so far as I could and still can judge, the desire to work in the field that seemed to contain most promise of discoveries conducive to human welfare. Indeed, in this age when we erect monuments to the boll-weevil, send up prayers for drought, pest and plague, and are chiefly concerned to make one ear of wheat grow where two grew before, it is difficult to retain enthusiasm for botanical research, unless one is a scientist of the peculiarly inhuman type.

The action filled me, I say, not only with admiration but

also with misgiving; for it appeared that I was in some measure unwittingly responsible. The Rhines, in pondering the question—What is most worth doing? To what cause can we give ourselves?—had come upon my *Body and Mind* and upon others of my writings, especially my plea for *Psychical Research as a University Study*;[1] and had determined to join forces with me at Harvard. Accordingly, Dr Rhine arrived on my doorstep in Cambridge, Mass., one morning in June 1926, at the moment when I had completed the bestowal of my family and worldly possessions in two taxicabs, with a view to begin a journey round the world, a journey which, owing to unforeseen alteration of my course, terminated in North Carolina. Nothing daunted, the Rhines spent the year at Harvard studying psychology and philosophy and in making acquaintance with Dr W. F. Prince and the Boston S.P.R. And in the autumn of 1927 they turned up at Duke University, as determined as ever to work in the field of psychic research, and, if possible, within the walls of a university. It was then I began to realize what manner of man I had to deal with. I found J. B. Rhine to be a ruthless seeker after truth, almost, I may say, a fanatical devotee of science, a radical believer in the adequacy of its methods and in their unlimited possibilities. He is one of those whole-hearted scientists for whom philosophy and theology are but preliminary skirmishings beyond the frontiers of scientific knowledge; one of those who will not admit a sphere of valuation in which philosophy must always retain her relative independence and prerogatives and responsibilities, no matter how greatly the province of science may be extended. When he comes into my room and finds me reading a book on metaphysics or religion, he scratches his head and (though he is too polite to utter his misgivings) wonders whether, after all, I, in my latter years, am becoming a renegade.

He has devoted much thought and study to the history of science and to the problem of scientific method. And he

---

[1] A lecture included in the Symposium published by the Clark University Press in 1926, *The Case for and against Psychical Research*, and reprinted in the recently published volume, *Religion and the Science of Life.*

manifests in every relation the scrupulous honesty and regard for truth that befit such a student. Yet, though a fanatic devotee of science, he is very human in the best sense. He has again and again shown that he is ever ready to share his resources of every kind with those who are in need; a multitude of students, both men and women, bring their troubles to him, knowing that they will receive tactful sympathy and sound advice. And this power to inspire and attract the confidence of young people has been of no little value from the point of view of the researches reported in this volume. For it has overcome the initial difficulty of inducing students to participate in and to give time and effort to research of a kind which is looked at askance by the world in general and by the scientific world especially. The manifest sincerity and integrity of Dr Rhine's personality, his striking combination of humane sympathy with the most single-minded devotion to truth, have induced in his collaborators a serene confidence in the worthwhileness of the effort, and have set a tone which, to the best of my judgment, pervades the group and contributes an important, perhaps an indispensable, condition of the striking successes here reported.

I cannot pretend to be intimately acquainted with all of those who have participated in the experiments. But I have some acquaintance with all of them and my impressions are entirely favourable. Four of those who have taken a prominent part have worked for some years in our department as senior and graduate students, and of them I can speak, with entire confidence, as students of the highest class, in respect of general training and ability, of scientific devotion and of personal integrity.

A question that must arise in the mind of many a reader of this report may be formulated as follows:—Granting that Dr Rhine is all that is here claimed for him, is it not possible that his collaborators have deceived or tricked him, perhaps with the benevolent desire to reward with positive results so earnest a seeker? My reply is that, if the experiments involved only some two or three collaborators and that during a brief period only, neither Dr Rhine nor I could perhaps

adduce any completely convincing objection to such interpretation; but in view of the considerable number of partici-
pants, often unknown to each other, and of the prolonged
period of participation (extending in some cases through
several years) it becomes wildly improbable that any such
conspiracy of deception can have been successfully maintained
throughout and under the constant variation of conditions,
without any trace or indication of it coming to light. To which
it may be added that the experimenters have been at special
pains from the beginning to exclude, by the conditions maintained, any possibility of deception, conscious or unconscious.

Finally, I would testify that I have 'sat in' at the experimentation on a number of occasions, and have in some
instances personally conducted the experiments, and have
failed to discover either any indication of lack of good faith
or any serious flaw in the procedures followed.

INTRODUCTION

By Dr Walter Franklin Prince

My acquaintance with the author of this book dates from 1926. I early learned that he was keen to discover the indicia of deception within the field of psychic research, and at the same time, while open-minded, only to be convinced of any of its claims by a slow process of evidence and sound reasoning. My estimate of the qualifications of an ideal psychic researcher is very exacting, and already in that year, before I had any idea that he would find opportunity as a psychologist to devote much attention to psychic research, I earnestly wished that he might be able and inclined to do so.

The momentous study here presented has what may be called, metaphorically, three dimensions. First, there is the unprecedently long period, about three years, during which experiments have been conducted until they reached a vast number. Secondly, we find that the co-operation, observation and critical judgment of many persons both within and without the teaching staff of the psychological department of Duke University have been applied to the experiments at various stages. Thirdly, we note the waxing rigour of the main stream of the experimentation, and the diversity of methods employed not simply to pile up proof to astronomical proportions, but to isolate telepathy and clairvoyance, each from the other, to find out what measures enhanced and what detracted from results, and to acquire data to test this and that hypothesis of the processes involved. Many admirable series of experiments for extra-sensory perception have been made by men of science and other men of university education and high mental endowment, especially since 1880, with some of earlier date. But in none of the particulars stated above can any of them compare with the great task accomplished at Duke University.

To be sure, some of the series of trials reported in this book rest, *prima facie*, upon the good faith of unwitnessed experimenters. The author could well have afforded to omit all of these, for the host of experiments witnessed under rigid conditions are enormously sufficient to bring the odds against chance to tremendous figures. But he wished to tell the whole story. Pearce's 15,000 witnessed trials under diversified conditions alone would have been abundantly ample upon which to rest the case as regards proof. But it is certainly worth while to know if some subjects can get results better when alone and others cannot and how the general progress under the two conditions compares. Besides, our confidence in the reported unwitnessed results in some cases is established by finding that their subjects did as well or better under inspection. And it is hard to discredit those persons whose unwitnessed results declined against natural wish or displayed under analysis, as will be shown, striking analogies, which could not have been foreseen by the subjects, with results received under inspection. But let the reader discard all these which he will, there remains a huge block of evidence against which it would appear that scepticism must batter in vain.

'Unconscious whispering' has had a larger place in psychical research discussion than it ever deserved, but in this report conditions under which, even though near the agent, the percipient could not have heard any such, and separation in different rooms and buildings, have banished this ghost. The discovery that some of the subjects did better at considerable distances is a noteworthy one. Some other writers have reported the reverse, but it may be that their subjects were too abruptly removed to a distance or that some other factor caused them to lose confidence.

This report agrees with most others in the effects of mental comfort, calm and abstraction in promoting success. But here much experimentation was done, expressly to measure the effects of various disturbances. So far as subjects were ill, their scores fell. But why should anyone not *guess* (that is, with all sensory data for judgment excluded) as well when ill as when well? Success declined when the percipient against his own desire was kept at the task until it was highly distasteful. But why should pure guessing be thus put at a disadvantage? At first, when conditions were suddenly changed as by the interception of a screen, scoring would fall, later to rise, and so also when a visitor was brought in while a series was in operation. A certain drug markedly and consistently lowered the ratio of 'hits', another drug tended to restore the ratio. There is no conceivable way by which pure guessing could thus be affected. There appears to be no explanation save that the various disturbances, including the administering of a certain drug, unfavourably affected that mental state most productive of extra-sensory perception, and that another drug mysteriously affected that state favourably.

The results of a single experiment may have great evidential force. Such an experiment has been lately reported by Mr Theodore Besterman, a very careful and conservative researcher.[1] The subject was Ossowiecki, with whom Dr E. J. Dingwall, an experienced investigator whose bent is toward scepticism, several years ago had a result almost equally amazing. Mr Besterman employed precautions the avoidance of which baffles the mind to imagine. The odds against chance in his case cannot be mathematically evaluated, but it is safe to say, after considering all the factors involved, that they could not be less than a million to one.

Nevertheless, probably many a scientific man, in spite of the critical character of the reporter, the precautions described, etc., will think there was some hocus-pocus in this case. But how can he suppose that a group of intelligent men, some of them belonging to a university staff, could, through a period of three years, all the while intent on sure conditions, where such conditions were so easy to devise and apply and where the described precautions were so multiplied and diversified, be all the time fooled by each other? Learned men have been obfuscated by tricks played in dark seances, with various crippling conditions prescribed by the medium. But

[1] *Proc.* S.P.R. Part 132, 1933.

the Duke University work was done in the light with all conditions under command of the experimenters. If the reader will peruse carefully, he will find that any explanatory suggestion which his imagination can furnish regarding a particular series of tests is effectually demolished by the conditions of many another series.

It is indeed extraordinary that so many good subjects were discovered. I am inclined to attribute this to three main factors: (1) the general harmony amid which the work was done from the first, the perhaps unprecedented fact that the President of the University, the entire teaching staff of the psychological department from Dr McDougall down, and other experimenters were open-minded and sympathetic to the unusual experimentation; (2) the tactful methods of approaching and dealing with subjects, maintained by Prof. Rhine and shared by others; (3) the gradual selection and segregation of hopeful subjects, and supreme patience in the continuance of tests with these.

Perhaps, in addition to Rhine's control experiments on the mathematics of probability, a specimen exhibit of what mere guessing can do will be worth while. I started out with the idea of discovering clairvoyant ability in my own office. After a number of non-significant experiments with another person, I set out to test Pure Clairvoyance on myself alone with one set of E.S.P. cards, shuffled after every five trials, and unseen. After one thousand, I had made 209 hits, an excess of only 9 above mean expectation, quite insignificant in so large a number of trials. My second thousand, done in the same way, yielded 201 hits, but 1 in excess of mean expectation. The first 500 of a third thousand was done in the same way, but, since nothing but chance seemed to be in operation, I then employed a device which guaranteed chance only, and the third thousand showed 199 hits, or 1 below mean expectation. The fourth thousand, with guaranteed chance results, resulted in 193 hits, or 7 below. It might now seem as though there had been a very slight clairvoyance in the first two sets, so I went through a fifth thousand, again by the method allowing clairvoyance to enter, through some hundreds working slowly, through others more swiftly, neither method showing an advantage. But my hits for this thousand were fewest of all, being 188, or 12 below. And the total for five thousand trials was 990, a deviation from mean chance expectation (below) of but 10, which for so large a number is quite insignificant of anything but chance.

There were, of course, groups in the course of the experiments where scores shot up, and other groups where they rapidly dropped, but in the course of a thousand, these vagaries, so to speak, nearly ironed out. Taking the hundreds consecutively, twice I made as many 'hits' as 35 in a hundred and once as few as 9. In the first thousand, five sets (that is, of the 5 cards) were guessed with entire accuracy, in the second none were, though both were done by the P.C. method. In each of the third and fourth thousands, I got one 5-card set entirely right, and in the fifth, two sets. Were there gleams of clairvoyance in the first thousand particularly? Possibly, but probably we have only high points of chance, which must be expected. At any rate, we have in five thousand a deviation of 10 from mean expectation, indicative of chance only.

Contrast these results with those of Dr Rhine's selected percipients! Even though there should come criticism of any results obtained by a higher order of mathematics announcing successively the mounting values of X, it would amount in the end merely to the exchange of one astronomical figure for another. The mere statistics in many tables giving the average number of successes per 25 through various long runs of trials, and not less the statistics of effects produced by various species of purposed disturbances and of recovery therefrom, given in the same terms of number of successes per 25, would seem to make the notion of chance entirely out of question.

While the chapters of this treatise are in proper logical sequence, I am tempted to suggest that some lay readers might, before reading the book as a whole, acquire a taste for its contents by first reading certain selected portions. Let them place a bookmark for reference at page xi in order that they may at any point consult the table for the meaning of abbreviations. Also, as one will find frequent evaluations of a series, or of total results to a date, in terms of 'X' (an arbitrary sign equivalent to 'D/p.e.') which signifies the odds against chance, I advise him (unless he is a mathematician) to keep a bookmark at page 41, so that when he finds the statement that X is 13 or 20 or 30 or a higher figure he can turn to that page and seeing that in the progress of X from 1 to only 9, it has already reached an anti-chance valuation of more than 100,000,000 to 1, he can better understand what the statement implies. Mathematicians think it rather silly to demand to know exactly the valuation of X 15, etc., for if one is not satisfied with odds of a hundred million by what would he be satisfied? Then let pages 149–154 be read, and then Chapter VII, describing the nature and analysing the results of Pearce's great number of 15,000 witnessed experiments. By this time, if not before, the reader should have acquired zest to carry him through the whole book, from the first to the last word.

Comments, questions and criticism from any readers, and especially such as are of scientific standing, are welcome, and may be addressed either to the author at Duke University, Durham, North Carolina, or to the Boston Society for Psychic Research.

PREFACE TO THE ENGLISH EDITION

The reception given this volume since it was issued about twelve months ago in Boston, has been most gratifying. Especially so has been the interest shown by many psychologists, most of them younger ones. The encouragement thus given to our efforts and the generous appreciation shown by many of the principal parapsychologists has induced new enthusiasm in our little group of workers here at Duke University.

During the year and a half since the book was written we have not been idle. The number of trials reported here has now been doubled, tripled and probably nearly quadrupled. And we have gone on in more than adding mere numbers. Several new lines of research have been opened up, and these will be presented in the reports to follow. Only one minor investigation has been reported at the time of this writing. I refer to a study of telepathic and clairvoyant capacity in the two-personality states of the British medium, Mrs Garrett. The good positive results obtained in this work are of interest, not only to the question of distribution of Extra-Sensory Perception, but even more to the problem of mediumship. The report appeared in the December issue of the journal, *Character and Personality*.[1]

No part of the huge bulk of data gathered since the first publication has been inconsistent with the earlier work appearing herein. On the contrary, it supports this report at every point where there is close enough similarity of conditions to make comparison possible. From outside the laboratory comes still further support and confirmation. Seven serious and systematic attempts to repeat our experiments elsewhere have been reported to me, and all have yielded significant positive deviations from mean chance expectation.

[1] Allen and Unwin, London.

That is, all are evidential, so far as excluding the chance hypothesis is concerned. Over a dozen others are planned, several of them in psychological laboratories. There may be still others I do not know of.

I have added a short appendix to this edition in which to reply briefly to the few criticisms that have been offered.

In closing, I should like to pay tribute to the great parapsychologist who wrote the Introduction to this book at a time when he was ill, and who died a few months after its publication. I have been proud to claim Dr Walter Franklin Prince as my teacher, and I strongly hope that his splendid critical poise and his ruthless logic will continue to influence the subject he did so much to advance along sound lines in America.

To English readers it is especially appropriate for me to acknowledge again the debt which this work owes to their great countryman, Professor William McDougall. So much of its inspiration, its support and protection, and its guidance has come from him, that it can well be said that in all probability, without him, it would never have been carried out.

PREFACE

There has been considerable deliberation prior to the publication of this work on perception-without-the-senses. It is three years since it was begun, and more than two years since the results began to be so striking as to move some of my interested friends to urge publication. These two years have been spent in making sure 'ten times over', in testing and retesting at every reasonable point of doubt, and in going on beyond the point of proof into the discovery of natural relationships or laws that will make the capacity for this mode of perception more understandable and acceptable to those who must understand somewhat before they can believe. Now that we are fast approaching the mark of 100,000 trials or individual tests—will doubtless be beyond it before this leaves the press— it seems entirely safe to publish these experiments. We need, of course, to have them discussed before a larger forum.

It is to be expected, I suppose, that these experiments will meet with a considerable measure of incredulity and, perhaps, even hostility from those who presume to know, without experiment, that such things as they indicate simply cannot be! But this inevitable reactionary response to all things new and strange, which is as old as the history of science, already shows many signs of decline, as the scientific world adopts a 'scientific attitude', one of open-minded but cautious inquiry, toward the facts. Even so short a period as the last ten years has been one of marked transition. In it we have had many features contributing to popular interest and enlightenment. There have been broadcasting telepathy experiments by radio in England and America; the popular presentation of some remarkable evidence in Upton Sinclair's *Mental Radio*, with introductions by William McDougall (in America) and Albert Einstein (in Germany), (and with a splendid analysis by Walter Franklin Prince in B.S.P.R. Bulletin xvi); popular tests for telepathy conducted by the *Scientific American* Magazine; favourable expressions by Freud, Whitehead and other prominent intellectuals in their lectures; and other features and facts that reach and impress the minds of the people at large. There is to-day much more natural inquiry as a consequence and less of the older blind intolerant credulity—for or against.

The work reported here is motivated largely by what may be termed an interest in its philosophical bearing—by what it can teach us of the place of human personality in nature and what the natural capacities are that determine that place. Ever since reading, ten years ago, of the telepathy experiments carried out by Prof. Lodge when he was a young Professor of Physics at Liverpool I have been bent upon this quest. The somewhat unknown and unrecognized features of mind such as are studied here promise more of such 'philosophical fruit' as that mentioned than any other inquiry I can conceive of. Hence their deep fascination for me. By a cautious study of the unusual we come most readily into an understanding of the more usual and common.

But it is a 'philosophy for use' that these studies are meant to serve. The need felt for more definite knowledge of our place in nature is no mere academic one. Rather it seems to me the great fundamental question lying so tragically unrecognized behind our declining religious system, our floundering ethical orders and our unguided social philosophies. This work is, then, a step, a modest advance, in the exploration of the unrecognized boundaries and reaches of the human personality, with a deep consciousness of what such steps might lead to in the way of a larger factual scheme for a better living philosophy.

It is the more general purpose behind this work to push on with caution and proper systematization into all the other seriously alleged but strange phenomena of the human mind. By proceeding always from already organized territory out into the phenomena on trial, never lowering the standards of caution in the face of the desire to discover or the need to generalize, the field of these unrecognized mental occurrences

can and will ultimately be organized and internally systematized to a degree that will simply compel recognition. How
long this may require one cannot estimate; but it is the only
truly scientific course to take.

I began using the term 'Extra-Sensory Perception'(E.S.P.)
at first with the more tentative meaning, 'perception without
the function of the recognized senses'. But as our studies
progressed it gradually became more and more evident that
E.S.P. was fundamentally different from the sensory processes,
lacking a sense organ, apparently independent of recognized
energy forms, non-radiative but projectory, cognitive but
unanalysable into sensory components—all quite non-
sensory characteristics. It seemed to extend the word 'sensory' ridiculously to use it to cover this phenomenon. Hence
the present interpretation is rather that E.S.P. is, frankly,
'perception in a mode that is just *not* sensory', omitting all
question of 'unrecognized'. I think we have progressed this
far with reasonable certainty.

'Extra-Sensory Perception' is preferable, I think, to
'Supernormal Perception' because of the ambiguity of the
term 'Supernormal' in psychology and because 'super' is
taken by many, in spite of careful definition to the contrary,
to imply an hypothesis of the explanation. In fact, 'extra'
(as 'without') includes 'super' (as 'above') and we do not
yet know if 'above' is what we want to state about the process; *i.e.*, 'above' may be the wrong 'direction' or rating.
'Metagnomy' is defined in much the same way as the use
here of Extra-Sensory Perception; but I prefer the more
obvious and simpler term, even though it is longer. E.S.P.
keeps the natural association with sensory perception more
before the mind as one reads; *i.e.*, it normalizes it as a psychological process more than does the strange and less obviously
associative term 'metagnomy'. There the need is to keep in
mind that E.S.P. is a natural mode of perception and an integral part of mental life, as this work helps to demonstrate.
'Cryptaesthesia', the name given by the eminent physiologist,
Richet, means a hidden sense, and for this there is no evi-

dence; it calls, moreover, for a vibratory theory of transmission which its author proposes. This, too, has all the facts against it. Let us merely say, if we wish to be noncommittal, as is safest, of course: 'perception by means that are outside of the recognized senses', and indicate this meaning by 'Extra-Sensory Perception' or E.S.P. We may then think of it, as I do, as a non-sensory type of phenomenon.

In the use of the words 'Telepathy' and 'Clairvoyance' I take their accepted usage of 'perception of the thought or feeling of another (telepathy) or of an objective fact or relation (clairvoyance) without the aid of the known sensory processes'.

The convenience of the reader will, it is hoped, be served by the arrangement of the chapters. Part I is introductory, general, historical and technical. Part II is a report of the evidence and the conditions followed, with little else added. If the reader is antagonistic to the field, he might better begin with Part II. Chapter III of this Part gives a narrative account of the experiments pretty much in the order in which they occurred and gives enough of the results to permit a sort of survey of the work. This may be as far as some readers will care to go into the data. But the careful scientific reader will find in the chapters of Part II that follow the full statement of the results and conditions, arranged around the individual subjects themselves. In Part III these results are generally discussed and, to a great extent, reassembled around the major points of importance, and their larger bearing is considered. This discussion is naturally the more debatable section of the report and the reader may judge for himself as to the acceptability of the suggestions and conclusions, since the supporting facts are given or else are referred to by table number and chapter.

Finally, I wish to give the strongest utterance to an expression of gratitude that these experiments have been permitted in a Psychological Laboratory of an American University. I am doubtful if there is any other Psychological Department on this side of the Atlantic or even, perhaps, in the world, where they would even have been permitted, much less encouraged and supported, as these have been. For this I have to thank Prof. William McDougall, Head of the Department, whom I might characterize as the 'presiding genius' in the work. But his own attitude of encouragement and interest has been shared by others of my colleagues in the Department, notably by Dr Helge Lundholm and by Dr Karl Zener, who have themselves, like him, given me valuable aid and counsel. Dr D. K. Adams, the remaining Departmental colleague, has kindly co-operated as a subject and given some promise of himself demonstrating E.S.P. ability.

It has, I think, been a unique and noteworthy feature that, from the sympathetic and enlightened interest of the President of Duke University, Dr W. P. Few, and of Mrs Few, down to the hundreds of students who kindly served as subjects, a very gratifying spirit of co-operation and open-mindedness has marked the trail of these three years of research, this spirit centring chiefly in the contributions and attitudes of the colleagues already mentioned, in the valuable work of certain of the graduate assistants of this Department, namely, Miss Sara Ownbey,[1] Mr C. E. Stuart and Mr J. G. Pratt, who have been my principal assistants, and of the major subjects who have spent hundreds of laborious hours in monotonous experimentation. At every point we have met only with friendly encouragement and willingness to give assistance. Thus the scope of the work was greatly broadened. It is with pleasure and gratitude that I acknowledge this help, the extent of which will be very apparent through the chapters to come.

The financial assistance given me from the Department Budget and the University Research Fund is also gratefully acknowledged.

To Dr Walter Franklin Prince, whom I am proud to recognize as my principal teacher in Psychic Research, I am grateful for help and criticism, especially from the standpoint

[1] Miss Ownbey has been married since the above writing, and is now Mrs George Zirkle.

of publication, and for his generous acceptance of this work for the Boston Society Series. My wife, Dr Louisa E. Rhine, has given me great assistance and encouragement throughout, but especially in the writing of this report. I cannot over-appreciate her share in whatever of merit it may have.

ABOUT THIS BOOK

From the Author in 1964

This is the book that started all the hullabaloo that, for more than twenty-five years, has been going on around the world over the subject of ESP, or extrasensory perception, and related topics. Its publication in 1934 started the movement that has brought parapsychology into the university laboratories in various countries and is leading to its acceptance as a proper branch of science, slow and irregular though this later development is in some countries especially.

Moreover, this is the only book that gives a blow-by-blow account of the early explanatory efforts of the group of workers at Duke University, who gave the subject its first permanent foothold in the academic world. I have written other more general reviews covering the program in the large, such as that in my book, *The Reach of the Mind,* but those first three strenuous, exciting, venturesome years of the Duke work have had no other accounting. We at the Laboratory have been too busy to go back. I had not even read this book in the last twenty-five years, and the world itself, that is, that part of it that pays attention to the new science of parapsychology, has been focusing attention on current developments. This is all as it should have been.

Why, then, turn back now? And whom should we expect to be interested? Is the book, indeed, mere history? I can at least give my own judgment.

I should place the main value of the book in the fact that it reports a unique situation that needs to be re-examined by the student and worker in parapsychology today, young or old. It seems clear, to me at least, and all the more so from a re-reading, that we had in those early years at Duke a very special situation and it was largely responsible for the unusual and unequalled production of results in ESP experiments. Where has there ever been such teamwork, a comparable spirit, a similar atmosphere?

Here was a young pair of scientists, man and wife, who had, with some determination, pulled up stakes in another university and another field, and had come to Duke University to set up under the distinguished founder of the Psychology Department, Professor William McDougall, a research center for work in the field known as psychical research. Here was a favorable university administration, and even some modest research funds, with working space, with the cooperative interest of the departmental staff, with the active cooperation of five and, later, twice as many graduate students in psychology, and the eager, enthusiastic assistance of large numbers of undergraduates, a tolerant university community that allowed, even in that day, the added attraction of the liberal use of hypnosis, the admission of interesting personalities, such as mediums, to the Department of Psychology; and, over it all, the protective sponsorship of departmental and administrative approval and personal interest. It was just about ideal. The enthusiasm was of course directed along scientific lines, the invention of new methods, the design of new test programs, but there was balance, too, judicious restraint, avoidance of sensationalism and publicity. The program was accepted, welcomed. It gave research training, intellectual excitement, and scientific adventure to hundreds of students. It was all in great good spirit and those who took part still look back upon those early days and retain a common bond.

It is true that probably no one who was not "there" will easily catch this spirit from reading between the lines in the book that follows; but I think it will not be hard for anyone to see that there must have been such an integrative influence, as I have suggested, to have kept these numerous young workers going through thousands of card-calling tests which, in some situations, can become boring in a few minutes. But for all of us concerned, this was a big thing we were doing, and every fresh score was a reminder of the magnitude of what we were discovering. We knew we had something by the tail that was too big for all of us, but we were having riotous fun pulling and holding on, twisting and prying, to get a better hold, a further advantage, a more complete capture.

The sober, reflective parapsychology worker of today well knows how important this kind of motivation can be; first, on the part of the one who administers the tests, because he needs to arouse it in the persons he tests if he hopes to motivate them to the effort and patience and persistence needed to bring out the elusive ESP ability.

In the early 1930's we hardly knew how fortunate we were in the atmosphere we had helped to create. There are glimmers of this realization to be found in the book, but the appreciation of it was easily lost when, following the publication of the book, other investigators undertook to do some sort of repetition. Arguments began, controversy followed, and aspects of the research came into prominence that over-shadowed the importance of the psychological atmosphere of testing. Attention concentrated on disputes over experimental precautions, interpretation of results, and the like; and, in the years of tension and contention, the wonderful good fun of the early Duke days was lost and forgotten. It never came back to the Duke Laboratory, where the ramparts had to be "manned for defense" for so many later years. Only in recent times have the older workers begun to call attention to the importance of the psychological atmosphere of testing, the prime importance of strong motivation in the subject, and to recall what has been lost over the years of shifting emphasis.

But can we take these early tests of the 1930's seriously? If there has been this long period of debate over the adequacy of test procedures, may not these early experiments have been so loosely conducted from today's point of view as to be relatively worthless? No, and I say it with emphasis! There have, of course, been many advances made since. In fact, it was through these early explorations that the advances were made possible. They were necessary steps, and the step-by-step advances can be seen. It is true, as I think every reader will see when all the details are given, those advances were made slowly. As one looks back, he wonders continually, "Why did we not see such and such a weakness?" Perhaps others in the same situation would have seen it. No one will ever know.

But here is just where the value of this early report comes in. It tells me, for one, what I want to know today—how in spite of the monotony of the procedure, how well the long we were able to keep those early subjects scoring well subjects responded to the new conditions introduced, and what sort of program we had that kept so many so productive for so long. What would we not give today for the like of that? I think any worker in the field today would say the same.

The point is, then, we do not read this book to see how good the evidence for ESP may be today. We want to know what made it so good then—so good in terms of performance level, so good at this crucial beginning. At the same time, I do not apologize for its quality. This is a story of progress, of advancement toward better control, and the evidence, especially that from the clairvoyance tests conducted with new cards, screened cards, with different rooms and even different buildings (as it ends up with the experiments with Pearce) would stand up very well even today for any reasonable mind. The main point is that, in any experiment, the evidence strictly needs to be only good enough to lead to the next advance; then, as each experimenter introduces an improvement or a modification, the advancement goes steadily on. So that any reader who is making up his mind about the case for ESP today, might better continue on through the progressive advances following the period of this book. But by the time this book was sent off to the printer (at the end of 1933) no one acquainted with the experiments could see any reasonable alternative to the ESP hypothesis. All were confident that there was a case deserving publication and further research. That is enough for one step to have provided. That started the ball rolling in ESP research.

But this book did another thing: It gave the field a framework of organization, showed how psychical research could be conveniently renamed and defined, suggested a system for its various problem areas and indicated where ESP belonged in it all. I do not see how I could do very much better today although if I were rewriting the first chapter I would trim it somewhat. For one thing our problems today are not primarily in terminology, due perhaps partly to this bit of organization introduced at that time.

It is also worth while to compare this summary of experimental parapsychology made in the early thirties with the picture of the field today. Since I laid myself out rather broadly in the commentary chapters at the end of this book, there are a great many points for comparison. In a general way, the succeeding decades have rather confirmed the leading points of that commentary.

What are some of these confirmations? The position taken that ESP was just not the sensory type of perception is one of these. Similarly, the nonphysical hypothesis of ESP has been considerably strengthened, and by the introduction of wholly new types of evidence as well. The unconscious level of operation has been more and more confirmed. The impression of the importance of motivation on the part of the subject is likewise strengthened. The lack of any association of ESP with ill health, mental or physical, has been firmed up strongly over the years. Also, the basic unity of ESP in its different phenomenal effects, telepathy and clairvoyance, has been further supported. It has been even extended, so that now it is in order to think of *one* basic parapsychical interaction between subject and object represented in ESP and PK (psychokinesis). We think of parapsychical phenomena as manifestations of this underlying reversible interaction between the person and his environment—extrasensory on the one hand and extramotor (PK) on the other.

Some of the tentative suggestions I made in 1934 have been strengthened. One of these emphasised the *primary* role or initiative of the percipient or receiver in telepathy tests. I stressed this "going-out" or active participation by the receiver as more likely than the view of a passive part in the transfer. Similarly, my hints regarding the energetic character of ESP have become bolder over the years, to the point where I would now say it makes little sense to talk about parapsychical operations without the assumption of a distinctive energy.

Where was I wrong in 1934? Had I known then what I now know about the evidence of ESP in animals, I would not have made the suggestion I did, even though tentatively, on the evolutionary position of ESP. It is now much more likely that ESP is something the animal kingdom possessed long before man himself evolved; but we must leave to future research a firmer answer to this important question area.

I thought too, perhaps naturally enough, that when a subject persisted in avoiding the target in ESP tests and giving significantly negative deviations from the expected average instead of the postive ones he was supposed to give, this meant he was unconsciously negative in his attitude. But, in the light of later studies, I have now abandoned this hypothesis of negative motivation for "psi missing," as it is now called. I am not, of course, saying that there is never negative motivation but that it is not the more general explanation of these significantly negative deviations.

LATER DEVELOPMENTS

What has happened since the publication of this book in the science of parapsychology? I will outline the main advances briefly under the heading of New Methods, New Phenomena, and New Events.

New Methods: First, I will speak of mathematics. Although the binomial method used throughout this book is still the principal method of appraising results, there are slight changes. Instead of using the probable error, we now use the standard deviation as the "yardstick." Also, when we combine critical ratios, by the use of the root-mean-square method we use the chi square tables. But there are a number of other convenient and useful methods of evaluation of test results now available to the parapsychological worker. The most useful of these are assembled in Chapter 9 of the introductory test book by Dr. Pratt and myself, called *Parapsychology, Frontier Science of the Mind.* Parapsychologists in this country have had no serious trouble over mathematics because of the extraordinarily generous cooperation of mathematicians; to give only one example, *The Journal of Parapsychology* has had throughout most of its existence two highly qualified mathematicians as statistical editors.

New test methods have naturally had to follow upon new problems. In the main, however, the methods have been built on or around the skeleton of test structure used throughout this book. The use of five targets, whether or not the standard ESP symbols, the run of twenty-five trials, and certain elemental test precautions in testing and recording have become fundamental. Again, these methods are summarized in Chapter 8 of the textbook just mentioned. Specific techniques had of course to be developed for the investigation of precognition, psychokinesis, and other distinct effects to be measured. There were also new telepathy tests to meet difficulties raised when precognition was introduced into the picture. For some of these more complicated methods the original articles in *The Journal of Parapsychology* should be consulted.

One main advance has been the introduction of test design to make it impossible for one of two experimenters to make a mistake without its being caught by the other. The two-experimenter test procedure is, of course, only used when the more conclusive or crucial type of experiment is conducted. A large range of research needs to be carried out under relatively free exploratory test conditions, much as most of the research reported in this book was done. For a discussion of the two levels of methodology, see Chapter 2 of the book, *Parapsychology, Frontier Science of the Mind*, mentioned above.

Heavy emphasis in present-day research in this field is on the provision of appropriate psychological conditions, aimed at favoring good ESP test performance by the subject. (Pratt and I have a chapter—no. 7—on this in our book.) Free exploratory conditions permit a wider range of possibilities for this important condition. Better controlled conditions can then be introduced when the stage is reached at which it is worth while and important to increase the precautions against counter explanations.

Another of the latest turns in research methods is the new look at spontaneous parapsychical occurrences. This is not for their value as evidence of psi but for the research clues they furnish. Some idea of this case approach can be had from Dr. Louisa E. Rhine's book, *Hidden Channels of the Mind*, and from her article in *The Journal of Parapsychology*.

New Phenomena: ESP of future events was next. In fact, at the time this book appeared in 1934, the Duke Laboratory had already begun its precognition tests, the first on record, and these had yielded positive results. It is true, many years of work were needed before the findings seemed sufficiently well-confirmed to warrant publication. They were not even mentioned in my first popular book on the ESP work, *New Frontiers of the Mind*, which came out in 1937. However, by 1947, in *The Reach of the Mind*, I did review this development and by that time felt justified in taking a fairly confident stand on this phenomenon.

Then followed PK. The evidence of psychokinesis or the direct action of mind over matter had just begun to accumulate in the Laboratory when the book was released in the spring of 1934, but it was not until nine years later

(1934) that the first article reporting the findings appeared in *The Journal of Parapsychology*. This work, too, based on the ability of the subject to influence dice without physical contact is reviewed in *The Reach of the Mind*.

New facts and findings of other types piled up through the mid and late thirties. ESP tests with children, both seeing and blind, both in the schoolroom and at home, came into some prominence. Personality types became the subject of study in the search for a "psychic type," and for fifteen years this search for personality correlates occupied major attention among a number of leading works. *ESP and Personality Patterns* by Schmeidler and McConnell reviews one large block of this evidence, and it is summarized in *The Reach of the Mind*. The original articles on personality and ESP mostly appear in *The Journal of Parapsychology*. But no personality type associated with ESP ability was found, though some states and traits do seem to affect adjustment to the test and determine whether a subject will go above chance average or below it. None of the personality abnormalities are related.

Much has been learned about the odd effects of the unconscious nature of ESP. In fact, some of the most revealing discoveries have sprung from this feature, which had little more than come to our attention when the first book was written. Now our knowledge of this lack of conscious control explains a lot of otherwise puzzling effects of psi (*i.e.* parapsychical) ability. Among these are unconscious missing (psi missing), displacement (hitting adjacent targets) and the various decline effects.

The work on ESP in animals, both through the collection of spontaneous or natural cases and experimental work, is new—too new, even, to have been covered in *The Reach of the Mind*. But it is reviewed in *New World of the Mind*, and the reports appear in *The Journal of Parapsychology*.

New Events: Most important to the scholar are new scientific publications. These will be listed at the end of this review. The new research centers too are of importance.

A number have opened up during the last twenty-five years, some of them associated with colleges and universities, a list of which follows.

Institute for Mental Hygiene and Borderline Studies, Freiburg, Germany.

Institute for Parapsychology, University of Utrecht, Holland.

Laboratory for Psychological Physics, University of Pittsburgh.

Parapsychology Laboratory, Wayland College, Plainview, Texas.

Parapsychology Laboratory, St. Joseph's College, Philadelphia.

Parapsychology Laboratory, University of King's College, Halifax.

Other research centers are being (favorably) considered, and two more in the U. S. A. are due to be announced before the year is out. At least a dozen doctoral degrees have been granted for theses in parapsychology by universities, mainly in Western Europe and the U. S. A. Several courses on the subject have been offered in colleges and universities in the U. S. A., Holland, Switzerland, and Argentina, with actual titles of Professor of Parapsychology being used at Utrecht for Dr. W. H. C. Tenhaeff and at the Universidad del Litoral by Dr. J. Riccardo Musso.

Scholarship funds for students wishing to prepare for research in parapsychology are being offered. A Parapsychology Scholarship Fund was established at Duke University for the aid of students, regardless of the place of study, and City College of New York has received funds for two graduate scholarships in parapsychology, to be handled by the Department of Psychology. Grants of research funds have been more generous in recent years than formerly. A number of the leading foundations have, at one time or another, aided research in parapsychology; for example, Rockefeller Foundation has aided the Duke Laboratory; the Mellon Charitable Trust supports work at the University of Pittsburgh; the Ittleson Family Foundation has made a grant to the Menninger Foundation for partial use in research in parapsychology, and the Human Ecology Fund of New York has made a grant for work in parapsychology at Oxford University. Other foundations too have made contributions to individuals or laboratories. And even government aid through contracts has entered to some extent into the support of parapsychological research.

The establishment of the William McDougall Award for Distinguished Work in Parapsychology (accompanied by a research grant) was set up by the Duke Laboratory to recognize work done outside of Duke. It is now in its sixth year.

The Parapsychological Association was established in 1957 as an organization of professional workers in the field, with a membership of more than 130 associates and full members, drawn from many different countries of the world. It is preparing to hold its fifth annual convention this year.

Perhaps the most important event in any field is the establishment and maintenance of an adequate outlet of scientific publications. *The Journal of Parapsychology,* established in 1937, with Professor McDougall as one of the founding editors, has completed its twenty-fifth year and now is affiliated with the Parapsychological Association. It is published by the Duke University Press.

New Problems: Progress itself brings new problems. As soon as money problems are reduced, shortage of adequate personnel to do the research comes into first place. Then, as more fully trained and sophisticated workers become the rule, the researches become more intricate and difficult, and progress may appear to be slowing down. Some of the sense of adventure and excitement evaporate. Fortunately, however, there are always new influences, new breakthroughs, fresh challenges to pull researchers out of these doldrums, off of these plateaus, and into new advances.

For a while we sought eagerly for the outer bounds, the far frontiers of our field. That was in the thirties. Then, from the late thirties on into the mid-forties, we were searching for the tie-up with personality features and types. The late forties found us heavily preoccupied with distinguishing one type of parapsychical phenomenon from another—precognition from psychokinesis and vice-versa, proving telepathy could be demonstrated without the possibility of clairvoyance producing the results even with precognition added, and so on. In the fifties we took up the search for a biological linkage in the form of the demonstration of ESP elsewhere in the animal kingdom—not without success. Then, too, emerged the long-view aim of trying to bring psi under control; this in itself embodied a number of approaches; the most outstanding was that of ESP tests in the schoolroom, which rather dominate the decade of the fifties.

The opening of the sixties finds stress on physiological measurements accompanying test performance. New efforts are going also into training ESP subjects through hypnotic methods, searching for advantageous effects through drug usage, and all the while there is the slow, too slow, recognition of the importance of psychological conditions, already mentioned. (*Parapsychology,* Chapter 7). But the future will place more emphasis on a search for just such conditions as we spontaneously developed in producing the results summed up in this book. The stress simply has to be on gaining improved control over the abilities.

So I say again, if the ESP research field is important, then this book is important; for it shows something that I, at least, have not seen anywhere else. Can the secret of it be learned and in some degree applied? Why not? Most likely it can be improved upon and extended to other situations.

SUGGESTIONS

Finally, a few practical suggestions to the reader of this book: I suggest putting two bookmarks in the book for permanent use—one with a List of Abbreviations and another at the Appendix to Chapter 2, which explains the mathematics used. If anyone reads straight through the book, he will see these items by the time he needs them. Most readers, however, will probably get ahead of these sections without having noticed them; so the markers will help.

I have another warning. As I look at it today, there is in this book too much emphasis given to the critical ratios (X-values) and the astronomical odds against the occurrence of certain results by pure chance. Of course, we are more relaxed today. We have lived with this thing so much longer that now we are not so overcome by these unusual results. Also, we do not so freely combine the results of one experiment with those of another. We do not need to.

I have left this book the way it was because it is part of the picture of the time. It belongs with the exciting climbers scaling one peak after another; if there seems to have been a lot of loud shouting back and forth over the phenomenal effects, that is the way it was. Life around this Laboratory was like that. Every bit of it. What would I not give if we could have kept it like that; or renewed it. But, of course, human beings simply cannot go on living on the peaks they scale. And the reception awaiting us from a naturally skeptical world helped us quickly enough to pull ourselves off the heights of enthusiasm.

All the same it is never to late to comment on it, criticize it, or inquire further about it. Dr. Prince, at the end of his introduction, directed readers to address their questions or comments to me or this Laboratory. I renew that invitation in our mutual interest. Today as part of our educational program we even have plans for the aiding of students (of whatever age) who want to turn their attention, in whatever degree, toward learning more about this still fascinating, still challenging, still enormously promising though far from easy field of inquiry.

J. B. RHINE, *Director*
Parapsychology Laboratory
Duke University

Box 6847, College Station
Durham, North Carolina

The More General Introductions

1961   Murphy, Gardner: *Challenge of Psychical Research.* New York: Harper. Selected researches are reviewed to introduce: Telepathy, clairvoyance, precognition, psychokinesis and the question of post-mortem survival.

1957   Rhine, J. B. and Pratt, J. G.: *Parapsychology, Frontier Science of the Mind.* A textbook, reference work, giving an introduction to the field, methods for testing, tables for evaluation, reading lists, and other research aids.

1947   Rhine, J. B.: *The Reach of the Mind.* New York: Wm. Sloane, 1947.

(1961)   (Also, New York: Apollo Editions, 1961. Paperback edition.) A step-by-step review of the first 15 years of experiments on ESP and PK, beginning with the Duke research and covering main advances.

1937   *Journal of Parapsychology.* Twenty-five volumes. Published quarterly by The Duke University Press, Durham, N. C. A technical periodical, but articles are preceded by abstracts in non-technical language. There is a glossary of special terms.

Special Topics

1961   Rhine, Louisa E.: *Hidden Channels of the Mind.* New York: Wm. Sloane. The author reports on the studies she has made on the large collection of spontaneous psi (psychic) experiences, using selected examples to illustrate.

1960   Soal, S. G. and Bowden, H. T.: *The Mind Readers.* Garden City, N.Y.: Doubleday & Co. ESP tests on two Welsh youths, carried out under a variety of conditions. Rewards of money were used, high scoring obtained.

1959   Schmeidler, G. R. and McConnell, R. A.: *ESP and Personality Patterns.* New Haven: Yale University Press. Deals first with general case for ESP, then with Schmeidler's ESP results correlated with subject's attitude toward ESP and certain other mental states.

1954   Soal, S. G. and Bateman, F.: *Modern Experiments in Telepathy.* New Haven: Yale University Press. Along with a review of other work on ESP, the authors report mainly on their own extensive ESP research done in England.

Some Publications on Parapsychology Since 1934

1938   Tyrrell, G. N. M.: *Science and Psychical Phenomena* (1938) and *Apparitions* (1953) (One volume, two books.) New York: University Books. 1961. The first is one of the clearer introductions to the earlier ESP researches (and mediumistic studies). The second is indicated by its title.

Criticism

1956   Ciba Foundation Symposium: *Extrasensory Perception*. Boston: Little, Brown. A critical discussion of ESP work held in London in 1955 by a medical foundation.

1940   Rhine, J. B., Pratt, J. G., Stuart, C. E., Smith, B. M., and Greenwood, J. A.: *Extrasensory Perception After Sixty Years*. New York: Henry Holt. (Reprint?) This sums up the experimental work on ESP up to 1940. It contains invited criticism and replies, as well as reviews of methods, tables for use in evaluation, and a bibliography on ESP to 1940.

Other Books — Since 1934

1961   Gudas, Fabian: *Extrasensory Perception;* New York. Charles Scribner's Sons. Written to aid college freshmen in writing papers on ESP. Contains a wide variety of types of articles, some critical, some philosophical, and some to aid in writing a paper.

1961   Heywood, Rosalind: *Beyond the Reach of Sense*. New York: Dutton. A non-technical review mainly of the English SPR's research history, with large coverage of the studies of mediumship.

1960   Murphy, Gardner and Ballou, Robert O.: *William James on Psychical Research*. New York: Viking Press. The writings of James on the subject with biographical and interpretative chapters by Murphy.

1957   Eysench, H. J.: *Sense and Nonsense in Psychology:* Baltimore, Md.: Penguin. One long chapter evaluates the case for ESP from the viewpoint of a neutral psychologist.

1954   West, D. J.: *Psychical Research Today*. London: Duckworth. An English psychiatrist who has worked in parapsychology reviews the field critically — giving much attention to mediumship.

1953   Flew, Anthony: *A New Approach to Psychical Research*. London: Watts and Co. One philosopher's critical review of the field.

Some Publications on Parapsychology Since 1934

1947   Tyrrell, G. N. M.: *Personality of Man:* Baltimore, Md.: Penguin. A review for the general reader of studies mainly in British psychical research.

1946   Carington, W.: *Thought Transference.* New York: Creative Age Press. An English (psychologist) research worker's review mainly of his own investigation of ESP.

Other Periodicals in English, devoted mainly to Parapsychology.

Journal of the Society for Psychical Research, 1, Adam & Eve, Mews, Kensington, London, W.8.

Proceedings of the Society for Psychical Research, 1, Adam & Eve, Mews, Kensington, London, W.8.

Journal of the American Society for Psychical Research, 880 Fifth Avenue, New York 21, N.Y.

Parapsychological Monographs, 29 West 57th St., New York 19, N. Y.

PART I

General Introduction

CHAPTER I

Clarification of the Problem

It is logically the first duty in making this report to bring into clear outline at once the particular field of study in which the work reported here has been performed, and to clarify at the start the special problem from this field which we are attempting to help to solve. It may well be that some readers will not agree with the outline drawn or with the statement of the problem given; at any rate, it is hoped they will understand the objective and orientation of the work after following the clarification, and be better able to evaluate it.

But, in outlining the field in which we are finding our problem, we are regarding it very tentatively. Since many claims in that field do not at present warrant great confidence, we are giving a minimum of credence at every point and are proceeding with extreme caution. The outline itself will be of use only as a reminder of what we may need to be kept aware of. It is a background of suggested possibility— so far as this work is concerned—just impressive enough at most points to justify inquiry; and conviction, which is quite a separate question, will depend upon the slow accumulations of inquiry.

We are concerned, of course, with the field of Psychical Research ('Parapsychologie' in Germany and 'Métapsychique' among the French). The general boundary-line that marks it off from other fields of problems for scientific study is that its phenomena seem, superficially at least, to escape in a significant way certain laws of the natural world as we know it through our sciences—laws that we have all come to regard with relative certainty as holding for the assumed conditions. Because we tend to think of our views of nature as complete, we think of any such apparent exception as almost a direct conflict. It becomes a conflict, then, in our system of beliefs. However, this does not mean necessarily a conflict in nature—a fact that is always hard to remember.

The phenomena of this field are not only radical in their aspect of escaping some acceptedly basic law of our science of nature, but this evasion or circumvention is always a purposive and intelligent activity, as of the nature of personality in function; *i.e.* the 'psychic phenomenon' is characterized by the suggestion of personal agency in some form. The field of Psychical Research may not be limited otherwise, I think; and it is, therefore, none too definitely bounded , like most other fields or problem-areas of Science. This personal and purposive characteristic of 'psychic phenomena' would, on the basis of any definition extant— even a Behaviourist's—bring it clearly within the field of Psychology.

Like any other branch of Psychology, Psychical Research naturally involves other fields of problems and laws— other Sciences, as they are artificially divided for the academics. If it is a common physical law that seems to be evaded, an accepted physiological principle that seems to be outdone or a well-known pathological law that seems not to hold—these Sciences are challenged and eventually must reply. And in their reply they will need to co-operate with Psychical Research in the interrelating of the fields for the solution of the common problem.

At this point it is urgently necessary to insert the statement again, that the concepts we are dealing with are not necessarily accepted ones. This outlining involves no expression of conviction of reality behind any claims for the branches outlined. The recognition accorded is merely that occurrences reported seriously by intelligent people offer problems for study. In outlining the field of these problems, we are as careful to protect against unguarded conviction as a good pathologist is careful with his deadly test-tubes. For a slip in the one case could scarcely be less terrible to contemplate than in the other.

4

One naturally outlines the field of Psychical Research on the basis of the neighbouring fields which are most involved; that is, on the basis the nature of the laws seemingly most clearly evaded in the phenomena. We find wide overlapping of these fields very often (since the universe failed to develop along college curriculum outlines) and there is consequent difficulty in any ideally clear-cut division. But at the present state of research only very broad lines are needed.

It has been customary to lump together the phenomena of the field under the headings of 'Physical' and 'Mental', with perhaps 'Psychic Healing' in addition. Under the 'physical phenomena', however, are included not only the seemingly more clear-cut exceptions of accepted physical law, such as 'levitations', 'psychic lights', etc., but also what are only secondarily exceptions to physical law (as this is academically distinguished), and are primarily physiological law, as for example, 'elongations', 'extrusions', 'stigmatization' and the like. As the subject becomes more refined by advance in knowledge there will be pressing need to clarify these problem fields. The branch generally known as 'Psychic Healing' would belong to the pathological subdivision because of its seeming escape from the laws of that science.

Under the 'mental' sub-heading of psychic phenomena are some that quite overlap with the 'physical', as in the case of 'thought-transference' at great distances with seeming evasion of the radiation laws covering the decline of intensity with distance. But there are the somewhat purer cases of the 'mental' type, as in perception of objects without sensory stimulation, *i.e.* clairvoyance. But even this has its physical side too, in the fact that apparently all the known ways of making contact with the object, all the sensorially intercepted energies, are excluded. Our tacit law that these are essential to perception is evaded. We may go on to other and still more purely 'mental' phenomena. The phenomena effected through sensitives and purported to have been caused by extra-somatic agencies, in

5

most of which evidence of the survival of personality after death is claimed, would, in the feature of survival, seem to be exceptions to the laws of psycho-physiology covering the role of the nervous system in mental life.

To designate these branches by acceptable names we shall have to wait for more agreement on the outline and this must await agreement as to observation of the facts. Tentatively, however, it seems reasonable to accept some terminology less confused and ambiguous than we are now accustomed to. The German usage of 'parapsychology' for the general field seems a little more generally appropriate than the others, if we do not use the prefix as implying that psychical research is outside the field of psychology—but simply that it is 'beside' psychology in the older and narrower conception. But the German usage of 'paraphysical' for the 'physical' and 'paraphysiological' for the 'physiological' phenomena of Psychical Research are, I think, not at all consistent with this use of 'parapsychology'. They have no reference to the essentially 'psychical' characteristic of all such phenomena. (We could as well call the psychophysical phenomena of psychology 'physical' instead of 'psychophysical'.) Rather, I think, should we use a term that clearly implies the fact of their being first of all parapsychological phenomena and indicate by adding to this term whatever other branch is involved. With this in view I propose to use the expressions 'parapsycho-physical', 'parapsycho-physiological', 'parapsycho-pathological' for these branches and to add on the same principle any others that are necessary. The 'parapsycho-' indicates the general connection with the field of parapsychology and the rest specifies the other field jointly concerned. The 'psycho' portion of every term used recalls constantly the connection with psychology, the fact that a phenomenon of personality is being dealt with. For the more purely and simply 'mental' phenomena of the field, the adjective 'parapsychical' is sufficiently distinguishing; quite as much so, indeed, as it is to say 'psychical' for the less 'physical' (*i.e.* less 'psycho-physical') of the phenomena of present academic psychology. The viewpoint is that all the phenomena of

6

the field are 'psychical' in some degree. When there is another scientific field very obviously involved by the apparent evasion of a law of its domain, there is ground then for making a hyphenated name, as 'Parapsycho-physical'. Those phenomena not thus described and given a hyphenated name are the more purely psychical ones and would be called 'parapsychical'. We have the following outline, then, as a tentative working adaptation of the more systematic German terminology:

*Outline of Parapsychology (i.e. Psychical Research) on the basis of the other fields most involved in the laws seemingly evaded or transcended.**

Parapsychological phenomena:

A. Parapsychical: Telepathy and clairvoyance, experimental and spontaneous; dowsing; previsionary and monitory dreams or hallucinations; 'psychometry', veridical 'spirit' communication, etc.

B. Parapsycho-physical: Telekinesis, levitation, 'psychic lights', temperature changes, 'apports', etc.

C. Parapsycho-physiological: 'Materializations', 'extrusions', elongations, stigmatization, extreme body-temperature changes, etc.

D. Parapsycho-pathological: 'Possession-pathology';[1] 'psychic healing' of organic disease, beyond effect of suggestion.

E. [Parapsycho-literary (and other parapsycho-artistic) : Creative writing or other art, clearly 'impossible' as result of natural training, *e.g.* Patience Worth, as reported.[2] (This may properly be regarded as a sub-heading of A, also.)]

[1] For instances of cures, using 'possession' as a working theory, see Dr W. F. Prince's report on page 36 of B.S.P.R. Bulletin VI, and Mrs Lambert's on page 5, Bulletin IX, as well as the work of Dr Titus Bull of New York.

[2] Dr W. F. Prince, *The Case of Patience Worth*, B.S.P.R., 2nd ed. 1929, Boston.

* I would today stop with A and B. "Parapsychical" has come to be a *general* term for the phenomena of parapsychology. See *Parapsychology*, by Pratt and me.

The outline, as thus far developed, deals only with the branching of the subject on the basis of the types of laws seemingly transcended, and consequently of the other subject or science involved. When we consider the other major features of the so-called 'psychic phenomena'—namely, their 'psychic' or personality aspect—we find that further outlining is required to express this feature and that the added lines cut horizontally across those already indicated. Among the phenomena reported, corporeality and incorporeality is the principal feature of personality condition that stands out. That is, the occurrences reported are supposed to be due to incorporeal agencies, called 'controls,' 'spirits', etc., or else are supposed to be produced by certain corporeal (or, as we say, 'living') agents who are specially sensitive and capable of these unusual performances. There seem to be four general cases possible on this principle: one corporeal agent may influence another, as in telepathy, or the one corporeal may be the only personality concerned, as in clairvoyance. The incorporeal agency (claiming to be a disembodied personality surviving death) may influence a corporeal one, as in the so-called 'mediumistic' experiences. Or, fourth, the incorporeal personality may seem to produce phenomena without the aid of a corporeal one with parapsychological capacities, as in the seeming 'invasions' called 'hauntings'. This gives us a small and simple working chart of the field, as it seems to lie in its more natural outline, from the viewpoints of the two main general characteristics of the phenomena as a whole. It is, I think, logically systematized on what seem to be consistent lines, and is capable of much extension and refinement along the same lines. There is no original element in it, of course, and the slight reconstruction is not a conspicuous feature. It is, rather, a restatement of established general usage that seems convenient. See the diagram opposite.

If it is remembered that we are merely dividing up a field of problems on the basis of reports of indeterminate value, and not a field of known facts or laws, the natural hesitation of many readers to accept such a working scheme will, I think, be much lessened. At least, this outline gives some system to the reported occurrences and enables us to hold them in mind as a whole, as the careful worker in the field needs to do. And it gives this simply on the basis of the two general lines of reference most characteristic. Such a general view of the field is essential, I believe, to the full evaluation of the work such as is reported here. In so far as the phenomena, mentioned here in connection with the outline, have been erroneously reported, the scheme will, of course, have later to be modified. But there is no reason to object to this or to expect it to be otherwise, in view of the way it is laid down.

A tentative diagram of the field of parapsychology

Subdivision on basis of fields involved, judged by type of laws 'evaded'.

		Para-psychical	Parapsycho-physical	Parapsycho-physiological	Parapsycho-pathological
Corporeal	Simple Corporeal Agency	1	2	3	4
	Inter-Corporeal Agency	5	6	7	8
Incorporeal	Incorporeal-through-Corporeal Agency	9	10	11	12
	Simple Incorporeal Agency	13	14	15	16

(Left axis label: Subdivision on basis of the state of the personalities supposed to be involved—chiefly as to corporeality)

The task of placing the occurrences and evidence types into the diagram just given is, however, one that I shrink from—since this would be to discriminate more than I can now do, especially on the question of how much of a role the supposed incorporeal personality plays in the reported occurrences, if (of course, we must say) any. Each reader or student who finds the diagram of help in the direction suggested can well place any phenomenon, according to its apparent features as it occurs or is reported to him. But even though the outline is recognizedly referring only to apparent phenomenal characteristics, one hesitates at this stage to do this fitting in of special cases for others—all the more so since it is so unnecessary. The framework is there ready for one to use as one will.

We are principally concerned in this report with that part of the parapsychological field that would be called corporeal parapsychical phenomena (Areas 1 and 5, in the above diagram). Only indirectly, and perhaps doubtfully, are the parapsycho-physical and the parapsycho-physiological divisions invaded. These possible invasions may have to be regarded when they are more clear; at present the problem setting, then, is only the parapsychical department, in its definitely corporeal branch. That is, we are dealing with the occurrences of parapsychological phenomena that apparently are more purely mental, and, as reported and described, involve only living individuals. This excludes those phenomena that clearly seem to involve incorporeal, *i.e.* 'spirit' connections, either as 'communicators' or as 'controls' or intermediaries. Accordingly, all mediumistic activities are outside; 'psychometric' work[1] also, in so far as it is described as the work of controls. But if it is not thus supposedly spiritistic, it becomes clairvoyance which belongs, then, to the designated branch. The spontaneous parapsychological occurrences such as hallucinations, dreams, etc., that are veridical and are purely psychical (not more obviously parapsychophysical, etc.), be-

[1] That is, work done by a parapsychic sensitive in which, seemingly with the aid of a 'token' or 'object of fixation', facts not normally or explainably knowable to the sensitive are expressed concerning the person, living or dead, to whom the object belongs — facts unlimited in range and nature. It is a sort of parapsychic 'free association' process. Wherever the term 'psychometry' is applied it has, rather commonly, though not necessarily, a connotation of 'spirit' agency in the process. Otherwise it would be simple unrestricted parapsychic perception with a 'parapsychogenetic' object present.

long here, too, if not plainly purporting to imply agency of incorporeal personalities. Automatic expression of extra-normal knowledge (through ouija-board, planchette, common script, etc.) is regarded in the same way, *i.e.* without the appearance of incorporeal personalities involved, the phenomena belong to the corporeal parapsychical department.

If there be any need to justify this laying out of the field at the beginning, it should be recalled that (assuming for the moment that these divisions are represented by actual phenomena) the subdivisions concerned here may be involved in part with all the others. It is almost certain that, if there be any foundation for a given department, its basic principles penetrate more or less prominently down through the whole parapsychic column, perhaps to the very bottom. Some lateral spread, too, may be reasonably expected, one would suppose. A second point is also strongly urgent; namely, no single problem department can properly be dealt with in any field—unless not only its boundaries are known, but—since no boundary really absolutely bounds—what it is that lies beyond the boundaries. He who studies, then, only one selected subdivision could not dependably study that in ignorance of what the field as a whole may be like. For these and other reasons, the place of the subdivision in the field as a whole has been worked out in this tentative fashion.

The central and primary problem of the subdivision of the parapsychological field indicated as Corporeal Parapsychical is: Are there really dependable evasions of psychological laws (as they are regarded to-day) by corporeal personalities? In other words, can we find persons able to demonstrate the more commonly reported sort of apparent exception to psychological laws—mainly, cognition of events without the usual sensory or rational experience required by our habitual concepts for the knowing act? Is this an actual principle of nature that such extra-sensory cognition can be done by normal individuals, as is so often reported?

The question or problem is a rather broad one, not limited to the perception, extra-sensorially, of mere objects or states, but is unlimited. It includes the perception of the mental states of other individuals, the facts of the past and of distant scenes, of sealed questions or of the 'waters under the earth'. The future, too, and its scrutability are within the scope of the general problems (unless previsionary parapsychics are cosmological enough in their evasion of time 'laws' to justify a separate branch of 'parapsycho-cosmology'. At present, however, the greater economy the better, or our big words will seem to mean more than the facts they cover). The manner of the operation of such parapsychic perception, too, must be broadly viewed in clarifying the problem; it might be in hypnotic trance or under the influence of a drug, with the aid of an 'object of reference' (associated in some way with the facts to be perceived), by the use of a crystal ball, a cup of tea-leaves, the ouija-board or a divining-rod. So far as the generalized problem goes, these are all included in the broad question, Is there a human function of extra-sensory perception?

This is the primary question, and once it is answered affirmatively (and the next chapter will show that there has long been a very considerable amount of valuable evidence available for so answering it), there comes next the task of exploring for its extent, its natural history, its duration and intensity in the individual, its racial and biological origins, history and value. But central among these, and basic to any scientific advance in the understanding and application of the principle concerned, is the logically next problem, What is the nature or more fundamental explanatory principle of this extra-sensory mode of perception? All the surveying of small facts will truly help in the solution of this problem, but, without continuous and clear realization of this major problem itself, the investigator will never get beyond the mere surveying of small facts.

The problem of the explanation of the simplest parapsychic principle calls first for a study of interrelationships within the corporeal parapsychic branch itself. What relationships can be found between, for example, clairvoyance, telepathy, dowsing, prevision, etc.? It is through the development of these interphenomenal studies made with different experimental conditions and correspondingly varying phenomena that progress in their explanation will be made.

Then, too, the expansion of relationships out into the more reliable neighbouring subdivisions of the field of parapsychology may be very enlightening as a procedure, at least, whenever there seems to be an interplay of the extra-sensory perception principle present. The variation it may undergo in these more foreign applications may be expected to help to reveal its own peculiarities and properties the better.

Outward, then, will the course of investigation go to the finding of still more general relationships of the parapsychic principle to be explained, to the more common psychological processes—to sensory perception, to higher cognitive processes, to motivation, integration, attention. The prevailing uncertainty among psychologists on these, their own supposedly 'known grounds', is, of course, no small handicap, and we shall have to avoid the peculiar dangers of 'school-affinities', and not map out our own uncertainties by lines that are themselves hypothetical and in danger of eventual obliteration.

Into the realm of physiology, too, the question must be taken if we hope to explain perception without the senses. Is the nervous system involved and, if so, in what way differently from the case of sensory perception? Do the usual nervous reactions from drugs that affect mental life affect E.S.P. in a like manner and degree? Is it a dissociation phenomenon or not? What part of the nervous system is receptive in E.S.P., if any?

Nor may we stop here. Physics has to give answer to several questions that an understanding of this process requires that we ask. It the E.S.P. function an energetic process, as is sensory perception? If not, how can we have causation that does work without energy (*i.e.* 'does work' in evoking responses; it always requires energy to direct energy, so far as energetics knows)? And, if so, what energy can satisfy the conditions under which we find that E.S.P. can function, the distance conditions, time conditions, the material relationships? Do the laws of radiation mechanics apply, with their distance-intensity formulation? Can the facts we have of penetration and differential absorption in connection with E.S.P. be explained by such mechanics? Does the purposive characteristic of E.S.P. clearly evade or transcend any mechanics conceivable for radiant energy, or can increased complexity along with the configurational view construct an energy mechanics hypothetically able to explain the facts? If forced to concede a new energy what can physics do—deny it as a 'physical' energy, or more wisely concede that there is still possibility for growth in the basic concepts of the field? But now we approach philosophy—*i.e.* *s*cientific questions too broad for one academic branch.

Yet need we stop short of philosophy? Certainly the general biology and evolutionary history, social implications, and general cosmology of E.S.P. are in line for being ransacked in the pursuit of interesting co-relationships. Anthropology and comparative religion have suggestive facts, possibly of considerable interest, if not of value. To say whither the study of the problem will or will not eventually lead us would be to anticipate rashly the results of a lifetime's research.

It will next be in order to survey the historical background for the special area we are engaged in investigating, the corporeal paraphysical; of this, only the experimental work will be dealt with at any length, since to do this fully would be to fill a volume in itself. The objectives in the literature survey are, first, to draw before the reader at the start some of the better evidence for E.S.P., along with the criticisms, and some of the failures, in order to permit a tentative solution of this first problem—does E.S.P. occur? The second objective of this survey is to sift out the points of value in past work that will help in solving the second problem of our special branch; what is the real principle underlying E.S.P.? At the close of the survey there will be reviewed the hypotheses that have been offered in explanation of E.S.P. phenomena.

It is the task of the investigation, after contributing independent proof of E.S.P. as a primary objective and justifying an interest in the problem of its nature, to go on to discriminate between the different hypotheses by testing them, and to add to the general factual accumulation that permits a logical evaluation of them and final choice among them. In a general way we have gone through this work along those lines. And it makes some definitely progressive steps, too, toward the second problem's solution, the explanation, although we can make no very positive general conclusions as yet. There is need, I think, at this stage to have a more exhaustive range of hypotheses for the explanation of E.S.P. and also, of course, practical proposals for testing them.

From this discussion, it is clear that, briefly stated, we are seeking to answer the following questions in this order: Is there E.S.P. and—What is E.S.P.? The first must obviously first be answered.

Comment in 1964: As I said in my introductory word, I would say less today about organizing the field if I were re-writing this. This is not because what is given here now seems wrong but rather that it appears now a little too "eager"; the field is not advancing as fast as I thought in 1934 it would. Perhaps, in any case, it is better to push these suggestions about terms and classification more slowly. *Parapsychical* (not paranormal) is the general term for the field. *Psi* is a sort of abbreviated equivalent. Psi phenomena consist of ESP or extrasensory perception, and PK or psychokinesis.

15

CHAPTER II

Historical Background

The evidence reported for Extra-Sensory Perception is very varied in character, especially if we include the less experimental and more complex types of phenomena. First of all in importance is the division of this evidence into perception of mental conditions (telepathy) and of physical objects (clairvoyance). And, secondly, these may vary as to the spatial conditions concerned, *i.e.* the images or objects may be distant or nearby. Third, there may be a time variable as well, along with either condition mentioned —the image or objective event may be a past, present or future one. Fourth might be mentioned the wide range of experiences and objective conditions that seem to be perceivable extra-sensorially; feelings and emotions; various cognitive states, of perceptual or imaginal origin; complex purposes and attitudes, or sentiments, along with objective effects of almost every conceivable type. And so on; the limits of evidential variety are not known because the principles are not known and recognizable.

There is also a large group of phenomena of parapsychic nature that are not easily determined to be due to simple E.S.P. They constitute most of the naturally or spontaneously occurring parapsychic phenomena, such as veridical dreams and waking hallucinations. For one thing, they not infrequently carry the suggestion of agency of an incorporeal personality—as in apparitional monitions, for instance. And, again, there is often possible question as to whether the senses may not really be involved and the event be indeed a parapsycho-physical one, as, for example, in collective and simultaneous hallucinations of a veridical nature. For these and other reasons, these uncontrolled parapsychical occurrences are not ideal material for a study into the questions we have undertaken here to investigate, although they are often most impressive and interesting. They have served, however, to awaken attention to the problems and, indeed, to direct interest considerably beyond our present questions to the other divisions of the parapsychological field.

In the early years of the Society for Psychical Research in England there were extensive collections made of reports of spontaneous parapsychic incidents and systematic study was made of the data obtained. Such material forms the basis of two volumes, *Phantasms of the Living*,[1] of Myers' *Human Personality*,[2] and, more recently, of Osty's *Supernormal Faculties in Man*[3] and of Dr Prince's *Human Experiences*, B.S.P.R. Bulletins xiv and xx. In these and other works literally thousands of individual experiences have been examined, classified and reported. The total effect is quite impressive in emphasizing the frequency and generality of distribution of such occurrences among the population; they range in the different studies from an estimated 1 for every 4 individuals, to 1 in 7 and 1 in 10 for the other larger surveys. Some other good suggestions and impressions stand out from these huge and laborious compilations; namely: many instances have seemed to be pure telepathy and have suggested what is for some students an adequate explanation for all; many cases of apparitions of the dying coincided with actual death to a degree significantly beyond chance expectation; friendship accompanied 32% of the spontaneous 'telepathic' impressions in the study reported in *Phantasms of the Living* and family relationship 53%; the occurrence of such experiences was found to be no more rare among the highly educated,[4] or even among the scientific, classes than among the general population—in fact, the estimate of frequency given by

[1] By Gurney, Myers, and Podmore; S.P.R. London, 1886.
[2] Longmans and Co., London, 1903.
[3] Trans. by Stanley De Brath; E. P. Dutton, New York, 1923.
[4] See *Human Experiences*, B.S.P.R. Bulletin xiv.

Dr. Prince, based on a questionnaire study of a *Who's Who* population of 10,000, is the highest we have had—1 in 4; there are other such points of interest. But, in spite of its considerable value, the survey method does not constitute the best approach to our particular problems, and we shall therefore have to refer the reader to the literature cited for any further interest he may have in the spontaneous occurrences. In any event, a summary of such data is impossible; a statement of cases studied, with statistical treatment of frequency and chance expectation, does not do justice either to the value of such material or to the more likely errors to which it is exposed. The reports are, however, well worth reading in full, at the same time that they baffle summary statement. Most fair-minded readers of these collections would, I think, be led, as were the investigators, to regard them as genuinely evidencing a parapsychic principle of some sort. But few would agree as to what it is. Hence the need to control the phenomena, if possible, or at least to approximate them under conditions of systematic observation; and as far as may be done, to vary conditions so as to isolate the factors involved.

Between these spontaneous parapsychic phenomena and the results of more definitely experimental investigation of the subject, there is an intermediate group of data which seems clearly to indicate an extra-sensory mode of perception. I refer to the results of systematic observation of clairvoyance mainly in its various forms of private and professional practice: dowsing, or clairvoyance with the use of the divining-rod; 'psychometry,' or clairvoyance with the use of an object of fixation connected with the situation in question; crystal-gazing, card-clairvoyance, and the like. If in such practice there are given facts not known by the recognized means, as many studies claim to show is true, we have in them somewhat better material for study than in spontaneous cases, due to the fact that precautions can be taken and conditions imposed that permit systematic observation and to some degree approach true experimentation. Much study has been done on such material, often with a more or less experimental procedure involved. The study of the divining-rod and its use in the location of desired underground substances—water, coal, oil, ores, etc. —has been pushed by Sir Wm. Barrett almost to the point of clear-cut experiment,[1] and he is convinced that the dowser can, for instance, parapsychically perceive water, and locate its depth, direction and strength of flow, and often its duration. But most of the data on dowsing have been obtained by following the practitioner and observing the conditions and results. Even this method furnishes a body of evidence worth examining.

There have been some apparently very carefully conducted studies reported on parapsychic sensitives of the type called 'psychometric mediums,' who appear to be able to give knowledge, parapsychically obtained, concerning absent and unknown persons (who may be living or not) when a token or 'object of contact' belonging to the person concerned is placed in their hands: Dr Pagenstecher's report[2] of the work of Señora de Z., Prof. Oskar Fischer's study of Rafael Schermann,[3] Tischner's cases in *Telepathy and Clairvoyance*[4] under the heading of (his suggested improvement of the name) 'psychoscopy', and Dr W. F. Prince's study of Mrs King.[5] In the last named of these studies the calculation of the probability on the chance hypothesis of obtaining the results actually given yields a

[1] See the interesting contribution in *The Divining-Rod,* Barrett and Besterman, London. Also Chapter IV, Richet's *Thirty Years of Psychical Research,* Macmillan, 1923. (Trans. by Stanley De Brath.)

[2] A.S.P.R. *Proc.* Vol. XVI, New York.

[3] *Experimente mit Rafael Schermann,* Urban, Berlin, 1924.

[4] Harcourt, Brace and Co., New York, 1925.

[5] A.S.P.R. *Proc.* XVIII, pp. 178–244, New York, 1924. Another great case that belongs perhaps halfway in this department of the subject but is somewhat more experimental than these is that of Prof. Gilbert Murray, as reported by Mrs Verrall, *Proc.* S.P.R. XXIX, pp. 64–110 and by Mrs Sidgwick, XXXIV, pp. 212–74. Prof. Murray usually requires a 'point of contact' (a hand-clasp), but not one connected with the situation in question, and his work seems to be more telepathic than clairvoyant also, though the writing and speaking by the agents are required, and we cannot, therefore, be sure of telepathy.

very impressive figure. And while I am here classifying this work among the observational, rather than among the more clearly experimental investigations, I wish to make clear at once that this is not to belittle it; for, with the sensitive concerned, it probably was the best way to proceed (certainly so at first) and, in view of the high quality of the observation and precaution, we may give great confidence to the work. So that, in so far as the sensitive's work, carefully observed, can reveal its own nature, this is done. But to discover underlying principles and inner relations we must vary the sensitive's ways of performing. We can, perhaps, for the open-minded scientist even answer our first question (Does E.S.P. occur?) by this intermediate or systematic observational type of investigation. For that matter, many intelligent students have been convinced of the existence of another mode of perception by the spontaneous parapsychic occurrences alone. There are, however, those more sceptical minds that demand some measure of experimental manipulation and even some artificial control of the phenomena in question before they venture credence. But to answer our second question, What is the nature of E.S.P., we have to experiment and doubtless to extend our experimental technique considerably beyond its present state of development.

When we turn to the more definitely experimental evidence for E.S.P., we shall see at once the advantages and the dangers of experimentally following one hypothesis without full recognition of the other possible hypotheses—perhaps the greatest danger point in all human thought. The early experiments grew out of the need to test what appeared to be non-sensory transference of thought from mind to mind. This was early given the name of 'telepathy' by Frederic Myers and it became for the English-speaking world, at least, the ruling hypothesis for all parapsychic perception. And experiments were framed to exclude sensory and rational cognition, but not any other possible parapsychic cognition. This is still true to the present day in parapsychic investigation. Experimental tests for telepathy, as

I know them, invariably fail to exclude the possibilities of clairvoyance. Our own at first failed to do so.

The early experiments, then, dealt with undifferentiated E.S.P., either telepathy or clairvoyance, or both. The fact that they were called experiments in 'thought transference' or a little later in 'telepathy' merely shows the pre-experimental belief of the investigators. But, in view of the fact that the foremost need at that stage was to discriminate rather between E.S.P. in general, on the one hand, and the sensory and chance hypotheses on the other, the work was of great value. The experimental design consisted first in the choice of material rendering computation of chance expectation easy and of making possible an estimation of the anti-chance value of the deviation from chance; thus, playing cards, lotto blocks, numerals of a chosen range and the like, were used, all with known probability in guessing. Second, various conditions were obtained for the elimination of sensory cues, such as separation by closed doors, by distance, by silence, by screening, position out of visual field, etc. Third, the range of thought-types transferable was worked at somewhat, using tastes, diagrams, pain localization, colours, melodies, etc. Fourth, the value of hypnotic trance, too, was tested. And there were other features.

On the whole and for the stage they represent, the early experiments in E.S.P. were admirably conducted (with the one limitation indicated above) as one would expect from the array of highly impressive names connected with them. The experiments with the Creery sisters, for instance, were conducted by Profs. William Barrett, Henry Sidgwick and Balfour Stewart, by Mrs Henry Sidgwick, Frederic Myers, Edmund Gurney and Frank Podmore. The Guthrie experiments, mainly carried out on drawings, led to other scholars being drawn into the research, among them Oliver Lodge, then a young professor of Physics at Liverpool, whose discussion of the results affords a fine display of scientific judgment.[1] Another lengthy and fruitful series is

[1] *Proc.* S.P.R. II, pp. 189–200, 1884.

what we may call the 'Smith Series', so called because Mr G. A. Smith was concerned in all of them as the hypnotist. He put the subjects into trance for the experiments and frequently acted as agent. In these exploratory experiments a wide variety of thought material for transference was used, and the condition of separation of agent and percipient by walls and by distance was instituted. It was found that walls and short distances (10 to 17 feet) did not prevent the transference, though the results were not so high as with agent and percipient in the same room. At longer distances the result was failure. Numbers were used for these tests and calculation of value from the anti-chance viewpoint was relatively simple.

In all this work the results were sufficiently striking to leave no doubt as to the exclusion of the hypothesis of chance. Even when the nature of the material was not such as to permit calculation of mathematical odds against the chance theory, the percentage of successes was impressive enough to discourage doubt. The explanation then was either one of E.S.P. or of some normal mode of perception, involving conscious or unconscious evasion of the conditions intended to eliminate the senses. The only seriously proposed alternative hypothesis was that of 'involuntary whispering' suggested by Hansen and Lehmann,[1] psychologists, of Denmark. In 1895 they offered this explanation of the results published in the *Proceedings* of the S.P.R., claiming to have demonstrated in the laboratory the adequacy of their view. But after Profs. Henry Sidgwick[2] and William James[3] pointed out the inapplicability of the hypothesis to the results in question and exposed its own intrinsic errors in logic, Prof. Lehmann withdrew his theory.[4]

[1] Hansen, F. C. C. and Lehmann, A. 'Ueber unwillkürliches Flüstern', *Phil. stud.* XVII, pp. 471–530, 1895.

[2] *Proc.* S.P.R. XII, pp. 298–315, 1896–7.

[3] *Psych. Rev.* III, pp. 198–200, 1896; IV, pp. 654–5, 1897; *Science*, VIII, p. 956, 1898.

[4] James, W. 'Messrs Lehmann and Hansen on Telepathy', *Science,* IX, pp. 654–5, 1899. Prof. Lehmann's words are 'not yet established (bewiesen)'.

Later,[5] While insisting upon the applicability of the involuntary whispering theory to certain of the results, he went so far in the other direction as to assert that, in the experiments in which agent and percipient were separated by a door and some distance, there was evidence of another, an unknown, factor at work and he appears to have accepted telepathy as a fact under those conditions.

Not all attempts made by investigators to demonstrate 'telepathy' in this early period, the 80's and 90's, however, were so strikingly successful. Prof. Charles Richet[1] of Paris in 1884 made 2,927 tests on ordinary individuals guessing card suits, and got very low results, still, however, above chance by a margin of 57. This is between 3 and 4 times the probable error, and slightly under the minimum commonly taken as a significant result. He made, however, an interesting observation—that those who were worked for long series of over 100 did not do so well. And if the shorter series (those of under 100) are taken alone, 1,833 trials give 510 successes, which is 52 above chance or over 4 times the probable error. Max Dessoir's experiments[2] with drawings for material are not nearly so striking as those of the Smith or the Guthrie series; in fact, to the ordinary judge they seem very poor. Yet, when an adequate method of evaluation was developed by Dr W. F. Prince (B.S.P.R. Bulletin XVI, pp. 104-14) the drawings became clearly significant. Large numbers of tests were made on ordinary citizens both in England and America with a view to getting at the commonness of the 'telepathic' ability. 12,130 trials were made in America, directed by Profs. J. M. Peirce and E. C. Pickering, with results only slightly over chance expectation. 17,653 were made in England and reported by Gurney; these gave 347 above chance. This is at a low rate of scoring, comparatively; but, due to the large number of trials,

[5]Lehmann, A. Aberglaube und Zauberei, 2nd ed. Stuttgart, Enke, 1908. This statement is based on Prof. Coover's Abstract, Experiments in P.R. pp. 33–5, Stanford, 1917.

[1] See Abstract, Gurney, E. Proc. S.P.R. II, pp. 239–64, 1884.

[2]Phantasms of the Living, 11, pp. 642–53, 1885.

it is significant, with odds against the chance explanation of 20 millions to one. Yet impressive as are such figures, they are small in comparison with the odds against chance attained in only 497 of the tests made with the Creery sisters and limited to the condition that none of the investigators knew the object selected. These 497 trials give odds of septillions to one against the chance theory.[1]

There is a very interesting group of experiments carried out mainly during the 80's and 90's in France by a number of eminent physicians and university professors, on a line that implies E.S.P. of some kind, as interpreted by some of the students of the parapsychic field. They have to do with hypnotization at a distance, under conditions that exclude sensory, mnemonic and rational cognition. The earliest case was reported by Esdaile, a Scotch surgeon in Calcutta. The names of Gibert, Janet, Hericourt, Dufay, and Dusart are most prominently mentioned in the later work. Frederic Myers made a study with Janet, with apparently excellent results—80% successes in 20 trials. Myers concludes that it is due to telepathy;[2] Janet acknowledges the facts but refuses to accept Myers's interpretation. He implies that he has a different view of the experiments but does not even hint to us what it is.[3] There we have to leave this most fascinating block of data, until someone else undertakes a repetition.

In France the Schmoll and Mabire series,[4] in Germany Schrenck-Notzing's,[5] in America the Rawson[6] experiments, and in England the Wingfield series[7] of 3,024 trials on number-guessing (with successes 10 times the chances expectation) and about half a dozen others of less importance

[1] *Phantasms of the Living*, 1, p. 25.

[2] For a review of this work consult Myers, *Human Personality* (2 vols), 1, p. 568.

[3] P. 125, Vol. 1, *A History of Psychology as Autobiography*, ed. by Murchison, 1930, Clark University Press.

[4] *Proc.* S.P.R. IV, pp. 324–37; V, 169–215.

[5] *Proc.* S.P.R. VII, pp. 3–22. See also Dr. W. F. Prince's review and criticism, B.S.P.R. Bulletin XVI, pp. 126–8.

[6] *Proc.* S.P.R. XI, pp. 2–17.

[7] *Phantasms of the Living*, 1, p. 24; 11, p. 653.

went on to strengthen the argument for a function beyond chance, fraud and malobservation—for a parapsychical mode of perception. As to what it was, what its relations might be to physics, to biology, to the rest of mental life, there was very little discovered. But the fact itself was amply proved over and over. (For a better and fuller review of the experimental work thus far mentioned see B.S.P.R. Bulletin xvi, by Dr Prince.)

Curiously enough, however, the facts seems to require proof over and over—many, many times. For we find in the twentieth century that Bruck,[1] a physician in Germany, Warcollier[2] in France, Coover,[3] and Estabrooks,[4] psychologists, and the famous novelist, Upton Sinclair,[5] in America (to mention only a few), have all produced fresh series of experiments primarily to answer the first question—Does it occur?—as if it were still an unsettled question. This will, I predict, be one of the more amazing facts for the future historian of science. And after reading Bruck and Warcollier and Coover and Estabrooks and Sinclair, as well as the more numerous and more varied series that preceded, still the students who would work in the field to-day must set out first to prove it all over again! Scientific method and systematic observation have meant so little that we dare not lean on them heavily unless we are already prepared, by *a priori* mental attitude, to accept their findings.

Yet there has been some progress; if not in conviction, at least in interest. At least three university laboratories have opened up to the problems and our own becomes a fourth. Coover and Estabrooks worked in psychological laboratories, at Stanford and Harvard respectively. The third laboratory study by Brugmanns[6] at Groningen (with Prof.

[1] *Scientific American*, May 1924.
[2] *La Télépathie*, Paris, 1921.
[3] *Experiments in P.R.* p. 640, Stanford, 1917.
[4] B.S.P.R. Bulletin v, p. 28.
[5] *Mental Radio* (Sinclair), p. 239, Los Angeles, 1930.
[6] *Compt. Rend. Off. du Premier Cong. International des Recherches Psychiques*, pp. 396–408, 1932.

Heymanns) is a double step forward, for it aimed to go beyond the first problem of proof and to try to find facts of natural relationships in the direction mainly of physiological measurements correlated with success in 'telepathy'. And the results of Brugmanns are striking also in proof-value, as well as contributing something to our knowledge of conditions. The 187 trials yielded 60 successes as against 4 for chance expectation. The conditions for exclusion of sensory perception were elaborate and appear highly satisfactory.

The Sinclair book, *Mental Radio,* does the great service, first, of reaching a wider public with very good and seemingly reliable results. It is rather of the systematic observational type than the more purely experimental. But there are some good distance experiments and an interesting introspective report by the percipient, who is Mrs Sinclair herself. The exhaustive analysis of the original materials by Dr Prince in B.S.P.R. Bulletin xvi adds a great deal to its value, and includes the independent and confirmatory tests on Mrs Sinclair made by Prof. William McDougall.

Prof. Coover seems to have regarded his own work as negative, and in many respects it was. But it seems pretty clear that he might have obtained more positive results and perhaps made considerable contribution by the very simple device of repeating the tests with those who succeeded best the first time. Even as it was, his 10,000 tests on 'telepathy' (undifferentiated E.S.P.) and clairvoyance yielded 294 successes as against chance expectation of 250 (p equals 1/40). This deviation of 44 is over 4 times the probable error and would be generally regarded as statistically significant. Prof. Coover does not appear to have discovered this contribution which he made to the subject. But, what is much more important, the bulk of this positive deviation was contributed by a few of his 100 subjects—eight in number —who were among the highest in both sets of the experiments—*i.e.* both in the pure clairvoyance tests and in the tests where both clairvoyance and telepathy were possible (loosely called 'telepathy'). Of the 12 highest scorers in the 'telepathy' series and the 10 highest of the clairvoyance series, 5 were the same subjects. This was indeed a doubly valuable discovery, had the investigator been aware of it. Without a doubt he would then have carried out the very experiments we have done in this laboratory fifteen years later. These results of Coover's work, if selected thus, become tremendously significant—20 times the probable error. Now this selection is permissible, of course, only if there is valid reason to suppose individuals may differ as to their 'guessing' ability, which involves the point in question—since on a chance hypothesis they should not. But it might well have suggested to Prof. Coover the need for long and careful testing of these more promising subjects —to ascertain if they differed permanently. Finding that 5 of the best subjects in either series were also best in both would suggest to any interested investigator the possibility of a good clairvoyant being also a good telepathic percipient—that, or else that in the 'telepathic' series it was really the clairvoyant function that operated. This would have been a valuable 'lead'. While, then, Prof. Coover did not prove anything at all, perhaps, he unwittingly opened up some very interesting suggestions, which might profitably have been followed up. (Especially so in view of the generous endowment provided at Stanford University for psychical research but not always used for it.)[1]

Dr. Estabrooks took the same type of subject, the average college student, and, using playing cards also, found some

[1] In the interest of completeness perhaps I should mention Dr Troland's short study of telepathy made at Harvard in 1916–17, including only 605 trials with a probability of $\frac{1}{2}$. It has no significance whatever and was too small a series to be important. There was also the negative report of an examination by Prof Stratton of a man who claimed telepathic powers and who invited the inquiry. ('The control of another person by obscure signs', *Psych. Rev.* XXVIII, pp. 301–34, 1921.) One can readily see that Prof. Stratton might have been right in his conclusion of sensory following of signals, but might equally well have been wrong—in having provided conditions unfavourable for abstraction, as I can see now was the case. The 'internal' field is even more important than the outer in psychological experimentation.

evidence of 'telepathic' ability in them. His conditions were excellent for excluding sense perception. The best points of his work were (1) some evidence of a lowering of the scoring rate with progress through a run of 20 trials, the last 10 yielding less than the first ten. And (2) the fact that one group ran considerably below chance expectation when asked to run a second series, at a longer distance than the first. These, too, are interesting leads had the investigator been able to follow them up. He explained the decline in the run as due to 'fatigue' (presumably of the 'telepathic' function) and the drop below chance in the special instance as perhaps due to space limitations.

Another variation of E.S.P. research is represented in the inclusion of other species in the range of 'subject material'. The more experimental of the animal parapsychic studies are those by the late Prof. Bechterew,[1] eminent Russian psychologist and physiologist, on Durow's circus dogs, and of Dr Louisa E. Rhine and myself, with the horse Lady as subject.[2] In both cases a tentative conclusion of 'telepathy' was announced after the investigation. There have been other cases brought before psychologists,[3] however, and for these I will refer the reader to the review in the report on Lady.

These animal cases have an especial interest for two reasons. One is the fact that in them the conditions often approximated pure telepathy as distinguished from the telepathy-with-clairvoyance-just-as-possible type of experiment which we have been reviewing thus far. Prof. Bechterew merely thought of the object in the room or in the adjoining room with which he wanted the dog to perform

[1] Bechterew, W. *Ʋeitschr. f. Psycho-Therapie,* VIII, pp. 280–304, 1924.

[2] Rhine, J. B. and Louisa E. *Journ. Abn. and Soc. Psych.* XXIII, pp. 449–66, 1929; and XXIV, pp. 289–92, 1929.

[3] The Eberfeld horses were doubtless best known among these. Krall was convinced that his horses were capable of telepathy but the demonstration of it has remained too debatable for definite conviction. Krall's own report in 1927 (*Zeitschr. f. Parapsych.* XXI, pp. 150–53), entitled 'Denkübertragung zwischen Mensch und Tier', lacks too much in completeness and detail to permit a safe judgment.

—*i.e.* he did not otherwise single it out. Supposedly it had no other isolation than the mental choice he exercised. There was thus, it would appear, an inadequate basis for clairvoyance. In the Lady experiments I looked at the blocks, with eyes screened. This is not so free from objective selection, then, as is the other case. The second point of interest is the fact that Lady, the filly, lost her ability to perceive or to be controlled extrasensorially (at least, as far as our tests could determine) after about a year of demonstration, and came to depend upon the rather obvious movements of the trainer for guidance, movements which, of course, we had had to eliminate during the earlier testing period. This loss of ability in an E.S.P. subject has had other examples, notably the Creery sisters, and Prof. Brugmann's subject, Van Dam, and perhaps others. It will be of especial interest in connection with this report.

Another diversion in type of experiment, while we are still dealing with undifferentiated E.S.P. conditions, is the condition of distance between agent and percipient. There was failure with increased distance in the Smith series and success with longer distance in the Sinclair tests. We have yet to review the Usher and Burt[1] tests made at a distance of from 120 to 960 miles, yielding in 60 trials with playing cards 4 successes complete and 14 right in value. This is at a very good rate of scoring but the number of trials is small for a conclusion. They did much better in the same room, getting 9 hits in 36 trials. The Miles and Ramsden[2] long-distance tests were made by having the percipient, Miss Ramsden, record daily and send to Miss Miles her impressions of what the latter was doing at a certain hour (7 p.m.). Miss Miles then got objective records, pictures, etc., for all of her setting that she could. Out of 30 trials, 13 were regarded as successful, barring what would conceivably be accidental. This series was not very experimental, it is obvious, but most critics have been impressed by it, in spite of its difficulty of mathematical evaluation. Another

[1] *Annal. Sci. Psych.* xx, pp. 14–21, 40–53, 1910.
[2] *Proc.* S.P.R. xxi, pp. 60–93, 1907; xxvii, pp. 297–317, 1914.

similar series is reported by Mr Wales and Miss Samuels,[1] and is likewise difficult to judge, although impressive in its totality.

The transatlantic series conducted by a Paris group directed by M. Warcollier and a New York group under Prof. Gardner Murphy of Columbia I have not been able to find in print, but critics who have seen the results seem to regard it as difficult to evaluate and inconclusive,[2] as are likewise regarded the results of the two radio-broadcast experiments in 'telepathy', the first conducted by Dr Murphy, broadcasting from Chicago, and the second by Dr Woolley,[3] from London. The sequel series of experiments following the Woolley broadcast that was carried out by Mr S. G. Soal[4] was negative. So we may say, it appears, that of the reported experiments in 'telepathy' with distance, the short Sinclair-Irwin series of seven drawings made at 30 miles from the agent is perhaps the best. (See B.S.P.R. Bulletin XVI, pp. 9–15.)

This brief sketch is far from complete, even in the mere mention of titles, so extensive has the literature become. Especially in reference to continental European work is it incomplete. The work of the Russians, Dr Kotik[5] and Dr Chowrin,[6] that of the French Dr Geley on Ossowiecki, of the German, Dr von Wasielewski[7] on Miss von B. (with whom Dr Tischner also worked) are examples of omissions. But there is great similarity in all this work, and we have given, I think, a fair notion of the field and its advance—or lack of it.

Similarity of work in this field does not mean any exten-

[1] *Proc.* S.P.R. XXXI, pp. 124–217, 1920.

[2] Soal, S. G. *Proc.* S.P.R. XL, p. 168, 1932. Dr W. F. Prince was very noncommittal in his review, p. 21, B.S.P.R. Bulletin VI, which I take as also an indication of the inconclusiveness of the experiment.

[3] *Proc.* S.P.R. XXXVIII, pp. 1–9, 1928.

[4] *Proc.* S.P.R. XL, pp. 165–362, 1932.

[5] *Die Emanation der psycho-physischen Energie,* Munich, 1908.

[6] *Experimentale Untersuchungen auf dem Gebiete des räumlichen, Hellsehens,* Munich, 1909.

[7] *Telepathie und Hellsehen,* Halle, 1921.

sive following of the work of others, but rather an ignoring of its conclusions and a starting all over again 'to establish the fact' first of all (a phrase that is repeated so often that it becomes commonplace after 50 years of research and almost as many researches; and the same ground is covered, with many of the same difficulties that others have had and with the same general degree of success, very often). In 1932, fifty years after the Creery sisters' investigation by the S.P.R., it publishes Mr Soal's long research made to prove the factuality of 'telepathy'—which ended negatively. There are two points that are worthy of attention in this situation: first, our evident lack of progress in 'establishing the fact' for society at large; this is obvious, and is the more remarkable in England, where the most of the work has been done. And, second, in these recent failures we have strong indication of real lack of progress in understanding 'telepathy'; its requirements and functions are still so little understood that we have these long negative series after a half-century of study.

The following general points seem to stand out as worth noting in the past contributions from these 'telepathy' experiments: first, the evidence is (to one who labours through it all) overwhelmingly convincing of some extra-sensory mode of perception. That this includes the perception of mental states of a wide range of variety is also clear. That the hypnotic trance is not necessary, but is a possible 'telepathic' working condition, seems also proved. Several interesting cases of loss of ability with lapse of time are recorded. Some decline of rate of success with length of the run is suggested by Richet and Estabrooks. Suggestion is made that certain drugs may help, but the only evidence is that of Brugmanns, who found improvement with alcohol (30 gms.), but only 29 trials are reported. The agent's greater tendency to fatigue and headache is referred to by several (Lodge, Guthrie, Sinclair), and the general need for passivity and serenity on the part of the percipient. Most of these points are fairly clearly indicated, if not established.

Strangly enough there has been comparatively little experimental work on the seemingly simpler phenomenon of clairvoyance. This is, perhaps, an effect of the large influence that spontaneous occurrences have had upon the course of parapsychological thinking. These more often seemed telepathic rather than clairvoyant in nature. Still it is a remarkable fact that clairvoyance has been so neglected that it has never been thought necessary to eliminate it by condition from telepathy experiments. Consequently all the phenomena of these have been possibly also clairvoyant in nature. Prof. Coover even used card guessing in the presence of the card as a control on the telepathic series—thus allowing clairvoyance to operate but being so sure it did not function that the results were taken as chance products. (They were, however, above, by about twice the p.e.) The same loose condition has existed in all the telepathy experiments I am acquainted with; but, of course, with no danger to conclusions so far as concerns the demonstration of extrasensory perception. While we have had this undifferentiated E.S.P. as regularly possible in the so-called 'telepathic' tests, there were some where it seems unlikely the clairvoyance played much part. In Prof. Brugmanns' experiment with Van Dam, he looked down through a glass-covered hole in the ceiling at the blindfolded subject, 'willing' the subject's hand to move to a certain square on a large checkered diagram before him. Here the looking was objective, of course, and there was an objective record of the choice to be 'willed', also; yet the conspicuous thing was the agent's act of willing. We can conclude nothing, but in fairness I think we can say that the mental activity of the agent was probably the guiding factor, rather than his objective behaviour or his record on paper. In Prof. Bechterew's tests of Durow's dogs, he sometimes did not even look at the object and we come still closer to pure telepathy conditions —perhaps close enough. But why not pure telepathy experiments by definite planning of the conditions?

Of pure clairvoyance we have had a few series of tests, rather similar to the 'telepathy' data in quality and in range. Prof. Richet deserves credit for the first systematic experimentation in clairvoyance.[1] His tests made in Paris in 1888 with Leonie B. in hypnotic trance, using playing cards enclosed in opaque envelopes, were very successful. Leonie got 12 cards correct (probability of $1/52$) in 15 trials and in a later series 5 in 25 (after having been transported to England and back, where a negative series was carried out). The odds against getting 12 hits in 15 trials on playing cards on chance alone is given by Richet as 1 quintillion to 1.

There were also the experiments of Dr Backman[2] of Sweden in the 90's, in which he put his subjects into hypnotic trance and commanded them to 'visit' specified points at some distance and report what they 'saw'. They were able to perceive parapsychically to a degree that, if the report is acceptable, leaves little doubt of the fact of E.S.P. The exclusion of telepathy is not as clear-cut as is desirable and his results are, unfortunately, not capable of definite evaluation. There is not sufficient experimental character to such observations to enable definite conclusions to be drawn regarding the successful exclusion of such factors as inferability, guidance by unconsciously given indications, laxity in observation and coincidence. One does not see in the text, however, any ground for these alternative explanations.

In 1895 Mrs Verrall[3] tested pure clairvoyance on playing cards, in conjunction with tests of hyperaesthesia and its possible functioning in parapsychic tests. She found that, under her conditions (which deliberately permitted it), hyperaesthesia of sight and touch could function to a degree, but that there was something more, presumably clairvoyance.

Tischner reviews Kotik's work on the clairvoyance of his subject Lydia, carried out in Russia in 1908. Tischner's review is inadequate for a judgment of the original work; but he states his conviction that some of the experiments 'are beyond criticism'. Tischner's own clairvoyance tests are not, as they are reported, explainable by any known alternative hypothesis. One has only the alternative of doubting

[1] *Proc.* S.P.R. vi, pp. 66–83, 1889.
[2] *Proc.* S.P.R. vii, pp. 199–220, 370–3.
[3] *Proc.* S.P.R. xxxviii, pp. 223–71, 1928.

the honesty or intellectual balance of the experimenter, and he quotes several witnesses in support. He used numbers of three or more digits, or words, written on slips of paper and folded up. He and the several witnesses testify to the exclusion of all trickery and, since the 78 trials gave 40 successes, the chance theory certainly does not apply. Tischner was on guard especially against 'pellet switching', since the sensitive claimed to have done this earlier in his career under different circumstances. Tischner's 'psychoscopic' observations ('psychometry') are likewise impressive, as described. Twenty-six witnessed experiments gave 61.5% positive results.

Miss Jephson published in 1928 the results of 6,000 tests for clairvoyant perception of suits of playing cards, made on 240 people, yielding results that average somewhat above mean chance expectation and, with the number of trials given, pass well beyond the minimum for significance. She obtained 1832 hits on suits or 332 above chance expectation, which would be approximately 14 times the probable error. Her results in pure clairvoyance compare roughly with those of Estabrooks on 'telepathy'—*i.e.* with both telepathy and clairvoyance possible. I quote the following figures of comparison from Miss Jephson's article:

	Dr Estabrooks %	Miss Jephson %	Chance %
Total colour right	56·5	55·1	50
Total suit right	28·5	30·5	25
Early guesses, colour right	55·7	57·9	50
Early guesses, suit right	30·6	30·9	25

It would be very doubtful then if Estabrooks or, perhaps, if anyone had actually demonstrated pure telepathy, in view of these results. For, if clairvoyance is possible, it must safely be excluded before telepathy can be inferred as the operative principle. I feel particularly indebted to Miss Jephson's work in that it helped to stimulate my own interest in clairvoyance. A second report in 1931, in conjunction with Messrs Soal and Besterman,[1] does not confirm the earlier

[1] *Proc.* S.P.R. xxxix, *pp.* 375–414, 1931.

work and its 'fatigue-curve' hypothesis. (This last point is discussed later in this report.)

If the more experimental studies of clairvoyance were regarded as the only 'pure clairvoyance' material, the evidence would not be at all overwhelming. I think it would be good but in need of much repetition. Even so, it is far ahead of the definitely experimental evidence for 'pure telepathy', for of such there is nothing on record, to my knowledge. And, if we accept provisionally the evidence from the 'telepathy' tests in which clairvoyance was not excluded, we may as well accept the evidence for clairvoyance from 'psychometry', in which telepathy (extended and generalized) is not often excluded. If we do, I am inclined again to give the odds of weight of evidence in favour of clairvoyance, especially if we include the dowsing or divination data under this heading. The long list of first class 'psychometric' cases is rather impressive: Señora de Z., Dr Prince's Mrs King, Dr Osty's Mme. Morel and Mlle. de Berly, Rafael Schermann, Wasielewski's Miss von B., Tischner's Mr. H., Dr Geley's Ossowiecki, Paschal Forthuny, to mention some of the more famous.

With practically no pure telepathy experiments and few pure clairvoyance tests, we have little or no basis of evidence for a study of relations between these two phenomena. Kotik's Lydia did both clairvoyance and telepathy (without excluding clairvoyance, so far as Tischner's review shows), and Wasielewski and Tischner's Miss von B. did likewise. Coover's subjects did card guessing in their barely significant way, under the same two conditions, pure clairvoyance and telepathy-plus-clairvoyance. But we cannot draw any conclusions about results from such conditions. The need for an experimental separation of the two is strikingly clear, all the more so since most students of the subject have had hypothetical views of some kind as to the relationship. In a very general way the Frenchmen, Richet, Osty and Geley, have preferred to think telepathy a special case of a general clairvoyance ('cryptaesthesia' Richet's term, 'metagnomy' Boirac's term). The English and American students have been slow to recognize clairvoyance, as is shown by the lack of any definite test of it in those countries until Miss Jephson's in 1928 and by their long ignoring the need for excluding it from telepathic experiments. There has been some bias against clairvoyance in Germany too, as is illustrated by Prof. Oesterreich's attempt to explain clairvoyant phenomena by telepathy—telepathy expanded to unlimited dimensions. Barrett and Myers have theories for telepathy, but not for clairvoyance. Both Myers and Mrs Sidgwick have suggested that there are probably connections between the two.[1] Tischner and Wasielewski are of the same mind.[2]

A final phrase of this review concerns the various hypotheses proposed to explain E.S.P. These fall into two groups in general—physical hypotheses and non-physical. The physical hypotheses are the more numerous and popular, as well as the more elaborated. But in a general way they are all radiation hypotheses, since this is the only physical principle available as yet for such theorizing. Even Forel's electron theory becomes as good a wave theory as any, since electrons are discovered to conduct themselves in an undulatory way.

A number of attempts have been made to offer hypotherical explanations for either telepathy or clairvoyance, but very few have tried to explain both at once. It is this attempt at a joint theory that gives the peculiar logical difficulty. Some find it easy to suppose brain-waves for telepathy but they seem to balk at supposing the same sort of waves to be emanating from all things clairvoyantly perceptible; and well they might! Others find it easy to suppose a 'magnetic', 'telluric' or 'rhabdic' emanation or force to be exercised by metals, waters—substances in general; but they likewise find a large gap between these forces and the thought-images of a telepathic agent's mind.

The physicist Sir William Crookes, perhaps the first general theorist of the field, proposed in 1897[3] the theory that

---

[1] *Proc.* S.P.R. xxxi, p. 377, 1921.
[2] Tischner, *loc. cit.* p. 206.
[3] *Proc.* S.P.R. xii, p. 352, 1897.

telepathy might be due to high frequency vibrations of the ether generated by molecular action of the brain of the agent and received by the percipient's. He was conscious of the difficulty his theory encountered in the inverse-square law of decline of intensity with distance, but felt that our ignorance might be cloaking some principle which covers this point of difficulty. Another eminent physicist, Prof. Ostwald,[1] has proposed a physical theory for telepathy, offering an energetic theory which assumes the transformation of known physiological energies into unknown forms that can be projected through time and space, received by the percipient and reconverted to known forms. But the great physicist of "energetics' had no evidence from his science to show that energies can be projected toward a goal, unless through a material channel. The energies radiate on a spherical front, so far as we know them. Sir William Barrett, another physicist, in argument against a physical theory of telepathy,[2] reminds us that the radiation theories would require, to reach 1000 feet, 1 million times the intensity of the transmitted telepathic stimulus that is required for one foot, and concludes that 'it is highly improbable that telepathy is transmitted by waves radiating in every direction, like light from a candle'. He quotes Myers, Mrs Sidgwick and other eminent students as of like opinion concerning telepathy—that it is a psychical, rather than a physical, phenomenon. Myers was especially opposed to a physical, and insistent upon a psychical, theory. But of what sort of a theory a psychical one is we have very little understanding, other than the fact that it is not physical.

Turning to the more comprehensive theories that embrace both clairvoyance and telepathy, we find three which are very wide apart in viewpoint and which will serve here to represent widely different possible approaches. These are hypotheses suggested by Hyslop, Forel and Tischner. Hyslop's[3] hypothesis (which he suggested without advo-

1 This mention is based on Tischner's review, *op. cit.* p. 206.
2 *Proc.* S.P.R. xxx, pp. 251–60, 1920.
3 *Life after Death,* pp. 137–42, E. P. Dutton, New York, 1918.

cacy) is the 'spirit hypothesis' applied to telepathy and clair-voyance. The incorporeal personality is supposed in this hypothesis to be a 'carrier' of the mental state or stimulus that the percipient receives, for both phases of E.S.P. It will be seen at once that this hypothesis would at best only pass the problem on to a stage of still greater complexity, since we wonder quite naturally how the 'spirit carrier' obtains his 'load', if not by clairvoyance and telepathy! Which is as bad as ever.

Tischner[1] invokes a theory of super-individual or collective mind, which serves as a common reservoir. He quotes E. von Hartmann as explaining telepathy through 'telephonic connection with the Absolute' and aligns himself with this view. The connection is, he believes, through the 'subconscious mind'. This hypothesis is less definite and, perhaps, less extravagant, as some would regard it. But, in essence, it leaves us no more advanced toward explanation than Prof. Hyslop's suggested hypothesis. For we have to explain the business of 'fishing' in the 'reservoir' of the absolute or the collective mind quite as inevitably as if we just omitted all that, and assumed a direct contact between agent and percipient or object and clairvoyant. If we should need to bring in these other complications, 'spirits', 'reservoirs', etc., as inferred *accessory* factors in telepathy and clairvoyance, it would be fully acceptable to do so; but let us not obscure the fact that they do not explain telepathy and clairvoyance at all. They only complicate it. For all 'absolutes' and 'spirits' would have to perceive extra-sensorially themselves. These two theories, then, leave us as we were.

Forel's theory[2] is a hard-boiled physical one, an electron theory. The electrons come either from the brain of the agent or from the object, and when they come off in certain complexes they convey to the brain of the percipient the stimulation which leads to perception. A given 'electron complex' can stimulate a corresponding 'engram complex'

[1] *Op. cit.* p. 211.
[2] *Journ. für Psychol. und Neurol.* 1918.

in the percipient's brain, provided the percipient has previously established such an engram complex through experience of the perception in question. This previous set-up is essential, because there is required the existing engram complex in the percipient's brain which through 'homophonous and synchronous' vibration may be aroused by an appropriate electron complex, and perception effected. Thus the thought of a card figure would give off from the agent's brain the same electron complex as would the card figure itself, both exciting the same engram complex.

But one need only remember that substances regularly emitting electrons—*i.e.* radioactive—are rare in nature. Physics is, of course, alert to this phenomenon. And, to secure intensities of the strength necessary for distance E.S.P. (a million times stronger radiation at a thousand feet than at one), there would be need for some remarkable electronic emission (indeed!), which could hardly have escaped physicists.

On the reception end of the E.S.P. phenomenon there has only been the vague inference of some hidden sense (cryptaesthesia), a 'sixth sense', as Prof. Richet, the leading exponent of this view, has called it.[1] The usage is not clear as to whether any reception whatever would be regarded as sensory, or whether the selective interception of a special energy pattern by a specialized and localized organ would be meant. No clarity has yet been achieved on this important end of the function of E.S.P.

For a summary of the chapter, one may say that the evidence for general E.S.P. is good but the theories are bad; and our knowledge of the phenomena needs refinement through variation and improvement of conditions. We need tests for pure telepathy and more of them for pure clairvoyance, made under conditions that enable easy evaluation of significance, provide safe exclusion of other modes of cognition, and introduce variation enough to suggest the relation of E.S.P. to other processes and lead to its natural explanation.

[1] *Notre Sixiéme Sens,* Editions Montaigne, Paris, 1928.

Mathematics of Probability used in Evaluation

From the beginning of the scientific period of parapsychology, the subject has had the aid of mathematical methods in its technique of evaluation. Prof. Richet first introduced the mathematics of probability into this field in his treatment of the results of his earlier work on 'suggestion mentale' or 'telepathy', in 1884.[1] And since then the names of Edgeworth and R. A. Fisher of England and of Hawkesworth in America have appeared frequently in connection with probability estimation in the parapsychic branch of the field.

I am no mathematician and must rely upon methods already developed, when they can be found. But in this work it is fortunately possible to make experimental method conform to easy computation of significance of results and this I have done. I have been able, by adhering to the use of five simple card-figures, to keep the probability of success by pure chance at $1/5$ for each trial. Where a straight run of consecutive successes is to be evaluated for anti-chance probability, simply raising $1/5$ to the power equal to the number of consecutive successes gives the value desired. This is established probability mathematics.

When, however, scattered successes are to be evaluated for anti-chance significance, the first step is to find the normal chance expectation. This is simply the number of trials (n) multiplied by the probability for success per trial (p), or np. With 1000 trials on 5-suit cards this would be 200. If more or fewer successes are obtained, the difference

---

[1] Richet, Charles, 'La Suggestion Mentale et le Calcul des Probabilités', *Rev. Phil.* 1884. For a full review in English see Gurney, *Proc.* S.P.R. II, pp. 239–56, 1884.

or deviation is found by subtraction. If 300 successes are given, there is then a positive deviation from np (or chance expectation) of 100. This can be evaluated in terms of percentages, if one merely desires to compare scoring rates. It may be expressed as percentage of the number of trials (n), or of chance expectation (np) or, of course, as fractions of these. Here we should have a positive deviation that is 10% of n or 50% of np.

But in order to get a more general evaluation—*i.e.* one that gives a value that measures the rate of scoring in conjunction with the number of trials at which such a rate holds—it is necessary to measure the deviation in relation to a standarized unit of probable deviation. The arbitrary unit I shall use here is the Probable Error (p.e.)[1] which, in this situation, is that deviation from the mean (chance) expectation at which the odds are even $(1:1)$ as to whether pure chance alone is operating or not. The deviation is then divided by the p.e., and the value $D/$p.e. or critical ratio is found. This is something of a more nearly absolute estimate of the anti-chance value of a given deviation than are percentage figures. Taking the data from Table LII of Gavett's *Statistical Method*,[2] I shall cite the odds against chance for the smaller value of $D/p.e.$ (Deviation divided by the probable error.)

$D/$p.e.	Odds against a chance theory
1	1 to 1
2	4·6 to 1
3	22 to 1
4	142 to 1
5	1,300 to 1
6	20,000 to 1

And adding higher figures adapted from R. A. Fisher's Table

[1] p.e.$=$·67449 $\sqrt{npq}$, where q is the probability of getting a failure. In the paragraph above, $n=1000$, $p=1/5$, and $q=4/5$. Hence
$$\text{p.e.}=\text{·67449} \sqrt{1000 \times 1/5 \times 4/5}=8\text{·}5.$$
[2] McGraw-Hill, New York, 1925, p. 180.

II, *Statistical Methods for Research Workers,*[1] I get approximately

7	100,000 to 1
8	nearly 1,000,000 to 1
9	over 100,000,000 to 1

Note the rapid rise of these figures for each unit of D/p.e. It is customary to accept a value of 4 as a signficant critical ratio. This implies odds of 142 to 1 against a mere chance expectation.

In this report I shall use X to indicate D/p.e., which will be given for nearly every set of data reported (*and all are reported*). X, then, for any particular lot of data, is its 'anti-chance index'.

Now these values of X for particular groups of results have a progressive effect upon the mind. That is, if there are three groups, each with an X value of 6, we can agree that these are more impressive than only one group with an X value of 6. How much more? And how determine this? I have searched in vain for authority on this point, and have finally attempted a solution which I submit here and use in this report. It is tentatively offered and may be later rejected for a better method, if such is pointed out to me. I have made certain that this method errs, if it errs at all, on the safe side. And it is not at all necessary to any major issue of this report to use it. The reasons for using it are: first, there is needed an easy way of summating the 'anti-chance' significance of an easy way of summating the 'anti-chance' significance of many groups of results, instead of pooling them all together and getting the value of X after each addition through the report. But, second and more important, in such pooling together the results made by the high scorers are merged with perhaps a greater number of the poor scorers, so losing the greater contribution they made in the general assumption of equal distribution

[1] 3rd ed. Oliver and Boyd, London, 1930.

over the whole lot. A short series of 1,000 trials by a good subject may well reach a higher figure for X than a poor scorer (only a little above mean expectation) over a series of 10,000 trials. For some purposes it is proper to pool these but for others it is proper to summate their joint effect against the chance-hypothesis by another method which gives proper weight to the scoring rates for each group. And, third, there is the reason that I have in some cases to deal with negative deviations, under conditions in which I tried to secure low results and succeeded. These, too, have their statistical significance and add, quite as well as the positive deviations, to the general weight of the conclusions. But if these were to be pooled with the totals, they would of course only detract from the total value. (Even this, however, would not at all destroy any of our conclusions, because of the large margin of safety.)

One may see the propriety of combining these values of X by remembering that each such value has a corresponding value (see Normal Probability Tables) representing the probability that the deviation it represents was due to chance alone; for example, for $X=3$, this is $1/23$; for $X=4$, $1/143$; for $X=6$, $1/20,000$. Now, three such values of X (for results given under conditions that permit generalization) can be combined by multiplying the three probability fractions and thus the total odds against chance be computed. (This is simple for low values but the needs of this report take in large values of X as well as small; and I have not found tables for the probabilities for large values of X.) Now, with the smaller probability fraction thus arrived at one may obtain an equivalent value of X from the normal probability tables, if they extend that far. Working thus within the range of the tables available, it was found that the product of the probability fractions of a series of X values came out roughly equal to the probability fraction for the square root of the sum of the squares of the X values concerned. In each case, however, there was a lower X value obtained by formula $X_n = \sqrt{X_A^2 + X_B^2 + X_C^2}$ than by the multiplication of the probability fractions. This is safe at least, if not exact.

I then reasoned in the following way for the deduction of a verifying procedure (for justifying the formula): each X is an independent value; it may represent a large number of trials with small deviation rate or a shorter series with a higher rate, and *vice versa*. If we can find a way of checking the formula for combined values of X, it must hold for X's derived from large and small deviation rates, or large and small numbers of trials. That is, like the probability fraction which it represents, it is independently manipulable.

Now it appeared possible to check this formula's reliability in the following way: assuming equally distributed deviation rates over a large number of trials, determine the X for the group as a whole (X_n); then divide the group into various subdivisions, large and small, and for each calculate the X values; apply the formula to these to find X_n by this method in order to test it. I did so and found that it worked closely, yielding an X_n equal within a unit to that computed the other way, from the group as a whole.[1] If larger X values can thus be calculated from smaller in this case (as was demonstrated) and if X values are independently usable values (as they logically have to be), the method must stand as checked, to the extent of accuracy claimed, which is all that is needed for this work.

The formula has, therefore, been used in this report and is in any case safe from exaggerative effect on the general results. And it will, I hope, serve at the same time to raise

---

[1] There is a similar practical check of the formula in Table XLIII, in the final chapter, in which the X value is given for the results reported in the various chapters. That value for the results reported in Chapter VIII is almost the same for both ways of computing the X value ($81 \cdot 9$ for the formula, and $82 \cdot 1$ for the computation based on the pooling together of all the results). Now, here the evenness of distribution of scoring rates for the five major subjects makes the pooling together do no violence to the resulting values. They would not have checked had the individual differences been great. Then the formula would have given the more correct value, as it does for the other chapters represented in Table XLIII.

the problem for those readers who may be on bet
with the 'Queen of the Sciences'.[1]

[1] On this point I have the following letter from Professor R. A. Fisher, of the University of London, whose authority could scarcely be exceeded:

UNIVERSITY OF LONDON, UNIVERSITY COLLEGE
GOWER STREET, LONDON, W.C.I.

Galton Laboratory

20 *August* 1934

Dear Professor Rhine,

Thanks for your letter of August 8th. I have read through the appendix to Chapter II and cannot see what ground there is for objection against the general use of the ratio $D/p.e.$ as you have done. With respect to obtaining a combined probability, from the probabilities obtained in a number of separate tests of significance, you might find it worth while to compare what you have done with the method I suggest in Section 21.4, page 97, of the fourth edition of my *Statistical Methods*. I forget which edition it first appeared in. I should judge that your method somewhat exaggerated the significance of the combined result, but not to a sufficient amount to affect your conclusions.

Yours sincerely,

(Signed) R. A. FISHER

So far as we have been able to check up on it as yet, we find that the formula errs slightly on the side of conservatism, rather than on that of exaggeration.

PART II

Experimental Results

CHAPTER III

A General Survey

The investigation of extra-sensory perception at Duke University has now been going on for more than three years, and has come to include well over 90,000 trials. To give a comprehensive report of these trials, with a proper account of procedure, conditions and results, would make a large volume. Much summarizing must, therefore, be done in order to present the results in a reasonably readable form. It seems best to present first merely a narrative sketch of the main lines of the research and to state the general results; and, following this chapter, to give more detailed accounts of the principal subjects who produced the results and of the special experiments conducted. Those who wish to skip these fuller chapters may do so by going on from the end of this one to Chapter IX.

Following upon our experimental interest in the telepathic horse, Lady,[1] during 1928 and 1929, considerable effort was made to find other infra-human telepathic subjects, but this was in vain. In the summer of 1930, then, I turned to the task of trying to find human subjects. I began by giving 'guessing contests' to some groups of children in summer recreation camps. The tests consisted simply in having each child guess the numeral (0 to 9) which was stamped on a card that I held concealed from him in my hand and looked at. Each child had a pencil and card, and noted down his guesses silently. From the thousand (approximately) trials thus made, no one indi-

[1] Rhine, J. B. and Louisa E. 'An investigation of a "mind-reading" horse', *Journ. Abn. and Soc. Psych.* XXIII, pp. 449–66, 1929, and the sequel, 'Second Report on Lady', same journal, XXIV, pp. 289–92, 1929.

vidual stood out well enough to seem to warrant further investigation.

During the autumn term following my colleague, Dr K. E. Zener, proposed that we try sealed envelope guessing tests on our own college classes. We accordingly prepared envelopes with numerals (or, in some classes, with letters of the alphabet) effectively concealed and sealed within. These were passed out to the students with instructions to guess the number (or letter) stamped inside, under certain conditions of quiet and relaxation. Of these trials 1,600 were carried out, also with quite insignificant results. The results of the five series as a whole were very close to the chance expectation, three of the groups coming out above chance and two below that figure. This, too, was then given up, partly because it was quite laborious, and partly because of indications of failure. Further detail will be furnished in Chapter IV.

The objective had been partly to measure the ability of the group and partly to discover individuals with special ability to perceive without the senses. The latter goal was achieved, since we did discover one able subject through these tests, Mr A. J Linzmayer. In the two group tests in which he took part he was the highest scorer. In the better of these, on envelopes containing figures chosen from 0 to 9, giving a probability of being right of 1/10 per trial, he got three correct in five trials. In the other, with a probability of 1/5 for correctness on each one, he scored four correct in five trials. From these results it was thought worth while to try further tests with Mr Linzmayer. These I will describe later.

At about the same time, the autumn of 1930, another colleague in the Duke Department of Psychology, Dr. Helge Lundholm, kindly offered to co-operate in an attempt to measure 'telepathic' perception (clairvoyance was not excluded) with subjects in a state of hypnotic trance. He assumed responsibility for providing the trance and we worked with, in all, 30 subjects, who made a total of 1,115 trials. These fall into three groups; they have a different probability basis in each and cannot therefore be thrown together. All are somewhat above the chance expectation but only slightly. The best groups, in which numbers from 0 to 9 were used as symbols, totalled 530 trials and yielded 65 right as against 53 expected on chance. This positive deviation of 12 is only 2·6 times the probable error (±4·66).[1] It might be said that, had we continued these tests for as many more trials with equal results, the data would have approximated the point of significance. But the procedure was slow and we discovered that such slight deviations as we got could be had as well in the waking condition. So we discontinued the series. The details of the various procedures, and the data, will be given some space in the next chapter.

A few tests in simple 'card guessing' made now and then upon individuals by Dr Zener and myself during the year 1930-31 seemed to give promising results. They were never high but seemed to favour the positive side to an interesting degree. These were mostly carried out on the basis of symbols suggested chiefly by Dr Zener, five in number; namely: circle, rectangle, plus, star and wavy lines (○, □, + ★,〰). We early began to use them in packs of five each, 25 in all. The subject usually called the top card, as the pack lay face down on the table before him. A series of 25 trials without any extra-sensory perception would yield, on the average, about 5 correct hits. But these odds tests we were making yielded around 6, on an average. And, keeping track of those of my own observation alone, I found after a while that they were becoming fairly meaningful statistically. From a total of 800 trials carried out during the academic year, 207 hits were recorded, which is a positive deviation of 47 and is more than 6 times the probable error. But this yield (around an average of 6·5 correct in 25 trials) was low in comparison with what was in store for us just ahead in the work of Linzmayer. Two more cases, however, came in chronologically before the real discovery of Linzmayer.

[1] See Appendix to Chapter II, page 41.

First is Mr Harvey L. Frick's interesting card-guessing experiment. Mr Frick, a graduate student, had demonstrated his ability in extra-sensory perception in work reported in his Master's thesis in 1931. Following this thesis work, he undertook to study the 'fatigue' effect on the results obtained by guessing a long run (100 playing cards) daily, supposing this would fatigue him. When, after 9 days, he reported his results, they showed a striking decline series. Totalling the results by order of 20's of trials per day we get for the total of the first 20's for the 9 days, 58 correct suits; for the second 20, 50; for the third, 48; the fourth, 38; the fifth, 36. If we subtract the chance expectation (*i.e.* 1/4 the number of trials) of 45 for each total of 180 (20 per day for 9 days), we get the following decline series in the deviations: $+13$, $+5$, $+3$, -7, -9. The results as a whole are not significant. They seem to cancel out at one end of the curve what they gain at the other. But the curve is significant; *i.e.* the difference in deviation of the high end from that of the low end is 4 times the probable error of the difference. The rest of the experiment and its conditions I leave for the reader to follow at greater length in the next chapter.

During the spring of 1931 another of my students, Mr Charles E. Stuart, now an assistant in our Department, carried out some observations on extra-sensory perception, mainly card guessing, sometimes with subject in trance and sometimes with one in the waking condition. In some of the experiments there was, as with those of Dr Lundholm and myself, a combination of the telepathic and clairvoyant conditions. He, too, used cards with 5 geometric designs as the basis for the guessing for about half of these tests. Out of a total of 1,045 trials made on 15 students, 495 were made on the geometric figures, with a probability of 1/5 per trial, giving a chance expectation of 99 in all. His subjects actually got 147 correct, a positive deviation of 48, which is 8 times the probable error and means an average of 7.4 per 25 guests. There were two other types of tests given by Stuart, also yielding above chance. But, again, with this brief item for the completion of the chain of development, we will leave the details of Stuart's work for the next chapter and for a later chapter entirely devoted to his more important later results with himself as subject.

Now we return to Linzmayer. Late in May 1931, he was given 45 card-guessing trials in very light hypnosis (which was as deep as he could go) and called 21 correct as against chance expectation of 9. In the few days we could work with him after this and before his leaving the campus with the close of the year, he brought his total trials up to 600, run for the regular test, with another 900 for a special test. The 600 regular trials yielded 238 hits, a positive gain over chance of 118; this is about 18 times the probable error. This figure can leave no intelligent question of the operation of a significant principle. In the average number of successes per 25 trials this rises to the unprecedented figure of approximately 10. In one series of 25 Linzmayer got 21 hits, 15 of them being successive. In this series he did not see the cards as they were dealt and called. But (and alas!), after three most exciting days of experimentation with Linzmayer, he had to leave. During the final hours I pressed him into a hasty experiment involving 900 trials, for a special purpose, the results and purpose of which will be presented in Chapter v.

Under the stimulation of Linzmayer's brilliant example, I set to work giving preliminary tests to many other students and acquaintances. My young sister-in-law, Miss Miriam Weckesser, then aged 15, could do fairly well if alone. In all, she ran 1,050 trials over a period of a year, yielding 266 correct calls, with a deviation 6.6 times the p.e. Then it appeared that she had lost the ability, at least temporarily. Her inability to work well when witnessed and her loss of the ability after 1,050 trials were points of value as suggestions, and they were evidenced later among well-authenticated results.

During the summer one of my students, Mr. A. E. Lecrone, a high-school teacher, became interested in this work and ran a series of tests with a friend (Miss A. A. P.)

as subject, and in another series served as subject himself, with the friend observing. The regular, 5-symbol cards were used, and the conditions allowed both telepathic and clairvoyant perception. Together they totalled 1,710 trials, he doing about half as well in deviation above chance as his friend. There were 392 correct, a deviation of 50, which is 4·5 times the probable error.

During the summer and autumn of 1931 my own odd tests, made on 14 'stray' subjects, totalled 835 and yielded 208 hits, which is 41 above chance. This is at the rate of 6·3 per 25. This little group is itself significant, being over 5 times the p.e.

In the month of October 1931, we were able to get Mr Linzmayer for a short period again and made 945 tests on clairvoyant card guessing as before. But this time he ran at a much lower rate. His yield was 246, which is 57 above chance expectation; this is about 7 times the p.e. The rate per 25 was 6·5. This is, however, still quite significant even though it was low in contrast with his first 600 trials.

The greatest event of the academic year 1931–2 was the work of Mr C. E. Stuart, who was mentioned above as conducting a number of tests on his student friends. Meanwhile he had added to the work already mentioned about 900 more, yielding 257 or 77 above chance, 9·7 times the p.e., with an average of 7·1 per 25. But Stuart had begun to test himself at card guessing. He worked alone but kept good conditions, not looking even at the backs of the cards. He ran, through the year, the very large total of 7,500 trials, which represents a great amount of patience and labour. What wonder if he perhaps got tired toward the end? For some reason, at any rate, he dropped in his rate of scoring until he ran only slightly above chance expectation toward the last and I advised him to stop for a while. His results over the 7,500 show an interesting, though somewhat irregular, gradation of decline. They yielded 1,815 successes, averaging 6·05 hits per 25. There is a gain over chance of 315, which is 13·5 times the probable error—enormously significant. While

Mr Stuart is himself a responsible investigator, it will do no harm to add, in view of the fact that most of the 7,500 trials were unwitnessed, that the 140 of them that were done in my presence yielded at the rate of 6·15 per 25 calls, slightly higher than the average for the whole series of 7,500.

In March 1932, we again had a short visit from Mr. Linzmayer and obtained 960 regular trials with him, as well as some more special tests. The 960 trials yielded 259 which has a positive deviation of 67, and this is 8·0 times the p.e.; the average per 25 was 6·75. (In the preceding autumn, it had been 6·5.) One of the special experiments was made at this time by giving the subjects 15 gr. of the narcotic drug, sodium amytal. By an hour after the ingestion Linzmayer was quite sleepy and dullwitted. He was 'thick-tongued', jolly and talkative. I kept him awake for 275 trials but he could not score appreciably above chance. The average per 25 was 5·1, having scored a total of 56 (as against 55 expected from chance).

Mr J. G. Pratt, an assistant in our Department, was engaged during the year to help in the necessary prospecting for more good subjects. He carried out 10,035 tests on 15 students with a yield of only 144 above the chance expectation; this, however, still more than 5 times the probable error. His tests on himself numbered 2,885 and yielded a positive deviation that is 3·9 times the p.e. But his main contribution lay in the discovery of Mr Hubert Pearce, Jr., a young ministerial student whom I had asked to submit to the tests, on learning that his mother was reported to have possessed parapsychical ability. Mr Pearce ran low for a few runs of 25 trials each, but soon picked up and then held fairly steadily at about double the chance figure (of 5 per 25). Pearce, too, was discovered at about the close of the school year, but he was able to stay over for a time and 2,250 witnessed trials were made in clairvoyant card guessing. The yield was 869 or 419 above chance. This means an average of 9·7 per 25. The huge deviation from chance expectation is 32·75 times the p.e., a figure of reassurance against the chance hypothesis that simply leaves no question of significance. The experiments were then interrupted by Pearce's appointment to ministerial service for the summer.

One of the characteristics of Pearce's work was the relative smoothness of the results from day to day. He would average around 10 per 25. He did not at this time seem to be helped by having the observer look at the cards. Curiously enough, he would usually drop in his scoring under this condition. However, almost any change whatever, unless he himself proposed it, seemed to throw him off his rate of scoring. Visitors disturbed him for a while but he would always get back to his level if they remained for a time. Also he would become adjusted to the changes in procedure in the course of time, so far as we tried to make him. But we did not want to induce too much strain and often yielded on a desired innovation. Certain changes were introduced by talking about their possibility indifferently and allowing Pearce to say if he wanted to attempt them. In this way we started the calling for low score; *i.e.* trying to make wrong calls. In 225 low-score trials made under this condition he scored only 17, which is 28 below the chance expectation, and this is 6·9 times the p.e. Highly significantly *low!* This averaged below 2 hits per 25 calls. He produced, for example, when asked to score 'high', a 10 in 25, then for 'low', a 1 in 25, then a 9 in 25 for 'high', and another 1 in 25 for a 'low'. It seemed a matter of choice!

Another new feature introduced into Pearce's work in a half-playful way, which was also successful immediately, was calling cards down through the pack without removing the cards until the finish of the run. This started off with scores of 8, 8, 12, 6, etc., per 25 for the beginning runs. The first 275 trials yielded 87 hits, a gain of 32 or over 7 times the p.e., and an average of 7·9 per 25. The value of these data is enormous, as we shall emphasize later, first in connection with alternative theories of hyperacute sense perception, and second in connection with theories of the physical basis of the process of extra-sensory perception;

i.e. the subject reads the cards under conditions to which no radiation theory seems applicable and no sensory perception seems adequate.

We repeated on Pearce the sodium-amytal experiment made on Linzmayer, using only 6 gr. this time. This would be equal to about half what Linzmayer had taken, allowing for weight differences. Pearce was not incoherent and irrational, but was quite sleepy. He could, however, keep himself awake and could converse intelligently. He made effort several times to reintegrate himself, once even washing his face with cold water. At the beginning his scoring fell off at once, yielding 5, 4, 3 for the first three runs of 25 each. Then he 'pulled himself together' and got 10 on the next. The average for 325 trials is 6·1 in 25, as against 9·7 for his regular scoring. This is a very significant drop. This ended the series for the summer, leaving the young minister barely time to 'sober up' for his first sermon.

During the summer months Mr Stuart was encouraged to try again and, to the surprise of every one, he 'came back' about as well as ever. During his first 400 he averaged 7·3 per 25, whereas his old average had been 9 in 25 for the first 500 but for the first 1,500 had been only 7·15. In 2,100 trials made by Stuart during the summer, he obtained 575 hits, 155 above chance expectation, which is 12·5 times the p.e. and represents an average per 25 of 6·8. But the same decline set in again with Stuart and after 2,100 trials his results showed that he might as well cease. Stuart carried out, however, one very interesting variation to the regular procedure. He did this independently in Rochester, N.Y., soon after we had made a similar experiment (of which he was ignorant) with Pearce here at Durham. He began giving a 'right' and 'wrong' call for each card, keeping the records labelled and separate. His results show for the 'wrong' calls about the same negative deviation from chance expectation that the 'right' calls show for the positive side. That is, when he tries, he can go high or low, in about the same degree. His decline curve based on the 'high' column became an incline curve for the 'low'. (For the full data see Chapter VI.)

In the early fall Mr. Pearce returned to Duke and we went hard at it again. We were particularly desirous of increasing the 'D.T.' totals. (These are obtained by calling down through the shuffled pack without touching the cards, leaving the pack unbroken until the end.) These soon reached the 1,000 mark and the significance rose still further beyond the range of question. At the '1,000' milestone, the deviation was about 12 times the probable error and the average run per 25 was 7.5. One feature of interest here was the apparent difficulty shown in scoring high in the centre of the pack, which kept the scoring lower than Pearce's other ('B.T.') work.

Another experiment of interest was the effect of the stimulant drug, caffeine. Under the influence of the drug treatments the deviation or gain above chance expectation was doubled over what it had been for the preceding part of the period. The rise of deviation was actually from 44% of chance expectation to 98%. (See Chapter XII.)

The effect of the presence of strangers upon Pearce's scoring was more carefully measured and found to be highly reliable; i.e. at first he would drop to 'chance'. But in every case he rose again, while the visitor waited, to his original level. He stayed down longest with a magician present, but he rose again before the magician left—and 'mystified the mystifier', who, himself, failed to score above the chance average in 75 trials given him.

A fatigue test was run with Mr Pearce over an 8-hour period, during which he called 900 cards. There were no signs of decline in scoring rate and no special fatigue evidence. The average for the day per 25 was 10.1, which is a little above Pearce's average. About a month earlier Mr Stuart had made 1,300 calls in one day, 700 for 'right' and 600 for 'wrong'. They were among his highest in rate of success.

There were some interesting experiments with screens with Pearce which will be given in detail later in the report. At the moment I will lump them off, 600 in all, with a yield of 215 or a gain above chance of 95, which is 14 times the probable error. The average per 25 is 9. These are especially interesting on the score of eliminating sensory cues.

But I was at this time pressing Pearce on the point of telepathic perception or thought transference. I mentioned above that he would drop in score when one tried to help by looking at the cards. I then began to work behind the screen so that he would not know when I did or did not look. The data came out about the same for a while, whether I looked or not. But all at once he seemed to be utilizing telepathic perception in the unscreened tests made in the same general period, since, when without the screen, I looked at the card, he got high scores, and fell lower when I ceased. He thereafter showed, even behind the screen, a marked advance in scoring with the added 'telepathic' condition. Then I gave him a 'pure telepathy' (P.T.) test, in which the agent merely chose at random an image of one of the five symbols on the cards. No cards or objective figures were used. This ruled out clairvoyance as commonly regarded. Pearce began, after some failures, to achieve real success with the P.T. ('pure telepathy') condition, with different agents. His first 950 trials yielded 269 or 79 above. This is 9·6 times the p.e. It is an average of 7·1 in 25, low for Pearce but not unusual for the beginning of a new experiment. This discovery in my best clairvoyant subject of a 'pure telepathy' ability also impressed me as of theoretical importance.

Meanwhile, the results were piling up at a rapid rate. With Pearce alone there were over 10,000, with Stuart another 10,000 and there were six others. Scepticism among colleagues was abating. They had only to come and see. And several students were becoming interested. During the autumn of 1932 a number of girl students very kindly tested themselves for extra-sensory perception and, out of perhaps 10 or 12, there were 3 that stood out strikingly. These were Miss Sara Ownbey, a graduate student in our Department, Miss May Frances Turner and Miss June Bailey. All three have since done dependably high scoring over long series.

Miss Bailey was first encouraged to try the tests because she had had parapsychical experiences in her childhood. She has now made 3,900 trials, at an average of 7.8 per 25. The value of the deviation over the p.e. is as high as 26. She does well both with 'pure telepathy' (P.T., no cards, only mental images) and 'pure clairvoyance' (P.C.; *i.e.* cards only—no agent). Her P.T. score (average 9.4) is somewhat higher than her P.C. (average 8.0) at present.

Miss May Frances Turner, during the academic year 1932-3, made the large total of 5,125 trials, mostly un-witnessed, with the average per 25 of 8.4 hits. This gives her work a value of deviation from chance expectation divided by p.e. of 35, which is a most remarkable statistical value. Her ability, too, lies in both types of extra-sensory perception, the telepathic and the clairvoyant. In fact, she has about the same standing for the two, an average of 9.0 for P.C. and one of 9.4 for P.T. She, like Miss Bailey, does not yet do so well at the D.T. calling (solid pack, un-touched) and this has lowered both general averages some-what.

The best subject on the D.T. work is Miss Sara Ownbey. Her average on 1,425 trials under D.T. conditions is 7.8 hits per 25 calls. On the total for the year of 1,975 trials, P.C. and P.T., she averages 8.9 per 25, and her positive gain ($+ 307 \pm 12$) is 26 times the probable error—again, a tremendous value. Miss Ownbey also does well in both branches of this mode of perception. Her P.T. average is 8.1, her D.T. 7.9 and her other P.C. work averages 11.6 in 25. (P.C. includes both D.T. and B.T.; in B.T. the card is removed from the top of the pack after being called.) She has hardly got well started on P.T. work as yet, however, and most probably will improve her P.T. score, bringing it nearer the P.C., as other have done. Her own telepathic perception has really been neglected, due to the fact that she is an excellent agent and has served mostly with others in that capacity.

Again in the spring of 1933, Linzmayer kindly gave us an opportunity to work with him further. But this time he fell still lower in his rate of scoring, averaging now only 5·9 per 25 on the 3,000 trials he took part in. This systematic decline is surprising, all the more so since he is so keen to improve in his E.S.P. ability. Even so his results are significant, the 3,000 trials yielding a positive deviation 7·5 times the p.e.

But the most interesting feature was the fact that Linzmayer yielded significant results on the P.T. condition also, averaging 6·0 per 25 for 1,000 trials. To find in this declining 'pure clairvoyant' subject a 'pure telepathic' perception approximately equal to the already weakened P.C. was a very stimulating discovery, since the possible relationships between P.T. and P.C. were becoming more and more fascinating.

The keenest interest then lay in getting at possible tests differentiating between P.C. and P.T., with distance. For instance, pure telepathy might possibly work at a greater distance than P.C. or *vice versa*. A long illness thwarted the plans for a time, but in June 1933 Stuart started working with Pearce on distance effect comparisons between P.T. and P.C. But somehow, to our surprise, Pearce did not do well even in ordinary circumstances and about all we got was the fact that, at short distances, Pearce scored the same on P.C. as on P.T., 6·3 in 25 on the one, 6·4 in 25 on the latter, both very low for him. This is in itself another link in the chain of comparisons that is seeming to unite these two phases of extra-sensory perception. One other curious feature showed up in this Stuart-Pearce experiment of June. Pearce did best on D.T., as did also Linzmayer, when he fell to his lowest. This would superficially seem to be the hardest, under ordinary conditions, and yet with a general decline it seems not to drop so easily. The data are as a whole, however, very significant, the total 5,400 trials giving a positive deviation more than 11 times the probable error.

Another excellent subject, one whom I had tested out over a year previously and who had scored 27 correct in the first 50 trials, appeared again on the campus in July 1933, Mr. T. Coleman Cooper. He made 4,850 trials in about 2 weeks, with Miss Dwnbey as agent and observer. His average per 25 was 8·6 hits, for P.C., and 8·1 for P.T. in the same room with the agent. He, like the others, seemed to be able to perceive both telepathically and clairvoyantly in about the same measure. Moreover, in his daily fluctuations, which were quite marked, he went up and down in P.C. and P.T., both together. Like Pearce, Cooper did not achieve any contribution to the distance question, now uppermost in mind, valuable as the results are otherwise. One other point of considerable interest came out clearly in this set of data. Mr Cooper worked with two agents in his P.T. work, Miss Ownbey and Miss Parsons. The results with Miss Ownbey averaged 10·9 in 25, those with Miss Parsons 6·5 per 25. This is a point of value as to the role of the agent. Miss Ownbey has herself marked E.S.P. ability. Miss Parsons has shown none as yet.

Then in July 1933, right in our midst arose a new and very successful subject, Mr George Zirkle, another graduate assistant in our Department. Miss Ownbey, his fiancée, discovered his ability to perceive telepathically. Working with her as agent, he has already got most striking results, averaging in P.T. through 3,400 trials, 11·0 hits per 25. Another peculiarity is his inability to work clairvoyantly as yet but, of course, this may develop slowly in him at a later period, as telepathic capacity did in Pearce. Zirkle's scoring is sometimes phenomenal. He several times has scored 22 correct in 25. Once in calling 50 in a series, 26 were found correct in unbroken succession. This was about equalled only once before in our experience with E.S.P. and that was by Pearce, who, in my presence, ran 25 straight hits by pure clairvoyance.

Still more to the point is the fact that Zirkle does quite

as well 12 and 25 feet away, with walls between him and the agent, as he does across the table from her. In fact, the averages are better with the distance and screening. The average per 25 in the same room when he is physically well is 14, at 8–12 feet away, 14·6 and at 28–30 feet, 16·0. Also, the conditions include the noise of an electric fan to exclude possible 'unconscious whispering' and thus give quite good conditions for safety. A telegraph key is used for signalling.

Under these conditions, fan going, wall serving as a screen, telegraph key as a signal, a constantly changing system of choosing imaginal figures, we carried out another drug experiment with Zirkle as subject. He was given 5 gr. of caffeine in capsule, not knowing whether it was caffeine or sodium amytal, and when tested an hour later rose from his pre-drug level of 12·5 per 25 to 14·7 per 25 for 12 series, 300 trials. The next day he was given sodium amytal (5 gr.) and dropped from 13·5 per 25 to 7·8 per 25 an hour after. Three hours afterward he dropped to 6·2. Then he was given 5 gr. of caffeine and came back up to 9·5. He did not know which drug he had until after the amytal made him very sleepy and he did not know what effect on E.S.P. to expect from either drug.

But the climax to our story, so far, consists of long-distance tests of the P.T. type, conducted by Miss Turner as percipient, at Lake Junaluska, N.C., and Miss Ownbey as agent, here at Durham, a distance well over 250 miles. They arranged to run series of 25 trials at certain hours, the trials five minutes apart. The first eight series run as follows, per 25: 19, 16, 16, 7, 7, 8, 6, 2. This is an average of 10·1 per 25, with a positive deviation of 41, which is 10·8 times the probable error. The first three series are enormously significant, as is obvious, reaching a value of well over twenty times the probable error for chance expectation based on 75 trials.

What now about distance and P.C.? This has become a most crucial sort of question, indeed. Later on in the summer, Miss Turner and Miss Ownbey arranged for a long-distance P.C. experiment (300 miles), Miss Ownbey simply selecting the card, isolating it on a table, but not looking at it. The cards are changed at regular known time intervals as were the images in the P.T. tests. These were to alternate daily with distance P.T. runs, conducted as those described above. The distance P.T. fell to chance average and stayed there for the 4 runs atempted. All we can say in explanation is that Miss Ownbey did not feel well for part of the period and was expecting to be married within a few weeks. What disturbance this might give to the necessary act of 'concentration' we can only conjecture. At the same time, Miss Ownbey was acting as agent in distance P.T. tests with Zirkle 165 miles away and these, too, yielded only 5.5 per 25 for 10 runs, which is not significant scoring. But in the distance P.C. Miss Turner was presumably alone responsible. She began with 4 in 25, 4 in the second run, then rose to 7, 8, 7. At this promising point they had to stop.

But just then Pearce began on distance P.C. Not so far away from the cards, it is true. But for some features 100 yards are as good as 100 miles. He began with a distance of 100 yards, from the Duke Library Building to the Physics Laboratory. He got an average of 9.9 for 12 runs, a deviation of 59 above chance in 300 trials, which is 12.2 times the p.e. He did better at the distance than he did in the same room, with all other conditions equal. As I wrote this he was just beginning to score high at 250 yards, after an initial adjustment period which he always requires.

If distance is no barrier, either to P.C. or P.T., what then, about time? Can these E.S.P. subjects evade that dimensional factor also? Only that factor itself has kept us from attempting to find out, but it cannot long do so now.

CHAPTER IV

Earlier and Minor Experiments

The twofold objective of the experiments in extra-sensory perception at Duke University is, as stated earlier, first, to answer, if possible, by mathematically indisputable evidence the question of its occurrence and of its range; and, second, to further its understanding by the discovery of its relationships to other mental processes and to the essential physiological and physical conditions. In the detailed accounts of the experiments given in this chapter and those immediately to follow (v to viii), the first of these purposes, concerned with the proof, will be given first consideration. Then in later chapters will be summarized those special experiments which were designed to help to explain rather than to prove. Those readers who are in danger of being bored by more proof for extra-sensory perception can well afford to go over to Chapter ix (unless perchance they may be interested in the personal accounts of the principal subjects given in the immediately following chapters).

In these chapters containing the more complete reports, all the available information that seems helpful to thorough understanding will be included and will be built up around the personalities of the major individual subjects. The reason for this is that in this work so much irregularity of conditions, procedure, and results is inevitable because of the great factor of human variability that it is hard to generalize over the whole range of subjects in any detailed fashion. However, in Part III, which follows this series of individual studies, there will be a general discussion of the main hypotheses, in which a summary will follow, and considerable generalization and summarization will be made from the results as a whole.

In the conduct of these experiments there has not been a

carefully drawn up plan of procedure right from the start. In work of this kind it is necessary to proceed as explorers, ready to adjust plans at every turn, flexible as to methods and conditions. Only the general objectives need be kept fixed, and the means and criteria of interpretation. Often a block of work is of little value because of poor conditions of security against possible errors or deception, but if thereby there may be a chance to develop a good subject for later improved conditions, we relax the conditions and record them as they actually are. The sensitive but powerful factors of mental atitudes and moods have to be regarded with care. One can seldom proceed directly to the point, as with test-tube work. Much of what may seem to many as the incredible stupidity of the investigator is due to these limitations. On the other hand, I see now several places where I might have done much better, saved time and improved a point, if I had known more. Naturally, the progress of the research as it has advanced has altered and improved the plans for the future. We are more given to following up the best leads, as they come, than to trying to elaborate a perfect experimental plan and following it strictly.

The first laboratory procedure was that of the trance-telepathy experiments of Dr Lundholm and myself. Our immediate purpose in this was to discover, if possible, any individual showing in the trance condition the striking telepathic capacity claimed for some of the hypnotized subjects in the 80's and 90's by French and English students in this field. We did not at this stage exclude clairvoyance as a possibility. We were using the hypnotic trance, however, merely as a presumably favourable condition. There was also the secondary purpose of measuring the total scores by the probability devices in order to reveal any minute and dispersed telepathic ability present. To state the outcome in a word, the first purpose was not satisfied by the experiment but the second did, I think, achieve a small degree of success.

The subjects were students who volunteered for the experiment. Dr Lundholm and I together worked with 12 and, after Dr Lundholm was unable to continue because of time limitation, I alone went on with 18 more. Six others were eliminated because of failure to attain the desired state of trance. With the 30 subjects in all we carried out a total of 1,115 tests, using three different procedures of testing for telepathic perception but with the same general hypnotic treatment.

The hypnotic trance was induced at first by Dr Lundholm, using mainly suggestions to relax and to become sleepy. After suggestions for muscular plasticity and rigidity had been effective, and suggested amnesia and post-hypnotic suggestion were found to succeed, the instruction was given that the subject would awaken on a given signal, would take a comfortable position in an armchair and would relax again. He would then be inattentive to general stimuli in the room but would be fully receptive to what the designated agent, Dr Lundholm or myself, would desire him to do, and he would be in close *rapport* with the agent. It was suggested that he would receive impressions from the agent's mental processes directly. Further instruction was given the subject after he was seated in the armchair, before a table.

There were a great many variations in the actual words used, the order of various tests of depth of trance and even in the instructions. We were exploring for a process, not quantitatively measuring one already known. My own hypnotic procedure, though I learned it from Dr Lundholm, soon varied considerably from his. But these are unimportant matters at this stage.

We began by using numerals, 0 to 9, printed on cards. These were shuffled and a figure selected by the agent by a random cut. The figure was shown to the other observer and both kept the visual image in consciousness for the span of the test. On a given signal, explained to the subject after he was seated in the armchair, he was to try to perceive which number from 0 to 9 the agent was thinking of and call it aloud. The regular run was 10 calls to a series and, as a rule, 2 runs were made for each individual during each experimental occasion. (I see now we might well have run much longer series.) There was no distinction here between clair-voyance and telepathy, since there were 'present' both the figure on the card and the thinking of it. Also there were no provisions aaginst possible 'unconscious whispering'. It was planned to progress to better conditions as results war-ranted. The subjects' eyes were, however, closed by sugges-tion. After the first 12 subjects had been tested there were, for this test, 210 trials with 30 correct, 9 above the chance expectation *(i.e. np, where n equals number of trials and p the probability of success for each trial, in this case 1/10; here np=21)*. This is only about 3 times the probable error and not to be taken very seriously. For the whole 530 trials made by the 30 subjects, the level of deviation is 23% above the chance expectation, and has still about the same ratio to the probable error, slightly less (2·6). This is, however, barely enough to encourage further work and not enough for a conclusion.

On one of the other techniques we had poorer results, not significant in any way. This was a simple test with 2 possi-bilities. The purpose in its use was to lessen the intellectual or rational element and come nearer to pure 'guessing'. The subject was given instructions that when the signal (2 laps) was given he would be impelled to raise one of his hands a little, which one being automatically determined by the corresponding one which the agent held raised. The order of this left or right sequence was determined by random card selection, using cards with L or R stamped thereon. The results of the 340 trials of this group were below chance expectation by 4 points; *i.e.* 166. This is, however, only about 0·6 of the probable error and is, of course, just 'chance' variation.

The third type of procedure involved a still more overt response. A circle 5 inches in diameter was cut in a piece of cardboard, with the circumference marked with pencil into octants. A drawing pin was stuck in the table at the centre of the circle. The subject was told that when the signal was given his second finger, which would be resting on the pin's head, would automatically move out to the circumference to that octant upon which the agent was fixing his gaze and was 'willing' him to touch. There were only 245 trials of this; it was very slow work and gave only a low positive deviation from np, chance expectation; namely, 4·4, which is 14% above np but only 1·27 times the probable error. We have, then, the following little table of results:

TABLE I

Extra-sensory perception in hypnotic trance
Lundholm and Rhine, Autumn 1930

No. of sub-jects	Test method	No. of trials	Prob. per trial	np or chance	No. of hits	Dev. from np	% of dev.	p.e.	X D/p.e.
1. 30	Numerals 0 to 9	530	1/10	53	65	+12	23 % +	±4·7	+2·6
2. 20	Raising hand, L.R.	340	1/2	170	166	− 4	2 % −	±6·2	−0·6
3. 13	Circle octants	245	1/8	30·6	35	+ 4·4	14 % +	±3·5	+1·3

The value of these results lay entirely in the encouragement they gave us to continue. It was clear that, unless they were unusual, the mere continuance at the same rate would soon produce considerable significance. For instance, in 5,000 trials at the rate of our 530 on numerals the positive deviation would raise to the very convincing figure of 8 times the probable error. The only way to ascertain if our preliminary tests were unusual or not was to continue.

Fortunately, we found that we did not need to use the trance, that it did not seem to help and, of course, made the work much more laborious. We continued then, using only the normal waking state. But to explain the circumstances of the change requires that we turn now to the work on pure clairvoyance which Dr Karl E. Zener and myself were carrying on during the same period in which the research just described was being conducted.

Dr Zener had suggested that we try tests for clairvoyance on a large scale, using our college classes for subject material. We adopted a procedure similar to that of Miss Jephson, of enclosing cards in opaque envelopes, except that we used cards on which the numerals 0 to 9 were stamped instead of playing cards. We chose the numerals as offering a simpler task, with a simpler problem in computation and evaluation. The 6 and 9 were distinguishable by the fact that all figures were upright and turned toward the face of the envelope with its marked corner to the right.

The envelopes were doubly sealed, once with shellac, and were given, 5 to each, to the students with instructions to choose a quiet occasion and try to guess the numeral from 0 to 9 on the card within. The record was to be made on the envelope. Out of the 495 returned envelopes there were 60 correct guesses, or a positive deviation of 10·5 or 22% above. It is only 2·3 times the p.e. Linzmayer was highest with 3 correct in 5 trials.

In the next experiment the letters of the alphabet were used. Only 170 envelopes were returned and of these only 8 were correct. This is 1·46 above the *np* or chance value (*i.e.* $170 \times 1/26$). It is 12% above chance expectation but, of course, quite negligible in probability value with this small number of trials.

Thus far the computation by the mean square formula of the total significance of the results from the different experiments (*i.e.* by taking the square root of the algebraic sum of the squares of the values for X, where X equals the deviation divided by the probable error) had risen only to 3·8, which is only of borderline significance. And the next three experiments added nothing to this reservoir of value. In fact, they even lowered it slightly (to 3·6).

In the three further experiments, conducted in much the same way, the symbols used were 5 simple designs: circle, rectangle, plus sign, star and wavy lines ($\bigcirc$, $\square$, $+$, $\bigstar$, $\approx$). These were mainly chosen (by Dr Zener, as already stated) with a view to avoiding undue overlapping, complication and difference in familiarity. They are still in use. (We have once since substituted a 'heart' for the 'waves' figure but later returned to the latter. I shall hereinafter call these cards the E.S.P. cards.) In the first use made of those there were 300 trials, and, although one subject got all five correct, the total hits were only 2 above *np* or chance. This is negligible. In the net series, 205 trials yielded only 35 as against 41 for *np*. This is 15% below chance expectation, the lowest percentage we have ever obtained in our regular experiments in a series of over 100 trials. This was, however, not significantly low at all, being only 1·4 times the p.e. The last series, 430 trials, yielded 82, when *np* was 86. This is within the p.e. itself.

The entire 935 tests on the E.S.P. cards came within the probable error range, on the negative side, with a deviation nearly equal to the p.e. As was mentioned above, this brought the total value of the positive deviation thus far gained in the extra-sensory perception tests down from 3·8 to 3·6. The 1,600 trials for pure clairvoyance may be compared in the following table:

TABLE II

Extra-sensory perception of the clairvoyant type class experiments Zener and Rhine, Autumn 1931

No.	Symbols	No. of students	No. of trials	Prob. per trial	No. of hits	Dev.		p.e.	X = D/p.e.
1	Numerals 0 to 9	99	495	1/10	60	+ 10·5		±4·5	2·3
2	Alphabet	34	170	1/26	8	+ 1·46		±1·69	+ ·86
3	E.S.P. cards	60	300	1/5	62	+ 2·0			
4	E.S.P. cards	41	205	1/5	35	− 6·0 }−8		±8·2	− 1
5	E.S.P. cards	86	430	1/5	82	− 4·0			

These 1,600 trials were enough, we thought at the time, to show that there was no highly appreciable extra-sensory perception in those particular groups under those particular conditions. We turned then to another line of technique. Neither trance telepathy nor class clairvoyance had been impressive, though both had held out faint promises of evidence—if we went on long enough. We began scouting for special subjects by the quick and easy method of having friends, students—anybody—call off the cards (E.S.P. cards) in a shuffled pack placed face down on the table before them. During the winter months I made a collection of these trial scores totalling 800, with 24 subjects, yielding 207 hits, with a positive deviation from chance expectation of 47. This deviation was our first really convincing result, since it was over 6 times the probable error and unquestionably significant. These results can be grasped most simply by many readers in terms of number of hits per 25 trials. These 800 trials averaged 6·5 in 25, while the chance average is 5 in 25.

These trials were all made in my presence, with fullest vigilance against deception, using cards that the subject had not had in his possession outside of my presence. Most of the subjects were friends or relatives or students from my class. The subject usually looked at the back, sometimes picked the card up, but often did neither. He had no opportunity to learn the cards by marks on the backs, even supposing there to have been present a general visual hyperacuity. The chief advantage here over the tests given before was that when a subject did well he was encouraged to go on, when he did poorly he usually was not. This helped to guard the score somewhat by selecting the better scorers. For instance, I myself made only 15 calls in the 800, since I got only 2 correct in 15 trials. Mr. Mann has 105, because he got 37 correct in all, an average of 8·8 in 25, as against 5 for chance. But there were exceptions to this rule of selection. If one seemed to want very much to continue, hoping to improve, he was allowed to. The following table will give some idea of the distribution. The average per 25 trials is given, since it is the simplest basis of comparison:

TABLE III

Pure clairvoyant perception, odd tests, Winter 1931–2

Name of subject	No. of trials	No. of hits	Av. per 25 trials	Remarks
Mann	105	37	8·8	6 times p.e. Eyes closed, no contact with cards
McLarty	115	26	5·7	Tried hard but never developed
Miller	70	19	6·8	
Stuart	60	12	5·0	He developed later into a good subject
Millican	50	13	6·5	Did these in hypnotic trance. Eyes closed
Buren	40	10	6·3	Eyes closed, relaxed. No contact
Joseph	40	13	8·1	Back turned. No contact. Good work since
Armstrong	40	13	8·1	In trance. No contact
Frick	35	5	3·6	Did work of some value before and after
Harrington	30	12	10·0	Did good work in class tests also
L. E. Rhine	30	11	9·2	Lost ability later
Linzmayer	20	4	5·0	Did brilliant work later
12 others	165	32	4·8	None of these 12 developed. Few were tried again
Total	800	207	6·5	+47 ± 7·6 = 6·2

Most of these figures cover more than one experimental occasion for the subject. We seldom ran over 20 trials per day per subject. Mr McLarty did; as did also Mr Mann.

In order to avoid repeating description of conditions, I mention here the later results of the 'Odds and Ends' that do not warrant individual presentation. Up to the end of the year 1932, there were 835 more odd trials at pure clairvoyance, yielding 208 successes, a gain of 41, which is 5.3 times the p.e.

Among this group were 100 trials by Dr William McDougall, yielding chance average, 150 by Dr D. K. Adams, also of our Department, giving 36 or an average of 6 per 25. Our greatest gain was the discovery of Cooper, who got 38 correct in 90 trials, a gain over np of 20, a deviation in itself 8 times the probable error. He has since done some most excellent work. For completeness, however, I must note that in these trials I did not myself supervise Cooper but asked another student, a friend of his, Mr Harriman, to do it. Mr Harriman, himself, got only 1 correct in 10, with the reverse arrangement. But if there were any doubt of Cooper's and Harriman's honesty, the further work of Cooper under supervision, reported in a later chapter, would adequately satisfy it.

We have, then, as a total of the odd clairvoyant tests 1,635 calls, yielding 425 successes, with a positive gain of 88, about 8 times the probable error. This is about an average of 6.2 hits per 25 trials. By these results the combined value of deviation over p.e. $(X=\sqrt{X^2+X^2...})$ has risen from 3.6, where we left it after the trance-telepathy and the class-clairvoyance tests, to the quite respectable and undoubtedly significant figure of 8.9. This figure would, I think, satisfy any mathematician, since the odds against a chance theory are here somewhere around 100 millions to one. But, fortunately, there is no need to raise the question. This value is soon dwarfed by the towering scores of later experiments.

In much the same manner and conditions as these tests just described, Mr Charles E. Stuart, one of my students, carried out a series of exploratory tests, using at first the hypnotic trance and the undefined telepathy-clairvoyance technique used by Dr Lundholm and myself. Later he adopted the waking condition and pure clairvoyance conditions we had come to use exclusively. At first, he used a set of symbols of his own $(\triangle, \bigcirc, \square, \bigstar, \math773{C})$ but he changed later to the E.S.P. cards. It is especially interesting to note that Stuart obtained better results than did Dr Lundholm and I —not with the same subjects, it is true, and any comparison is based on all the uncertainties of individual differences. But it is easy to see now that Stuart, himself a student, working with fellow students who knew him well, did not induce the restraint and self-consciousness which Dr Lundholm and I undoubtedly did with many student subjects. Stuart's results also warrant the detail of a tabular statement. (See Table V.)

TABLE IV

Trance-telepathy tests, conducted by C. E. Stuart, Spring 1931

Name of subject	Raising L. or R. hand			Cards, numerals, 0–9			Five symbols		
	No. of trials	No. of hits	Dev. from np	No. of trials	No. of hits	Dev. from np	No. of trials	No. of hits	Dev. from np
Sykes	70	43	+8	70	10	+3	25	10	+ 5
D. A.	40	24	+4	70	10	+3	215	54	+11
Holt	60	29	− 1	60	8	+2			
Powell	30	22	+7	30	2	− 1	20	7	+ 3
Whitehead	30	18	+3	30	4	+1	25	9	+ 4
Armstrong	30	16	+1	30	3	0	20	7	+ 3
Totals	260	152	22	290	37	8	305	87	26

$X = D/\text{p.e.} =$ $+22/\pm 5 \cdot 4 = 4 \cdot 1$ $+8/\pm 3 \cdot 4 = 2 \cdot 3$ $+26/\pm 4 \cdot 7 = 5 \cdot 5$

For a description of the technique of the three procedures used see the experiments of Dr Lundholm and myself above. Instead of the circle-8 test Stuart used the 5-symbol test mentioned above. It will be noted that the best results were obtained with the 5-symbol cards and this has been pretty much the general case. The values of X or deviation divided by p.e. are, in order, 4·1, 2·3, and 5·5. When combined by taking the square root of the sum of their squares, we have 7·24. Combined with our last figure of accumulated value against 'chance', 8·9, we get the root mean square, 11·5, as our more advanced fortification against the chance theory.

Following the experiments of Table IV Stuart went over to the pure clairvoyance tests, using the E.S.P. cards. The procedure was essentially the same as that used by me in the exploratory tests for clairvoyance, except that Stuart used to shuffle the deck after each 5 cards, unless the calls were checked only after the entire 25 were called. In these exploratory tests I myself seldom did this, since few subjects tried to keep track of the cards already called off and checked, and seldom were all of a given symbol drawn. At worst, however, the probability would very occasionally be increased a little for the last 5 calls. It was, however, a point in favour of Stuart's caution. He, himself, in running did not look at the cards; he held them behind his back in his own calling. See Table V for the results up to the autumn term, 1931.

TABLE V

Pure clairvoyance, by Stuart as observer, Spring and Summer 1931

Name of subject	No. of trials	No. of hits	Dev. from np	Remarks
Scott	520	150	+46	Nearly 8 times the p.e.
Stuart	250	76	26	Unwitnessed; over 6 times p.e.
Mintier	100	26	6	
D. A.	85	29	12	
Miller	45	15	6	
Stiger	30	9	3	
Whitehead	25	7	2	
W. P.	20	2	− 2	
C. E. F.	15	3	0	
Total	1,090	317	+99 ± 8·9	$X (D/\text{p.e.}) = 11·1$

The last figure given for the combined value of the ratio of positive deviation to p.e. was 11·5. Stuart's results in Table V alone contribute a value for X of 11·1. Combining these, then, in the proper manner, we arrive at 16·1, a value that renders the alternative theory of 'random distribution' or 'chance' still more hopelessly unacceptable.

Mr Harvey L. Frick, a graduate scholar in our Department, had in May 1931 just completed his Master's thesis on the subject 'Extra-Sensory Cognition', in which he presented evidence from telepathic and clairvoyant drawing tests carried out with considerable distance between the agent and himself as percipient. He undertook, then, to do some pure clairvoyant work as well. He was interested in the decline curve suggested by the work of Richet,[1] Jephson,[2] and Estabrooks,[3] and decided to run 100 clairvoyant trials per day for a time, calling suits on playing cards, and then total the results in order of 20's in the hundred. That is, he added up the results by the various 20's for all the runs made. He totalled after 9 days and secured a very striking decline curve. There were in all 900 calls, with 180 in each of five sections into which the run of 100 was broken. Chance expectation for 180 trials in calling the suits of playing cards would be 45. The hits actually scored were 58, 50, 48, 38, 36. Subtracting 45 from the five totals of the hits in the serial 20's, we have left $+13$, $+5$, $+3$, -7, -9. The total deviation from chance for the entire 900 is not significant but the extremes of the decline are significantly separated. From $+13$ to -9 is a difference of 22. The probable error of the difference (p.e. diff. $\sqrt{\text{p.e.}^2 + \text{p.e.}^2}$) is 5.5. This gives a ratio of 4 for the difference over the p.e., which is regarded as just barely significant.

Mr Frick was urged to continue with his laborious task and he generously did. The curve, however, lost some of its smoothness and developed more irregularity. Naturally, since it must in any case be the expression of some form of mental configuration and since such configuration must be regarded as highly labile, we must not be surprised at the changes. In any case Frick's work contains an interesting suggestion. He ran a total of 3,120 trials, with a total positive deviation of 49 suits. This is only 3 times the p.e. But the internal comparisons are somewhat more significant. They can best be displayed in a table. See Table VI. Frick's

[1] Richet, Charles, 'La Suggestion Mentale et le Calcul des Probabilités', *Rev. Phil.*, 1884.

[2] Jephson, Miss Ina, 'Evidence for Clairvoyance in Card Guessing', *Proc.* S.P.R. xxxviii, pp. 223-71, 1928.

[3] Estabrooks, G. H. *A Contribution to Experimental Telepathy*, B.S.P.R. Bulletin v, 1927.

3,120 trials in clairvoyant card guessing, interesting though they are in their decline relationship, raise the ratio of positive deviation to p.e. only slightly, from 16·1 to 16·4.

In the spring of 1931 Miss Miram Weckesser, my sister-in-law, then 15 years old, found she could do clairvoyant perception, if left alone, but did not do above chance with the telepathic condition added. She was encouraged to work at it from time to time through the succeeding year and totalled 1,050 trials, yielding 266 hits, which is 56 above np; this is 6·6 times the p.e. None of these was witnessed by anyone else, but they are interesting for certain points. First, is the fact that she could only work when alone. The suggestion of the inhibiting effect of divided attention was a very good one and is brought under experimental treatment in Chapter VIII. The second point of value is that Miss Weckesser lost her ability after those 1,050 trials. She declined through the last 475 trials made from December 1931 to June 1933, averaging only 5·8 per 25. Divided into 3 parts, her results are as follows: 1st 350, average 6·4 hits per 25; 2nd 350, 6·9 per 25; 3rd 350, 5·8 per 25. At the time of decline she was offered, with a view to its effect, what was for her a substantial reward for scoring at her usual height but this had no deterrent effect upon the decline.

TABLE VI

Clairvoyant perception of playing cards, H. L. Frick, Spring 1931

Date	Total trials	Total deviation from (np) chance by order of 20's					Remarks
		1st 20's	2nd 20's	3rd 20's	4th 20's	5th 20's	
15. v. 31– 24. v. 31	900	+13 (±3·92)	+5	+ 3	− 7	−9	+13 to −9 − 22 ± 5·5 (D/p.e.) $X = 4·0$
25. v. 31– 29. v. 31	600	+12	+4	+ 7	− 3	+7	+27 ± 7·15; $X = 3·8$
Totals	1,500	+25	+9	+10	−10	−2	+32 ± 11·3; $X = 2·8$
29. v. 31– 13. x. 31	1,300	+ 1	−3	+ 9	+ 6	−3	+10 ± 10·5; $X = 1·0$
Broken runs	320	7					
Total	3,120	+33	+6	+19	− 4	−5	+49 ± 16·3; $X = 3$

Again reporting largely for completeness, we should give the details more fully of Mr A. E. Lecrone's experiment in general extra-sensory perception, not differentiating between telepathy and clairvoyance. Mr Lecrone, a student in my class during the summer of 1931, become deeply interested in my results, yet was courteously but frankly sceptical. He therefore (as one could only wish all sceptics would be spurred to do) set to work to give the question a fair test. He used the E.S.P. cards and followed the procedure of having the agent look at the card while the subject attempted to perceive it. Mr Lecrone's conditions were not perfect but they served after 1,710 trials to convince him of the reality of extra-sensory perception. The most important point in his work, however, is the fact that, assuming that telepathy was primarily involved, the function from Lecrone's mind to his friend's worked about thrice as well as when reversely directed.

TABLE VII

Lecrone's experiment, telepathy plus clairvoyance, Summer 1931

Condition	No. of trials	No. of hits	Av. per 25	Dev. and p.e.	X, or D/p.e.
L. to A. A. P.	890	216	6·0	38 ± 8·0	4·7
A. A. P. to L.	820	176	5·35	12 ± 7·7	1·6
Total	1,710	392	5·75	50 ± 11·2	4·5 (4·97 computed from $\sqrt{(4·7)^2+(1·6)^2}$)

One more large group of data belongs in this miscellaneous collection, namely, that supervised during the year 1931–2 by Mr J. G. Pratt, an assistant in the Department. Using the regular procedure already described for pure clairvoyance testing, with the E.S.P. cards in packs of 25, and with the checking done either after every 5 calls or after the whole pack of 25 was called, Mr Pratt collected data on 10,035 trials with 15 student subjects, including himself. Mr Pratt also supervised 1,975 trials with Mr Hubert Pearce, but these results will appear in the chapter devoted to Pearce's work. The other 10,035 trials were for exploratory purposes, although they went beyond the limit needed for this purpose. The total yield was 2,151, only 144 above $np.$, 5.3 times the p.e. The most interesting feature here is the fact that Pratt himself declined in his capacity for clairvoyant perception, as did Miss Weckesser. Both of these worked alone. Both, also, had strong interest in continuing and even in raising their scores. Pratt's results are partly itemized in Table VIII.

TABLE VIII

Clairvoyant perception tests, by Pratt as observer, 1931–2

Name of subject	No. of trials	No. correct	Dev. and p.e.	Value of X	Remarks
J. G. Pratt	2,885	634	$+57 \pm 14.5$	3.9	Investigator. Av. per 25 = 5.5
F. M. Pratt	1,975	403	$+ 8 \pm 12.0$	0.7	
Robertson	1,150	245	$+15 \pm 9.1$	1.6	
Sapp	950	219	$+29 \pm 8.3$	3.5	
Miscellaneous	3,075	650	$+35 \pm 15.0$	2.3	
Total	10,035	2,151	$+144 \pm 27.0$	5.3	Av. per 25 = 5.4

There are no other large 'batches' of data except those about to be reported in the chapters named for the subject producing them, with the following exceptions (this laborious explanation must be given since many will want to know if anything is omitted—especially of the lower scores); for a year and a half, now, we have followed the policy of giving a new subject a preliminary test, the results not to be taken into the record no matter what they are. When the subject gets 3 hits in 10 or better, the record can be started on the next trial following but must be so designated at the time. If, during the performance for record, the score drops below 6 in 25, it is legitimate to quit scoring for the time. These preliminary test data have been rejected. My estimate of them, from memory and my own experience, is that they were on the whole above chance average anyhow, and probably represent only a few hundred trials with those subjects who later came into good scoring. But there have been a few subjects who have 'practised' for thousands of trials without getting above the chance expectation (np). No conclusion of this report would be changed or appreciably weakened by including these practice data. For that matter, no amount of failing to score above chance by any number of other individuals can seriously affect our judgment of the results of those who succeed, since an individual ability is in question.

Also, I have lost a few small records by mislaying them. I remember them in general but cannot state them exactly. I should estimate from 300 to 500 as a liberal total for these. They were mainly data taken at odd moments with a neighbour and his wife. She ran fairly consistently above chance expectation and he ran below a great deal of the time. More I cannot recall; there are probably other lost bits, but they can in no event be of consequence here.

I have finally a number of scraps of data for record that do not fit in anywhere. Some of them are very good and some are poor. I cannot be sure, of course, that to-morrow or next year I shall not find a sheet of data stuck away absent-mindedly in a book I was reading or holding at the time. There may have been through the course of conducting or directing these 90,000 tests such lapses as these. But I am fully confident that there is no batch of forgotten and unreported data that would alter the final 'anti-chance' value (D/p.e.) by so much as half a unit. That is safe, and there we will leave it. The remnants are given in Table IX.

TABLE IX

Clairvoyant perception, odd data, 1932–3

Period	Subject	No. of trials	No. correct	Dev. from np	Remarks
Spring, '33	Burling	450	120	+30	Unwitnessed
Spring, '33	H. Johnson	300	124	+64	Witnessed. Subject's eyes closed. 10 feet away
Spring, '33	J. Ellis	200	44	+ 4	Witnessed. Regular clairvoyant conditions
1932	5-word test	70	16	+ 2	
1932–33	J. B. Rhine	235	63	+16	Unwitnessed
1932–33	L. E. Rhine	90	26	+ 8	Unwitnessed
Totals		1,345	393	124 ± 10	$X = 12.4$

Someone may be interested in the cumulative value of X for all the data (23,550 trials) reported in this chapter; it rises to 22·7, a value of indisputably great significance.

None of the data reported in this chapter is essential to any single point made in this report. On every score better results under better conditions are available. Why then, the labour and expense of publication—if, indeed, the answer is not obvious? To give the reader the opportunity to see the whole of the case, in its infancy as well as later, at its worst and most doubtful levels as well as at the most striking stages; and to reassure him that no important block of facts is omitted. Also, some of the weaknesses of these beginnings one has only to read here to avoid. They may help to guide those who will repeat these tests.

CHAPTER V

A. J. Linzmayer

M r Linzmayer was our first really striking subject, and it is perhaps only natural that we should especially appreciate him and his work. Also he has been very patient and co-operative in this work over a period of almost three years under conditions that were often very trying.

Linzmayer was an undergraduate student in Duke University when he began to work with us. He is of German-American stock, has excellent health, and is a normal, alert and intelligent young man. He is fairly sociable and makes friends easily. Although he is very dependable and even somewhat methodical, there seems to be a dash of the artistic, too, in Linzmayer, pretty much undeveloped. He seems to be, on the whole, a quite well integrated personality. He is not especially religious, and is not given to unnatural or mystical interpretations of things. But it is interesting to note that he states that his mother has had monitional experiences which made her aware in some extra-sensory manner of the death or other trouble of relatives and friends, in several instances. He himself has had no unusual parapsychological experience, except that he plays cards with marked success and has many good 'hunches'. He was only slightly hypnotizable and was somewhat negatively suggestible in his relaxed condition. His jaw set and protruded with a distinct show of resistance, and suggestions brought contrary responses. This point will be of special interest later and is mentioned for that reason.

There has been no slightest indication of dishonesty in Linzmayer. He has been scrupulously careful to avoid having any undue advantage given him. He responded properly to temptations deliberately put in his way when he was under the influence of the narcotic sodium amytal. But, although I am fully convinced now, after years of acquaintance, of his excellent character, he was under continual surveillance during all the experiments in which he took part. There was no chance given for any effective deception.

As state earlier, Linzmayer was in two of our group tests for clairvoyant perception and was the highest scorer of both groups. He was tried in the trance tests for telepathy but could not go into a deep trance. And at first in the waking condition he did not do very well (4 hits in 20 with the E.S.P. cards, which is just chance average). The next trial he was given was on May 21, 1931, and in this he gave the very high score of 21 hits in 45 trials. These were made in the waking condition, with undifferentiated telepathic and clairvoyant possibilities. In these he got nine correct calls in succession under most excellent conditions. He was not even looking at the cards in these series; his face was turned towards the window, I held each card face down, under my hand, after first looking at it. Also I visualized the figures in such conditions, without verbalization, as anyone may do with deliberate effort. The image, not its name, was in consciousness; so the 'involuntary whispering' ghost need not, I think, haunt us at this point. The chance of his getting, as he did, nine straight hits is alone so small as to be convincing; namely, one in about 2 millions. He did this three times.

Unfortunately, Linzmayer had examinations during the ten days following and could give us only three days' work before leaving the campus for a summer appointment. During these three days he ran 535 more trials for the regular purpose of evidence, which occupied most of the time, and 900 in a special experiment during the last few hours. 360 of the total 600 regular trials were still under the same conditions; *i.e.* undifferentiated E.S.P. with the observer looking at the face of the card. The other 240 trials were made as pure clairvoyance (P.C.) tests. The scoring was about the same under the two conditions, as may be seen from Table X.

Apparently the added telepathic condition did not help

Linzmayer to score. In fact, he expressed a preference for the pure clairvoyance condition. It seemed clear to me after questioning him that when I was looking at the card he was making no effort to perceive my images, but was striving merely to perceive clairvoyantly the card figure itself. The cards were held or the backs of the cards were seen, or both, by Linzmayer in 250 of the 600 trials, and these yielded 88 successes, 38 above the chance average. This is 8·8 per 25 trials and is lower than Linzmayer's average for this period. Holding and seeing the cards did not appear to help this subject; they may even have been a distraction and have caused the drop in rate.

TABLE X

Comparison, pure clairvoyance with undifferentiated E.S.P.
A. J. Linzmayer, 1931

Conditions	No. of trials	No. of hits	Dev. and p.e.	Value of X	Av. for 25
Undifferentiated E.S.P. Telepathy and Clairvoyance	360	143	$71 \pm 5 \cdot 1$	13·9	9·9
Pure Clairvoyance	240	95	$47 \pm 4 \cdot 2$	11·2	9·9
Totals	600	238	$118 \pm 6 \cdot 6$	17·9	9·9

Of the total 360 telepathy-plus-clairvoyance tests, 145 were carried on with a motor going that would effectively submerge any conceivable 'involuntary whispering'. And in 120 of these (145) the cards were screened and Linzmayer's eyes turned away. These yielded, for the 145, a score of 68 or 11·3 hits per 25, and for the 120 trials, 57, which is about the same (11·4). These are very significant scores and, under such conditions, none of the sensory modes of perception were at work. The 120 trials, just referred to above, alone yield a positive deviation of 33, which is 11·2 times the p.e. ($\pm 2 \cdot 95$). This excludes the 'mere chance' hypothesis by odds of safely over a trillion to one. (The tables available to me do not go so high and it is not necessary to quote such odds for the ratios of deviation to p.e. that exceed 10. Such a value is, in any field of science, taken for a practical certainty. In fact, we never require such high odds for acceptable significance in the general sciences.

Of the pure clairvoyant tests only 55 were made with cards screened from the subject's view, but these 55 yielded 22 correct trials, a doubling of the chance average of 11. 50 other clairvoyant trials, however, were made with perfectly new cards, in which no opportunity was given for relating the figures on the face to possible back markings or other features. These 50 give 17 correct, 7 above chance average. In the total 105 just described we may regard the conditions as not in any known way allowing for sensory perception. They yielded 18 above chance average, about 7 times the probable error, which gives odds against the hypothesis of mere accident or chance, of about 100,000 to 1. The mode of screening here used was that of simply covering the back of the card with the hand, and laying it down still covered on the table or a book. The cards then used were $2'' \times 3\frac{1}{4}''$; my hand is large enough to cover the card pretty thoroughly.

The 120 trials described in the second paragraph back, along with the 105 of the last paragraph, make 225 trials under very good conditions for the exclusion of the senses, in the perception of the card images. They yielded so unquestionably impressive a total deviation, too, that no one who comprehends the high value of $X = 13$, which was given, can accept the view that there is nothing here but happy accident.

On the occasion in which Linzmayer got his largest series of consecutive successes, 15, he also got 21 correct in the whole 25 trials. He was seated in my car with the engine going. We had been driving for the purpose of resting him. He was leaning back over the seat so that his eyes saw only the roof of the car—no mirrors, no shiny surfaces in line or at the angle necessary for him to see. I held the pack out of sight face down, shuffled it several times as we ran the series and drew the cards with my right hand over the pack, keeping the drawn card concealed as I leaned forward, tilted it a little, glanced at it and laid it on a large record book which lay across Linzmayer's knees. Linzmayer called the card about 2 seconds after I laid it down, and I said 'Right' or 'Wrong', and laid it on the appropriate pile. We counted and recorded at the end of the 15 calls, and then at the end of each 5 calls after. Ordinarily we recorded each call when made but on this occasion we continued through the first 15 in order to avoid a break in the unusual scoring; and after the break there *was* a drop. The easy informality of this situation may have made the brilliant run of 15 unbroken hits possible. But there was no lack of caution, nevertheless. The probability of getting 15 straight successes on these cards is $(1/5)^{15}$ which is one over 30 billion. And 21 in 25 is, of course, still less probable.

Now for a very different set of results: during the 600 trials just described, Linzmayer would sometimes run 5, 10 and even 15 trials without a success. He said his mental attitude had a lot to do with it. When he had no confidence in himself he would do poorly. What gave him confidence or took it away he could not say, beyond the belief that success gave him confidence and failure discouraged him. If, because of a mere mental attitude, I reasoned, we could throw him down in his scoring, that would give us an excellent check on the extra-sensory character of the perception. This is, it would be a control test on the point of possible deception, conscious or unconscious, if we used the same cards and conditions. Then too, the validity of the belief of Linzmayer that his attitude mattered was an intriguing question.

When on the afternoon of June 3, then, Linzmayer was about to leave as per arrangement—and the last results had been poor (4 hits in 20) due possibly to general fatigue or waning of interest with eagerness to be off—I urged him strongly to continue for a little longer, stating that I had just thought of a good experiment for which I needed some more data. His disinclination was obvious, since he had planned to leave with a friend the following day and had packing yet uncompleted. But his courtesy and good nature prevailed. We sat down, he a bit reluctantly and I enthusiastically, and I pushed through 500 trials of 'pure clairvoyance' tests with Linzmayer handling the cards himself, looking at their backs when he cared to. I even omitted to cut the pack between runs most of the time in order to allow every loophole for an alternative hypothesis. In the first 100 he dropped from his previous level of about 40 hits, all the way down below chance average (which is 20) to 14, a negative deviation of 6, twice the p.e. On the next 100, still below, he got 16. On the third 100 he rose to chance average exactly, but plunged down again to 17 on the 4th 100 and again down to 14 on the 5th 100.

Here was a negative deviation of 19 in 500 trials, which is more than three times the p.e., almost consistently below chance. Heretofore we had gone very slowly, taking time out when Linzmayer did not feel like going on. Since he felt he could work only in a certain mental state, we endeavoured not to endanger that by haste or disregard for his feelings. Now, on the other hand, we pushed ruthlessly on. When Linzmayer protested against the low scores and evidently felt badly about them, I urged him, none too sympathetically, to keep on and they would improve. I extracted a reluctant promise from him to work a short time the next morning and, at that time again, went at my heartless task. But Linzmayer's unhappiness over the low scoring, which he did not know was equally valuable to me, spurred him to a renewed interest and effort. The 6th 100 rose to 27. I should have stopped then until I had him down again in a more depressed condition. But his approaching departure stimulated me to go on through a 7th, 8th and 9th 100. These ran 21, 23 and 14. He then insisted that he had to leave; there was a limit to my own willingness to press him and we had to stop the interesting series at a very promising point.

The 900 trials yielded 166 hits, 16 below np. This is less than twice the p.e. and is not independently significant. In later visits I have had the opportunity, on odd occasions, to raise this 'negativism series' to 1,650 trials, with a yield of 291, a drop of 39 from the np (330). This is 3·6 times the p.e., which approximates significance. The only point I make in this low-score work is that it suggests a new feature for further investigation, one that tends to relate this mode of perception to other mental processes. One further small but striking point in these data is that, while ordinarily the first calls are highest, here they are lower than average. Selecting the first calls of the runs or series, we find that Linzmayer, in his regular work, tends to run higher in percentage of hits on the first call than on any later call. Over the regular work he averaged on 'firsts' the score of 10·4 hits per 25, while his general average for the same period (to 24. iii. 32) was 7·5. But in the low-score experiment, where the average per 25 on the whole data was 4·4 hits per 25, the first dropped to 2·1 in 25. While not perhaps finally proved, there appears pretty clearly to be some definite reversal of the function, a kind of negativistic clairvoyance. (It should here be recalled that under light hypnosis Linzmayer shows distinct negativism; in the waking state this is, however, not noticeable.)

TABLE XI

'Lowering-score' clairvoyant tests, A. J. L., 1931–2

Date	Conditions	No. of trials	No. of hits	Dev. from p.e.	Value of X
3. vi. 31	Tired, anxious to go, trip planned, reluctantly stayed overtime	500	81	−19 ± 6·0	−3·2
4. vi. 31	More determined; ashamed of low scoring	400	85	+ 5 ± 5·4	+ ·9
15. iii. 32	Danced night before till late. Sleepy, wanted to be excused	500	83	−17 ± 6·0	−2·8
22. iii. 32	Tired, opposed to working. Said he would be no good	100	14	− 6 ± 2·7	−2·2
23. iii. 32	Had lost confidence; did not care to work	150	28	− 2 ± 3·3	−0·6
Total for Lowering Score		1,650	291	−39 ± 10·96	−3·6

Mean square of other values of X gives X = 4·7

These data were of course taken under special conditions and are not to be pooled with the regular records. But even if so included, the work of Linzmayer would still stand out with a high value, as may be seen at the close of the chapter.

We have been able to get Linzmayer to visit us several times, even though he did not return to the college for study. In all, we have had four periods of experimentation with him, two in 1931, one in 1932 and one in 1933. But his extra-sensory perception ability has gone through a marked decline from the beginning. The regular experiments are summed up in Table XII. The conditions are very much the same from period to period. Note the rate of decline as shown in the 7th column, 'Average per 25'. By P.C. is meant pure clairvoyant perception, as distinct from P.T. or pure telepathy, with no object present, or Gen.E.S.P., which combines the two conditions experimentally.

TABLE XII
Decline of ability in extra-sensory perception, A. J. L.

Date	Conditions	No. of trials	No. of hits	Dev. and p.e.	Value of X	Av. per 25
4. iv. 31 to 3. vi. 31	P.C. and Gen. E.S.P.	600	238	118± 6·6	17·9	9·9
Oct. '31	P.C.	945	246	57± 8·3	6·9	6·5
Mar. '32	P.C.	960	259	67± 8·4	8·0	6·7
Mar. '33	P.C.	2,000	469	69±12·1	5·7	5·9
Totals		4,505	1,212	311 ±18·1	17·18	6·7

The total value of these 4,505 clairvoyant trials is best measured by combining the separate values of X in column 6. This gives 21·82, a relatively large value. The average per 25 is 6·7 or 1·7 above np.

The decline of Linzmayer's ability is here more long drawn out than that of Miss Weckesser or Mr Pratt. But the similarity of the declines in scoring rate is obvious.

Before dismissing the regular clairvoyant data of Linzmayer, there is one special condition in the last series (March 1933) in Table XII that deserves emphasis. In the work with Pearce we introduced the D.T. testing technique, in which a shuffled and cut pack of the cards is put before the subject and he calls off the whole 25 without anyone touching the pack or removing the cards as called (as is done in the B.T. procedure.) Until the end of the run the calls are recorded as made and are checked up at the end of the run of 25. This sweeps away all possibility of using the normal vision of the backs of the cards (except one) as a guide to calling. Linzmayer was given 1,000 trials under this condition, as well as 1,000 with the B.T. procedure. The 2,000 in Table XII are made up of these B.T. and D.T. trials. With a value of $X=4.6$ we have, even at the low rate of scoring, a significant case for clairvoyant E.S.P. But the most valuable feature is, I think, the fact that Linzmayer did better at D.T. that at B.T. We have other cases of this. It may be better not to give the senses a 'chance to get in the way.' (*Cf.* Chapter XII, on the point of abstraction.) One suggestive relation of the D.T. scores of Linzmayer is shown by the comparison of the total number of hits he got in the various layers of 5's down through the pack. He seems to succeed better in the top 5 and the bottom 5, and the worst of all in the 2nd 5 and next worst in the center. This will be chiefly interesting in comparison with other similar curves to be presented later.

But at the same time that we introduced Linzmayer to the D.T. condition, we tried him for the first time on the P.T. or pure telepathy condition. This requires the use of images by the agent, without any objective record in existence *until after the trial is over*. No cards are held or looked at, not even little pencil sketches; but the same E.S.P. symbols are for comparison used as images in the mind of the agent. The order of choice of image is deliberately varied from one run to another, with freedom to repeat or vary in any conceivable way. The 1,000 P.T. trials gave a positive deviation of 41, 4.8 times the p.e. and slightly better than the P.C. (clairvoyance) of either type. To find Linzmayer capable of both modes of E.S.P. was at this time a most interesting result. The nature of the relationship between P.C. and P.T. is an old problem in the field, still unsolved, and will become one of our most important points of attack as we go on. The data just referred to are presented in Table XIII.

TABLE XIII
Comparison of D.T., B.T., and P.T., A. J. L., 1933

	No. of trials	No. of hits	Dev. and p.e.	Value of X	Av. per 25
D.T.	1,000	239	39 ± 8.5	4.6	6.0
B.T.	1,000	230	30 ± 8.5	3.5	5.8
P.T.	1,000	241	41 ± 8.5	4.8	6.0

In March 1932, in the midst of the work for regular scoring, which averaged 6·8 in 25, I asked Linzmayer to take 6 gr. of the narcotic drug sodium amytal. (This is twice the usual dose for aiding sleep.) He willingly did so, but a half-hour later insisted it had no effect upon him. It appeared not to, and so I added another 6 gr. capsule, making in all a really large dose. He still, by exerting strong effort, resisted any marked signs of dissociation and I finally added 3 gr. more. The 15 gr. made him quite jolly, a bit incoherent in speech, frank and talkative but thick-tongued, and unable to walk fully straight. His senses still were relatively clear and perception not impaired to a degree that incapacitated him. But his E.S.P. was entirely unable to function. His clairvoyance capacity was gone. In this condition I put him through 275 trials, with a total score of 56 or 5·09 per run. Before and after this he ran at a level of 6·00 or more. The amytal appeared to destroy for the time all capacity to perceive extra-sensorially and to do so before it destroyed the perceptual capacity of the senses.

There are a number of fragments of data with Linzmayer that are not of great value, because incomplete. One of these I shall mention because of its interesting curve effect. In order to work with Linzmayer at a distance, I sent to Miss Helen Turner, Librarian at Navesink, N.J., who kindly offered to assist, 50 sealed and numbered envelopes containing E.S.P. cards. These were called by Linzmayer 6 times in an attempt at clairvoyant perception. The conditions were apparently unfavourable (the work was done in a public place—the library), as I think I can now better understand. He scored only at the level of mean chance expectation. But, like Frick's experiment, there is an internal relationship of importance in the form of a decline curve in the number of successes per sections of 10 in the daily runs of 50. The rate of scoring fell off with the order of 10's in the run. Totalling the first 10 calls in the 6 times over the 50 envelopes, we find 19 correct, where 12 is expected. The hits in totals, by order of 10's in the 50, are 19, 13, 15, 9, 4. This makes a pretty fair decline curve, suggesting that Linzmayer, as he went, got off the track to the point even of going well below chance, almost significantly below. The result, 4, for the last ten of the 50, is a deviation of $-8 \pm 2 \cdot 1$, nearly 4 times the p.e. And again, as with Frick, the extremes of the decline, with a positive deviation of 7 and a negative of 8, give a difference (15) that is significantly large (5 times) in its ratio to the p.e. of the difference, which is 3.

The other fragments of our work with this major subject I shall, for reasonable brevity, include in a group, along with the data just described, labelled briefly and of necessity incompletely as Table XIV.

TABLE XIV
Scraps from the Linzmayer workshop

Date	Observer	Trials	Hits	Dev.	Remarks
9. x. 31	With Dr Zener	144	30	+1	Cf. with initial adjustment period required for Pearce, Chapter VII
20. iii. 32	J. G. Pratt	300	68	+8	Same as above
20. iii. 32	Helen Turner	300	60	0	Conditions not favourable
7. x. 31	J. B. Rhine	175	41	+6	Attempt at reducing score by negative suggestion; not successful.
7. x. 31	J. B. Rhine	375	78	+3	Prediction tests. Record taken of L.'s prediction of general rate of scoring. Not impressive
Totals		1,294	277	$18 \pm 9 \cdot 7$	$X = 1 \cdot 86$

In order to strike a total estimate of the 'anti-chance-theory' value of the whole Linzmayer work, including the entire 8,724 trials, we compute the value of

$$X = \sqrt{(17 \cdot 9)^2 + (6 \cdot 9)^2 + (8 \cdot 0)^2 + (5 \cdot 7)^2 + (1 \cdot 9)^2 + (4 \cdot 8)^2 - (3 \cdot 6)^2},$$

from the various values from the separate experiments. The 'Low-Score' value is subtracted, merely as a concession to any who may question our grounds for regarding this low-scoring as a purposely induced negative deviation. Rather, it should be added, since it, too, shows an 'anti-chance' factor, presumably, I think the same as that which usually works positively. But it matters little either way. We arrive, then, at the imposing value of 21·9. Even if we grossly neglected distribution and diverse conditions, and lumped all together, the value of X would still be 13·2; this leaves nothing against which to complain in our principles of grouping of data. Taken either way, whether lumped off or labelled, they are still safely behind the value of 13·2 for X. This makes the odds in favour of the E.S.P. factor, and against chance, away up beyond the trillions again, and well into the zone of entire safety. Combined with the final figure for X from Chapter IV, we have, as the accumulated value against the explanation of mere 'chance' for the 32,274 trials thus far covered,

$$\sqrt{(22 \cdot 7)^2 + (21 \cdot 9)^2} = 31 \cdot 5.$$

CHAPTER VI

Charles E. Stuart

M r Stuart rose to prominence as a subject after Linzmayer, but as an investigator he antedated Linzmayer's best work. The experiments made by Stuart with
other subjects have been reported in detail already in
Chapter IV and need not be repeated. In these tests he included some trials of himself and was encouraged by these
results to go on to an extended series. It is of his own extra-
sensory perception, then, that we shall write in this chapter.

Stuart is now a graduate assistant in this Department of
Psychology and has been, through the years I have known
him, one of the ablest students within my acquaintance.
His own experiments were, I believe, very carefully conducted. He always impresses me as being very cautious and
responsible. I think no one of our Departmental staff would
have the least hesitation in taking his report of his own unwitnessed experiments in E.S.P.

Stuart is of Scottish-American stock, one of a pair of
identical twins. He has the capacity to be more positively
suggestible than Linzmayer and can go into good hypnotic
trance. He is perhaps not quite so stably integrated as Linzmayer; he is a little more imaginative, more emotional and
more expressive. He is somewhat more sociable and has a
fairly altruistic disposition. He is religious in an active but
very liberal way, and has a definite interest in art. He even
does some work in two different forms of fine arts and shows
appreciation in several.

Although Stuart has had no definite psychic experiences,
he has occasional 'intuitions' in small daily affairs that may
well be clairvoyant. His mother and aunt have had veridical psychic experiences; in his mother's case there was a

visual hallucination of a wounded relative on the battle-field, correctly coinciding in time and detail so far as knowledge went. The aunt has had veridical premonitory dreams.

Stuart was a subject of Dr Lundholm and me in the trance-telepathy series. He scored, at that time, just a little above chance average. That is the level also of his first 100 trials witnessed by me alone, or more exactly at an average of 6 hits per 25 calls (with 5 expected). The other 40 trials I have witnessed raised the average for the whole 140 trials to 6.15 hits per 25. All the rest of his work is unwitnessed but, since he does not on the whole rise beyond the level of these witnessed results and since he is the responsible man he is, I feel that we may unhesitatingly offer his work to the public as fully worthy of consideration.

Beginning in the autumn of 1931 and continuing through the school year, Stuart ran the huge sum of 7,500 trials. Marvellous patience indeed! These were not very high but, on account of the large number of trials, they take on great mathematical significance. The ratio of the positive deviation to the $p.e.$ rises to 13.5. The average per 25 for 7,500 was 6.05. Table XV will show these results in details of 500's. In his procedure Stuart held the cards behind him, cut the pack there at the start, and held each card by the corner between thumb and finger, recording each call when made and checking up after every 5 calls (and then reshuffling). (If the value of X is worked out from the separate values for sections of 500, which to a certain extent represent varying mental conditions, we get for X the increased figure of 18.14.)

The most remarkable feature of Table XV is the decline of the rate of scoring. Taken by 500's this is less gradual than with the larger groupings. With 1,500's the decline is steadier, the average per 25 being respectively 7.1, 6.1, 5.7, 5.9, 5.4, while with 2,500's the decline is abrupt. The last 150 trials were slightly below chance and, after discussing it with me, Stuart discontinued for a time. We were interested in preserving his full capacity. He agreed with me that his interest had somewhat declined.

TABLE XV

First series, pure clairvoyant perception, by Stuart, 1931–2

Serial No.	Trials	Hits	Dev. and p.e.	X	Dev. per 1,500	Value of X	Av. per 25	Dev. per 2,500 p.e.	X	Av. per 25
1	500	180	+80 ±6	13·3 }						
2	500	132	+32	5·3 }	+128 ±10·4	12·3	7·1 }			
3	500	116	+16	2·7 }				+180 ±13·5	13·3	6·80
4	500	139	+39	6·5 }						
5	500	113	+13	2·2 }	+67	6·4	6·1 }			
6	500	115	+15	2·5 }						
7	500	119	+19	3·2 }						
8	500	124	+24	4·0 }	+42	4·0	5·7 }	+70 ±13·5	5·2	5·70
9	500	99	− 1	−·2 }						
10	500	113	+13	2·2 }						
11	500	119	+19	3·1 }	+55	5·2	5·9 }			
12	500	123	+23	3·8 }						
13	500	105	+ 5	0·8 }				+65 ±13·5	4·8	5·65
14	500	102	+ 2	0·3 }	+23	2·2	5·4 }			
15	500	116	+16	2·7 }						
Total	7,500	1,815	+315 ±23·4					X value 13·5		

During the summer of 1932 I wrote Stuart, asking him to try some more E.S.P. work with the cards. His rate of scoring was found to be quite good again, averaging 6·8 in 25 for 250 trials. He continued for the summer, until 2,100 trials were made. These were about on the same scoring level, averaging 6·8 per 25 trials. They alone have a value of 12·5 for the ratio of deviation to p.e.

But again the decline set in as before and, at the end of the 2,100, Stuart's scoring had fallen down almost to chance average. This effect can be shown best in the following table, XVI, in which the data are grouped in 400's in order to spread the decline effect out over more points. The falling off of the rate of scoring is apparently in the last 1,000 trials; the first 1,000 keep at a fair level. This second decline is much more abrupt than the first, but the better scoring period is longer (in point of number of trials) and more consistent scoring characterizes it.

TABLE XVI

Second series, clairvoyant perception, Stuart, Summer 1932

Serial No.	Trials by 400's	Hits	Dev. and p.e.	Value of X	Av. per 25	Dates, 1932
1	400	117	$+37 \pm 5 \cdot 4$	6·9	7·3 }	2. vi.–14. vii.
2	400	117	37	6·9	7·3 }	
3	400	116	36	6·7	7·2 }	15. vii.–21. vii.
4	400	110	30	5·6	6·9 }	
5	400	96	16	3·0	6·0 }	21. vii.–28. vii.
7	(100)	19	$- 1 \pm 2 \cdot 7$	·4	4·8 }	
Total	2,100	575	$+155 \pm 12 \cdot 4$	12·5	6·8	

Stuart introduced an interesting technique into the tests reported in Table XVI. He began on July 21 to make 2 calls for each card, one for 'correct' and another that he thought was 'incorrect'. The two records were appropriately labelled and kept distinct. Pearce had been asked to do a short series of runs with the deliberate purpose of getting as many calls as possible incorrect. But he was afraid to complicate the procedure by making both 'correct' and 'incorrect' calls on one card. Stuart found no difficulty, and, his positive deviation on the high scoring and negative deviation on the voluntary low scoring are about equal. They likewise decline together at about the same rate. Comparison of the two is made in Table XVII A with the data grouped in 400's for the purpose of comparing the decline. The columns showing the percentage of deviation from the np value (chance expectation) bring the close similarity to a focus. Note also the closeness of the various values for the total in the 5th line.

Another interesting accomplishment of Stuart was his huge day's work of July 21. He called 700 for high record and 600 for low. This is perhaps not equal to 1,300 scores for high record but it is a huge day's work beyond doubt — the longest on our records; Zirkle is second with 950, and Pearce comes third with 900, for straight record. No one seems to have suffered, or have become fatigued especially. In all cases the scoring was up to par, even to the last. This evidence is directly contrary to the 'fatigue theory' as proposed by Miss Jephson.[1]

TABLE XVII A

Comparison of low-score and high-score calls on same cards, Stuart, Summer 1932

	Low-Score Calls by 400's				Serial No.	High-Score Calls by 400's				
Trials	Hits	Dev. and p.e.	Dev. per 25	% of Dev. from np		% of Dev. from np	Dev. per 25	Dev. and p.e.	Hits	Trials
400	52	−28±5·4	−1·8	−35	1	+45	+2·3	+36±5·4	116	400
400	52	−28±5·4	−1·8	−35	2	+38	+1·9	+30±5·4	110	400
400	61	−19±5·4	−1·2	−24	3	+20	+1·0	+16±5·4	96	400
(100)	17	− 3±2·7	− ·8	−15	4	− 5	−0·3	− 1±2·7	19	100
-3,00	182	−78±9·7	−1·50	−30	Totals	31	+1·56	+81±9·7	341	1,300
	(X=8·0)							(X=8·4)		

At present the most interesting phase of Stuart's work is his development of P.T. scoring, *i.e.* pure telepathy. He has only relatively lately got started at it and he does it with just about the same level of ability as he now shows on the P.C. work. On the 500 trials of P.T. he averaged 5·8 hits per 25. His regular B.T. trials, the 950 made since the work of Table XVIIA, gave only 5·7 hits per 25. This is quite naturally a most interesting comparison to follow up.

Stuart has tried D.T. clairvoyance but has not done it very successfully in all his 2,100 trials; but, in all of his work he has been scoring lower than formerly for nearly a year. In the 2,100 trials the average is only 5·3 per 25; and is not 'significant' as yet—it is less than twice the p.e. But it shows the same type of curve which we found in Linzmayer's D.T. data, and have also found in the distribution of D.T. scoring by others; *i.e.* a curve showing greater frequency of successes near the top and the bottom of the pack.

His totals of all the hits made in the 1,000 trials of D.T. test data examined, obtained by superimposing the results by 5's and totalling, then, for each ordinal in the 5, yield the following: 46, 37, 37, 31, 51. These 1,000 trials are not

[1] Jephson, Miss Ina, 'Evidence for Clairvoyance in Card Guessing', *Proc.* S.P.R. XXXVIII, pp. 223–71, 1928.

selected; they happened to be at hand and convenient. They show in total yield very little deviation from chance, only 2 above, but are interesting for this internal peculiarity, the distribution that produces the difference of 20 points between the 4th and 5th sections. This suggests a factor of internal motivation of the percipient.

TABLE XVII B

Summary of E.S.P. results by Stuart, himself as subject, 1931–2

Date	Condition	No. of trials	No. of hits	Dev. and p.e.	Dev./p.e. or X	Av. per 25	Remarks
Spring, '31	B.T.	250	76	+ 26 ± 4·3	6·2	7·6	
1931–32	B.T.	7,500	1,815	+315 ± 23·4	13·5	6·1	
Summer, '32	B.T.	2,100	575	+155 ± 12·4	12·5	6·8	
Summer, '32	'Wrong'	1,300	182	− 78 ± 9·7	8·0	3·5	Purposely 'wrong'
1932–33	D.T.	2,100	440	+ 20 ± 12·4	1·6	5·3	
1932–33	P.T.	500	115	+ 15 ± 6·0	2·5	5·8	
1932–33	B.T.	950	216	+ 26 ± 8·2	3·2	5·7	
Totals		14,700			21·16		

Total value of X or D/p.e. $\sqrt{ = (6\cdot2)^2 + (13\cdot5)^2 + (12\cdot5)^2 + (8\cdot0)^2 + (1\cdot6)^2 + (2\cdot5)^2 + (3\cdot2)^2} = 21\cdot16$

We have reported now a total of 17,400 trials made by Stuart, which represent great labour on his part and which also make a valuable contribution to the subject. They alone give a value of 21·16. This is in itself much in excess of the requirement for the thorough exclusion of the 'chance' theory for these results. Stuart's results alone, then, would be an adequate basis for the dropping of the hypothesis of accidental or random distribution. They are summarized in Table XVII B.

The cumulative value of the 'anti-chance' index (X) for the 46,974 trials reported thus far is now equal to

$$\sqrt{(31\cdot5)^2 + (21\cdot2)^2} = 38\cdot1,$$

with the heaviest scorers and half the scores still to come.

CHAPTER VII

Hubert E. Pearce, Jr.

Of all the eight 'major subjects' Mr Pearce has done the greatest amount of work and has been put through the greatest variety of conditions. He has been relatively very stable in his scoring in spite of these conditions, and has been very co-operative throughout. In fact, he has sportingly entered into new ventures and conditions whenever they have'been proposed.

Pearce is a young Methodist ministerial student in the Duke School of Religion, very much devoted to his work, though fairly liberal in his theology. He is very sociable and approachable, and is much interested in people. There is also a pretty general artistic trend to his personality, expressing itself mainly in musical interest and production, but extending into other fields of art as well.

Pearce has not, himself, had any striking parapsychological experiences other than numerous 'hunches' and 'intuitions', but he reports that his mother and others of her family have had certain clairvoyant experiences. It was on learning from him of these experiences of his family that I asked him to try our clairvoyance tests with my assistant, Mr. Pratt.

All of Pearce's work has been carefully witnessed; but I wish to state in addition that I have fullest confidence in his honesty, although in this work the question of honesty arises in my mind with everyone, preacher or no.

In the beginning of his clairvoyant work, in the first 50 trials, Pearce got only chance average and rose very little above on the first 100 trials. But he kept on rising until very soon he had reached a level of 9 correct per 25 trials and has held close to this average ever since—now over a year, and well over 15,000 trials—except in experimental situations definitely produced to work against E.S.P. capacity and a few other occasions (illness, etc.). Even including special experiments in which he was handicapped and including his one short ill period, his totals up to April 1, 1933, were 11,250 trials with an average of 8·9 hits per 25. Such results as this are positively breath-taking, when one calculates their mathematical significance. These alone sky-rocket the value of X up above 60, with odds against chance now enormous beyond our capacity to appreciate.

During the late spring of 1932 Pearce ran 2,250 calls under pure clairvoyance conditions and with the remarkable average per 25 of 9·7, almost double the chance average. Some of these (275) were witnessed by me alone, several hundred by both Pratt and myself, and the rest by Pratt alone. The working conditions were these: observer and subject sat opposite each other at a table, on which lay about a dozen packs of the E.S.P. cards and a record book. One of the packs would be handed to Pearce and he be allowed to shuffle it. (He felt it gave more real 'contact'.) Then it was laid down and was cut by the observer. Following this Pearce would, as a rule, pick up the pack, lift off the top card, keeping both the pack and the removed card face down, and, after calling it, he would lay the card on the table, still face down. The observer would record the call. Either after 5 calls or after 25—and we used both conditions about equally—the called cards would be turned over and checked off against the calls recorded in the book. The observer saw each card and checked each one personally, though the subject was asked to help in the checking by laying off the cards as checked. There is no legerdemain by which an alert observer can be repeatedly deceived at this simple task in his own laboratory.[1] (And, of course, we are not dealing even with amateur magicians.) For the next run another pack of cards would be taken up.

[1] 'Wallace the Magician' (Wallace Lee) was asked to work under these conditions, after watching Pearce work. He did not score above mean chance expectation, and frankly admitted that he did not see how Pearce did.

Further reassuring features on the point of deception are: first, when Pearce got to running well, he seldom looked at the backs of the cards; later we asked him, as a rule, not to do so. On the whole, results under this condition are as good as before. We later added the request to call the top card before lifting it off the pack. And this, too, was successful after a period of adjustment. Then we brought in new cards many times, without there resulting any change in the level of scoring. We had Pearce follow the procedure of working with the cards held behind a screen and this, too, succeeded after the low period at first, that accompanies nearly every innovation. And, finally, he did very well under the remarkable D.T. condition, in which the pack is left unbroken on the table while the subject makes the 25 calls in succession for the cards before him. Most of the time in working at D.T. Pearce closes his eyes and takes a posture of strong concentration; it seems as if this were a more arduous task for clairvoyance than the ordinary conditions.

On all the points mentioned in the last paragraph above the evidence is amply significant, as may be seen in the following table (XVIII) summarizing the data just referred to. It is a table packed, I believe, with tremendous meaning, the most evidential of the entire series.

It does not seem possible that any reasonable and honest doubt can exist in the mind of the reader who accepts this table as reliably presented (and if it is clear to him) that there is amply demonstrated in these tests an extra-sensory mode of perception, of the type popularly known as clair-voyance. It did not, therefore, seem profitable to spend more time and effort in the mere pursuit of evidence for the existence of E.S.P. What more, indeed, can be asked for simple proof's sake? With a value of X, the anti-chance index, of 61·5, such that the door is 'slammed' on the chance theory; and with the D.T. data, the screen data, and the new-card data together removing the weakened remains of the 'sensory-cues' theory from the realm of rational possi-bility, what alternative to E.S.P. is there left, except to suppose that we are *all* (a dozen or more are involved) playing a deeply complex game of deception, or else are thoroughly irresponsible and unreliable?[1]

TABLE XVIII

Clairvoyant perception, conditions guarding against sense perception

Serial No. and conditions	No. of trials	No. of hits	Dev. and p.e.	Value of X	Av. per 25	Remarks
1. General B.T. as described above	5,000	1,834	+834 ± 19·1	43·7	9·2	
Special Conditions						
2. S. looks away from cards	650	279	149 ± 6·9	21·6	10·7	Not much change in conditions, but 1st runs low
3. Same as 2, plus calling before removing	475	236	141 ± 5·9	23·9	12·4	Little real change; 1st low
4. Same as 3; no contact with cards	275	74	19 ± 4·5	4·2	6·7	Great change; first 4 ran below chance. Last 4 average 8·5
5. Same as 3, plus *new cards*; data on first 3 times used	1,675	626	291 ± 11·0	26·5	9·3	1st use runs as high as 3rd use of cards
6. (*a*) Screen, concealing cards (B.T.)	300	99	39 ± 4·7	8·3	8·3	
(*b*) Same, plus P.T. (*i.e.* gen. E.S.P.; Agent screened)	300	116	56 ± 4·7	11·9	9·7	Began very low
7. D.T., pack left unbroken till end of run	1,625	482	157 ± 10·9	14·4	7·4	
Totals, P.C. (except 6 (*b*))	10,300	3,746	+1,686 ± 27·4	61·5	9·1	

On the point of reliable witnessing and judgment, then, there is a set of data on observations that were witnessed by other mature and responsible persons, some of them professional men. Each one witnessed, along with me, the production of the data set opposite his name in Table XIX and in no case raised any question as to the genuineness of the effectual exclusion of sensory perception of the card symbols. The data of columns B and C were doubly witnessed in their entirety, the visiting observer seeing as much as he cared to and taking any part or position desired. The magician, Mr. Wallace Lee, tried a few series himself with only chance average results. He said frankly that he was

[1] The striking data obtained lately with Pearce at some distance from the cards (100 yards, for example) may be taken as perhaps a further step.

Hubert Pearce (left) calling down through a pack of twenty-five E.S.P. cards (five sets shuffled), before taking a card off. The author recording his calls.

Pure clairvoyance. Mr Pratt handled (did not look at) cards at B, afterwards at A. Mr Pearce got his surprising results at C. Both made independent sealed reports to the author.

convinced. It appeared that he was, at least as far as we all are, 'mystified'. Pearce was somewhat ill with tonsilitis on the day the magician was present, hence (as I think) his low scoring, even for the period before the entrance of the visitor. Note the high value of X for these results, 23·5. With these doubly witnessed results, we will dismiss for this chapter the question of proof and move on to the special experiments made for the purpose of throwing light on the nature of the process.

The data in Table XIX were originally collected for the purpose of measuring the extent of the inhibitory effect of visitors upon the clairvoyant function. We had noticed earlier that when someone dropped in to watch Pearce work the scores at once dropped down. We began to take down the evidence, sometimes inviting a visitor for the purpose, sometimes availing ourselves of a casual caller. We recorded the time of entrance and exit of 7 visitors, one being present twice. They all produced a drop in Pearce's scoring. The results taken before the entrance will be stated in Column A and then in Column B will be given results taken from the point of entrance, continuing until there is an upward turning of the score curve that remains above mean-chance expectation for at least 2 runs, with the remainder of the series averaging above chance. The curves are all sharp enough to make decision easy. Column C, then, contains the scores made after the up-turn of the curve described as the stopping point for B, which means after Pearce had become adjusted to the visitor's presence. The number of runs in B is evidently indicative of the difficulty experienced in adjusting to the visitor's presence. Notice it is larger (11 runs, 275 trials) for the magician, whose vocation Pearce knew, than for Miss E. C. (1 run), a young lady, or for Dr McDougall (2, 5), who he knew was sympathetically interested in the results. In consulting Table XIX for this point compare especially the 3rd column under the headings A, B, and C, giving the average hits per 25 trials as a basis for comparison.

We have in A and C about the same scoring level, showing eventually complete adjustment to the new situation. This would seem to mean that visitors are not inhibitory except in the strain excited in the subjects. Naturally, subjects would differ in degree of this, as visitors would differ in their effect. We have here an average drop of 4·1 in 25, a very significant figure with the large number of trials given.

TABLE XIX

Showing effect of visitors on Pearce's clairvoyant perception[1]

Date 1932	Visitor	Before Entrance			Visiting Witness Present					
		Control Period A			Lapse Period B			Recovery Period C		
		Trials	Hits	Av. per 25	Trials	Hits	Av. per 25	Trials	Hits	Av. per 25
16. ix.	Dr K. E. Zener	50	23	11·5	75	15	5·0	225	89	9·9
13. x.	Dr J. F. Thomas	100	41	10·3	125	26	5·2	50	30	15·0
20. x.	Dr Wm. McDougall	75	34	11·3	50	13	6·5	75	28	9·3
9. xi.	Dr H. Lundholm	100	39	9·8	50	10	5·0	75	29	9·7
10. xii.	Miss Edna Cousins	100	43	10·8	25	7	7·0	100	44	11·0
1933 2. ii.	Dr Wm. McDougall	350	132	9·4	125	33	6·6	250	105	10·5
16. ii.	Miss June Bailey	—	—	—	100	24	6·0	75	33	11·0
23. ii.	Wallace Lee, the Magician	150	45	7·5	275	55	5·0	125	37	7·4
Totals		925	357	9·6	825	183	5·5	975	395	10·1
		$X = 21·0$			$X = 2·4$			$X = 23·8$		

Following along on the theme of disturbing factors, we may properly take up next the illness effect shown in the results opposite the name of the visitor, Wallace the Magician.

Pearce had not done well even before Wallace came in. The difference between the average of 7·5 and 7·4 and those

---

[1] Another major subject offers an exception to the rule evidenced in this table. Miss Turner, whose work will be given in Chapter VIII, once went to Dr E., one of her genial but sceptical psychology teachers on the campus, and offered to demonstrate E.S.P. to him. She ran 100 trials with Dr E. holding the cards behind a notebook and got scores of 8, 11, 7, 7, which gives a deviation of 13 or 5 times the p.e. Dr E. gave me an independent confirmation of the demonstration. This is exceptional, and is due, I think, to the fact that she proposed the venture herself and that she did not stand in awe of Dr E.

of 10·5 and 11 on days preceding is a significant one for the number of trials made. This was the only illness the records show for the time we have worked with Pearce, but the result is in harmony with the results of other subjects. So it seems plausible to agree with Pearce's own judgment and connect the illness as a causal factor in the production of 375 results with a drop from 10·5 per 25 to 7·5, which is an average of 3 per 25. On 375 this would be a drop of 45, which is over 6 times the p.e. diff. (7·4).

Another factor that upsets Pearce's scoring, as a rule, is any change that he does not easily and spontaneously accept as likely to work. A few changes he has taken without a considerable drop, those apparently in which he has taken part in the planning and in which he felt sure of success. Among these were the use of very small figures on the cards (about 2 mm. high) which he suggested, the D.T. procedure which he partly originated himself and the calling for low scoring, voluntarily proposed half playfully. These all succeeded at once. But most changes meet with a drop to chance scores. To illustrate this point, I have collected the

TABLE XX

Showing effect of changes of techniques on P.C., Pearce

Nature of change	A Transition to new technique			B Same technique after transition			
	Trials	Hits	Av. per 25	Trials	Hits	Av. per 25	
1. Possible Telepathy added to regular B.T. condition; Observer looked at card figure	175	42	6·0	175	95	13·6	
2. Introduction of P.T.	175	38	5·4	175	58	8·3	
3. B.T. subject not seeing backs of cards, and calling before removing	50	12	6·0	50	19	9·5	
4. B.T. no handling of cards by the subject	100	19	4·8	(100	28	7·0	
				100	34	8·5)	next 100
5. B.T., Screen, 11 in. high, concealing cards.	25	6	6·0	25	13	13·0	
6. B.T., Screen, 24 in. high, concealing cards	50	9	4·5	50	18	9·0	
7. Screen, 15 in. high. Subject ignorant whether or not observer looks at card.	125	30	6·0	125	51	10·2	
Totals	700	156	5·6	700	282	10·1	$X = 19·9$

data on the introduction of a number of new techniques, with the results taken during and after the transition, grouping them into Columns A and B. For a fair comparison, I have taken equal numbers of runs made next after the transition to that made during it. Compare especially the 3rd column under A and B.

Compared to the high recovery level of 10·1 in 25 Pearce is shown here to have dropped almost to chance, 5·6 per 25. This drop in average score of 4·6 in 25 leaves no doubt that the introduction of new procedures may be a quite disturbing thing to the E.S.P. function in Pearce. There is some evidence that this may not be as much the case with some subjects, but, again, may be still worse with some others.

Still following the matter of disturbing factors, we come to another line of influence on E.S.P., this time a more physiological one. I refer to the work done with sodium amytal on Pearce, simply repeating the amytal experiment carried out earlier with Linzmayer. Pearce was asked to take 6 gr. of the drug (he is light in weight), and a half-hour later was tested on the cards in the usual way and found almost to have lost his ability, as had Linzmayer. He had averaged 14·5 hits per 25 in 50 trials just preceding the taking of the drug. Now that the effects of drowsiness were showing, when he was tested he got only 5, 4, 3 in succession. He had become careless, fumbled the cards, spoke dully and mostly kept his eyes closed. It may be interesting to follow the variations of the data in Table XXI.

This phenomenal fall from his usual average per 25 of about 10 down to 6·1 is even more striking than Linzmayer's drop from 6·8 to 5 and confirms the earlier result. In both cases we ran enough trials to recover from the possible novelty or new technique effect. One feature that is rather well brought out as an incidental observation is the factor of effort. No one could have failed to see the coincidence of intense effort at attention to the task, with better scoring, in this series of runs with the amytal.

This interesting experiment invites quite naturally a comparable one with a drug having the opposite effect—

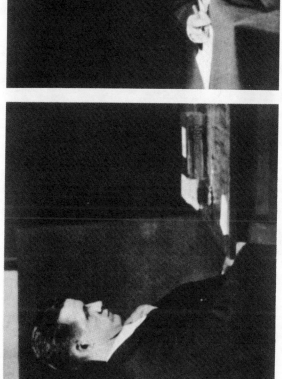
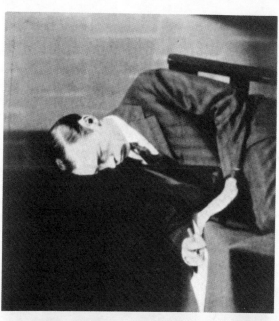

Mr J. G. Pratt (left), as he handled the cards in long-distance B.T. clairvoyance with Mr Hubert Pearce (right) as percipient (E.S.P.). Distance, 100 yards and 250 yards. The card, kept face down, lying on the book, is the one 'exposed' at the moment.

that of integration. We used caffeine for this purpose in 1-grain tablets of citrated caffeine. The effect of caffeine was tried on Pearce on five occasions, using 5-grain doses. The general aim was to give it when Pearce had been running low (hence the low pre-caffeine score quoted), since it has been caffeine's 'defatiguing' effect that is most recognized. Under those conditions it raised his scoring very considerably. We may compare the records of work just preceding the drug taking with those following for the experimental period. The data are fragmentary, due to the cutting-in of other experiments which were usually brought in as soon as the scoring level rose again. The results are summarized in Table XXII.

TABLE XXI

Effect of sodium amytal on clairvoyant perception, Pearce

	Trials	Hits	Remarks
1	25	5	
2	25	4	Very drowsy; sat listless, eyes closed
3	25	3	
4	25	10	Realized lowness of score; seemed ashamed. Tried to pull himself together
5	25	5	
6	25	6	Washed his face to help waken up
7	25	8	Tried hard to reintegrate
8	25	5	Fell into lethargy again; no response to jokes
9	25	5	Fully serious
10	25	8	Rather boastfully offered to 'Run the Pack' (D.T.) and worked
11	25	10	hard at it. Seemed to pull him up
12	25	5	Wanted badly to stop. Very sleepy
13	25	5	
	325	79	$(+14\pm4.9)$ (Av. per 25 = 6·1)

TABLE XXII

Effect of caffeine on clairvoyant perception, Pearce

Date	Conditions	Before drug			After drug			Rise in % of np
		Trials	Hits	Av. per 25	Trials	Hits	Av. per 25	
8. ix.	B.T.	125	42	8·4	175	75	10·7	46 %
10. ix.	D.T.	125	36	7·2	75	26	8·7	30 %
13. ix.	D.T.	50	8	4·0	150	42	7·0	60 %
13. ix.	B.T.	25	11	11·0	75	38	12·7	34 %
26. ix.	B.T.	50	15	7·5	175	76	10·9	68 %
30. x.	B.T.	75	18	6·0	100	43	10·8	96 %
Totals		450	130	7·2	750	300	10·0	56 %

From these data it is evident that we have got a rise following the drug ingestion from 7·2 to 10·0 hits per 25. Now, this latter figure is just about Pearce's normal rate. What we have done, then, is to pull him back up to his usual running score, taking him at a time when he is scoring low to begin with. It will take more experimentation to ascertain if he can be raised above his own past level significantly by the use of caffeine. There is, however, not the reason to expect this that we had for the results just stated. (For the important condition of the subject being unaware of the nature of the drug and of its effect, see in Chapter VIII, the experiment carried out with Mr Zirkle).

It was of interest to test the process of E.S.P. for fatigue in itself, especially since in certain long series there is always a question concerning the possibility of fatigue coming in as an unknown and uncontrolled element. We had Pearce go through about 8 hours of steady E.S.P. work and in that time he made 900 trials. They show, however, no significant signs of decline and he showed at the end no unusual signs of fatigue in general. Of course, it was confining and tiresome, as any such work must be, but nothing more. We did a mixture of experiments, contributing data to a number of minor lines of inquiry. This variation was superficial, however, since it was all genuine E.S.P. of the P.C. condition. His average for the 900 trials was 10·1. It was only slightly (1·4 in 25) lower in the afternoon than in the forenoon; this difference is not significant for that number of trials.

I have mentioned earlier the purposively low-scoring tests carried out by Pearce. He showed that he could alternate high and low scores on request, actually giving on one occasion 9 in 25 when asked for a high-score run, followed by 1 in 25 for low; then a request for high brought 10, and one for low another 1 in 25. He has, on the one hand, *called 0 in 25* by calling 'wrong' purposely, and, on the other, once called *25 correct in 25* in my presence when I playfully dared him, bet with him and thereby aroused special effort with him over each card. (I, myself, held the cards.) Of the low-scoring record there are 275 trials, yielding only 20 hits, 35 below chance average. This is in itself a valuable bit of evidence of the purposive principle of E.S.P. at work, since X for this negative deviation equals 7.8.

So far we have said little about Pearce and telepathy. He took rather slowly to it, as the data in Table XX have shown. But eventually he emerged from the transition level of scoring and began to do fairly good P.T. work. We undertook first to introduce a telepathy test into the P.C. experiments for comparison of P.C. with the combined or general E.S.P. test. While at first Pearce dropped off considerably if I looked at the card, he came eventually to do even somewhat better than when I did not look at it. Omitting, then, the first 175 transition trials which gave an average per 25 of only 6 and which belong under 'New Technique Data', we have 350 trials of the combined conditions (allowing both telepathy and clairvoyance), giving an average of 14 hits per 25. This is an extraordinarily high average for Pearce or anyone else, and is significantly elevated above Pearce's usual level of about 10 in 25. It may well be the effect of the combined extra-sensory activation from the two sources (the card and the agent), or, of course, may result from the possibly greater attention stimulated in the percipient by the combined possibilities. Or, again, it might have been the effect of suggestion arising out of the expectation that such results would occur. At any rate, a refinement of test procedures was necessary.

To get at the question, then, of whether or not the telepathic condition really aided the clairvoyant, we tried having the agent work behind a screen so that Pearce, the percipient, would not know when the agent looked at the card and when we had the simple P.C. conditions alone. Here again we had transition troubles but they were, of course, equal for both conditions, P.C. and general E.S.P. From a total of 600 trials made behind a screen which concealed the agent's face and the cards from Pearce, we still got quite better results for the combined telepathic and clairvoyant conditions. See Table XVIII, 6, (a) and (b).

The 300 P.C. were so interwoven with the 300 general E.S.P. that Pearce could not have inferred any order in them. Usually I changed conditions after every 5 calls. The difference is considerable, yet it is not quite up to the requirement for significance, with this number of trials. The difference is only 2.6 times the p.e. of the difference; but, supported as it is by the greater difference found without the screen, it would at least suggest that the telepathic condition may help clairvoyant perception to higher proficiency.

On P.T. itself Pearce showed a steady rise for a time. His first 250 P.T. trials averaged only 6.4 per 25. The next 250 rose to 7.3, and the third to 7.8. His first 950 gave an average per 25 of 7.1 and a value of X of 9.6. We can now say without any question, so far as the mathematical significance of the data is concerned, that he, too, possesses both P.T. and P.C. capacity.

In the 950 P.T. trials referred to above, the agent and percipient were in the same room. The percipient sat with closed eyes, waiting for the uniform tap of a telegraph key as a signal. At the time of the signal the agent would be holding in consciousness the image of one of the symbols of the E.S.P. cards, but actually had no cards present. The choice of order of images was planned by the agent for each 5 trials, avoiding any naturally expected order, and varying, repeating, in a mentally determined 'random' fashion from one five to another.

Four agents served with Pearce. With Stuart he averaged 7; with myself as agent, 7.3 (omitting the transition period); but with two charming young ladies he averaged 8.7!

And now for what is at the moment one of the most fascinating points of the Pearce study. In the work to be described he too produced P.T. scoring at approximately the same rate as the P.C. done at the same time and with the same conditions. The time and circumstances are most important, and we need to have the control data from the same situation and time period as the primary data. And from our results it is now clear that when we compare P.C. and P.T. with Pearce under the same conditions, we get, as with most other subjects, about the same rate of scoring in the two phases of E.S.P., P.C. (B.T.) and P.T. There are two sets of data to offer in this connection, the first from the P.T. data already presented, merely omitting the transitional data of the first 175 trials as not properly comparable. These P.T. trials are quite similar in score value to the B.T. data taken during the same experimental periods. In the one case there is an average of 7·7 hits per 25; in the other, 8·1. The second set of data come from an experiment to be described below, made by Stuart and Pearce in the summer of 1933 on the comparative effect of distance upon P.C. and P.T. The results under distance conditions were but little above chance expectation for even the relatively short distances introduced and in these tests they show mainly the fact that they both dropped together (B.T. to 5·3 and P.T. to 5·7). See Table XXIV. The scores made across the table are also quite comparable, averaging in the one case 6·4 and in the other 6·3. The details are shown in Table XXIII. It should be said in explanation that, in giving the detailed results in the table, the point is to show the fluctuations from day to day, since these run predominantly in the same direction for both the P.C. and P.T. columns.

TABLE XXIII
Comparison of clairvoyant and telepathic perception, Pearce

Dates	Clairvoyance			Telepathy			Agent
	Trials	Hits	Av. per 25	Trials	Hits	Av. per 25	
1. 3. xii.	100	49	12·3	100	33	8·3	J. B. Rhine
2. 10. xii.	125	51	10·2	150	46	7·7	Miss E. C.
3. 10. xii.	75	28	9·3	100	27	6·8	J. B. Rhine
4. 13. i.	50	13	6·5	(25	14	14·0)	Miss J. B.
5. 2. ii.	100	24	6·0	75	19	6·3	Miss J. B.
6. 16. ii.	100	35	8·8	75	25	8·3	J. B. Rhine
7. 6. iii.	150	42	7·0	100	28	7·0	C. E. Stuart
8. 6. iii.	125	26	5·2	125	39	7·8	C. E. Stuart
Totals	825	268	8·1	750	231	7·7	
9. June, '33	950	239	6·3	475	121	6·4	C. E. Stuart
Grand total	1,775	507	7·1	1,225	352	7·2	(107 ± 9·4; $X = 11·4$)

Nothing could be at this state more interesting than to see so large a group of data turn out such similar score averages for the two different conditions of experimentation, 'mind-to-mind' and 'card-to-mind' transference. The fact that Pearce has on the whole scored much higher in clairvoyant work does not bear on this point here. Perhaps, under different conditions, he might also score higher on P.T. The data for the two phases cover the same general conditions and the same periods. There is, too, the general similarity between P.T. and P.C. in the direction of fluctuation from day to day. If we leave out the 4th and 8th lines, all the rest of the 9 show a rise or fall of both clairvoyance and telepathy together, both taking the same direction. In the 4th line, at least, we have a peculiar atypical instance, with only 1 run to deal with under P.T., and with the 8th line we just have an exception.

It is true, this latest experiment, conducted by Stuart, did not yield the usual rate of Pearce's scoring. Pearce's scoring was at the lowest average it has ever been. There is no reason to think there was anything in the combination with Stuart that inhibited him. Pearce, himself, thinks it is because he had been somewhat exhausted by the year's school work and was not in his usual state of vigour. The purpose of the series was to test the relative effect of distances upon the three main modes of testing in use, P.T., B.T. and D.T. It is probable, I think, that the elaborate conditions and plans laid down (three conditions multiplied by the three distances make a somewhat complex design in this work) were inhibiting, as new techniques usually are with Pearce. The distances were to be short at first and they did not get beyond these short distances. The results are presented in the three conditions at three distances; the three columns represented the distances: A, close range, *i.e.* across the table; B, 8 to 12 feet away from the agent or the card; and C, 20 to 30 feet away. In all there were 5,400 trials made under the three conditions, with all three distances. During the experiments an electric fan was kept going and any 'unconscious whispering' sounds during P.T. work must have been effectively drowned by its noise. The telegraph key was used for giving signals from agent to percipient. The results, I think, do not warrant any greater detail in presentation. Later work has already 'outshone' them considerably. Probably only one point further is of sufficient interest to mention, and it is not at all adequately substantiated. It will be seen that the D.T. results under A are the highest. Yet this D.T. work scores lowest with distance, as shown in columns B and C. It simply raises the question whether the precision required to read the cards packed closely together can be achieved at a distance even of 10 feet or whether this is an effect of the mental attitude of the subject, an 'expectation effect'; *i.e.* he cannot because he thinks he cannot.

It was pointed out above that in the P.T. and B.T. work of the Pearce-Stuart series, the results obtained with the percipient in the same room with the agent or the cards were remarkably similar. Now, at the distances used, 8-12 feet and 28-30 feet, both D.T. and B.T. together do not show enough positive deviation to reach mathematical significance $(1,525:322:17 \pm 10.5; X = 1.6)$. Whereas the P.T., which in the same room yielded less than the D.T. and about the same as the B.T., yielded at the shorter distances (8-12 feet) a positive deviation over 5 times the p.e. and the whole distance-P.T. data have a value of X (4.3) above the usual requirement for significance (4). This naturally raised the question as to whether there was a genuine difference between P.T. and P.C. on this point of distance testing, or whether we had here to do again merely with mental attitudes that offered different limitations for the two conditions.

In Tables XXIV and XXV will be shown the results just described. The entire 5,400 results are really very significant, giving a gain over chance expectation (np) that is 11.4 times the p.e. But for Pearce they are very low, giving an average of only 6.0 per 25 instead of his usual level of 10 or thereabouts. The points of interest lie chiefly in the column of 'average per 25'. The contrast of these averages in general columns A and D in Table XXIV are worth attention, as are the 5th and 7th columns in Table XXV. These bring out the point of the difference between P.T.

and B.T. results with distance, and their similarity at close range, suggesting that while P.T. can clearly be done at such distances, it may be that B.T. cannot. It is still more strongly suggested that D.T. may be limited to close range.

TABLE XXIV

Comparison of P.T., B.T., and D.T., at short distances, Pearce, Stuart as agent

Con-dition	A Across Table			B 8–12 feet way			C 20–30 feet away			D Both distances, 8–30 feet		
	Trials	Hits	Av. per 25	Trials	Hits	Av. per 25	Trials	Hits	Av. per 25	Trials	Hits	Av. per 25
P.T.	475	121	6·4	850	209	6·1	625	129	5·2	1,475	338	5·7
B.T.	950	239	6·3	450	91	5·1	250	56	5·6	700	147	5·3
D.T.	975	282	7·2	625	135	5·4	200	40	5·0	825	175	5·3

The values for X (*i.e.* Dev./p.e.) for the totals for each condition are in column 3 below. The values for the data taken across the table (A above) are in column 5 and those for the total distance data are in column 7. (Note that in this case the distance data are combined for contrast with those taken across the table.)

TABLE XXV

Values of X in P.T., B.T., and D.T. comparison, Pearce

Condition	Totals		Across table		Total distance	
	Trials	X	Trials	X	Trials	X
P.T.	1,950	4·8	475	4·4	1,475	4·3
B.T.	1,650	5·1	950	5·9	700	1·0
D.T.	1,800	7·5	975	10·0	825	1·3
	5,400	11·2				

The fact that in D.T. work at close range Pearce did almost as well as usual, but fell off in his B.T. and P.T. suggests, of course, that the inhibiting factor was more operative under B.T. and P.T. conditions. This leads one to look for some distracting set of circumstances in the procedure, in the change to Stuart's conditions, since B.T. and P.T. naturally allow more opportunity for disturbance than does the D.T.; *i.e.* in the D.T. work the subject is most independent of his surroundings.

And, finally, the curves! Pearce's work is full of interesting relations that can be drawn up in graphic form. But these will be presented in later chapters, and are omitted here because they do not involve any other data than have already been given and were not the result of planned experimentation. Pearce's D.T. curve shows the same dip for the central part of the pack that the others showed (Linzmayer and Stuart). He has a very marked curve of calling on his B.T.-5 trials (*i.e.* made 5 calls at a run, followed by a check-up). There are regions of relative emphasis in his other work as well, all pointing to the lawfulness of the processes of E.S.P. and their natural interrelationship with other functions.

We have in Pearce's work no adequate estimate of its importance in the mere index of the value X, but this is in itself a figure so large in significance that we can no longer appreciate it. It is, for the 17,250 trials performed by Pearce since the Spring of 1932, 64·9. When this is merged with the value left at the close of the last chapter, the figure vaults now to 75·3 for the entire 64,224 trials reported to this point. We must all agree that after reaching this point it would be almost a deliberate waste of time to try to add to the mere significance or weight of the evidence for E.S.P. The principal blocks of Pearce's data are indicated in the following summarizing table:

TABLE XXVI

Summary of Pearce's work in E.S.P. to August 1, 1933

Date	Condition	Trials	Hits	Dev.	p.e.	X	Av. per 25
1. iv. 33	B.T.	8,075	3,049	1,434	24·2	59·3	9·4
1. iv. 33	D.T.	1,625	482	157	10·9	14·4	7·4
1. iv. 33	P.T.	950	269	79	8·3	9·5	7·1
1. iv. 33	Screened E.S.P.	600	215	95	6·6	14·4	9·0
1. iv. 33	B.T. (Amytal)	325	79	14	4·9	2·8	6·1
1. iv. 33	B.T. (Vol. Low Scoring)	275	20	35	4·5	7·8	1·8
1. iv. 33– 1. viii. 33	Stuart-Pearce Series	5,400	1,302	222	19·8	11·2	6·0
To 1. viii. 33 total		17,250				64·9	

In order to give a correct picture of the state of progress and constant flux of these E.S.P. experiments, I will simply add to this chapter as it is being copied the latest fruits of Pearce's work. It is in many respects the best yet and answers several important questions at once. The experiment is conducted by Mr. Pratt and is a long-distance B.T. test.

In a room in the Physics Building at Duke, Pratt picks up a card from the shuffled pack before him at the rate of one per minute. He lays it face down in a book in the center of the table without looking at it.

At the beginning of the same minute, Pearce, in the Duke Library, over 100 yards away, tries to perceive the card then 'exposed' by Pratt. He has succeeded remarkably well in doing so. At first he failed, as he nearly always does with a new condition procedure. But the scores mounted as he went, as follows: 3, 8, 5, 9, 10, 12, 11, 12, 11, 13, 13, 12. The total 300 at that distance average 9·9 per 25; $X = 12·2$ and excludes the chance hypothesis. In his B.T. with the same technique, carried out in the same room with the cards but with the latter invisible—conditions the same as reported just above, except that Pearce was a few feet from the card instead of 100 yards—he obtained only an average of 7 in 300 trials. At any rate, distance does not seem to matter in this mode of perception, so far as these results go to indicate. Then the cards were taken to the Duke Medical Building, with over 250 yards between cards and percipient. Again there was the low-scoring adjustment period at first. This lasted over more runs this time but was followed by good scoring, which is now going on daily at this distance. After a time the distance will be still farther extended.

These long-distance results with P.C. were most crucially appropriate, as will be seen later in the report. The point was that with P.T. we already had some evidence that distance was not a limiting condition. We are keenly searching for possible differences and similarities.

What then will distance do to the scoring in P.C. tests? This point will be followed up with vigorous interest.

CHAPTER VIII

Five Other Major Subjects

I t will be convenient to complete the presentation of the other five principal subjects as something of a single unit of contribution, partly in the interest of economizing space and partly because they have, because of their relative new-ness, each one contributed fewer data than the three already reported on, but chiefly because these subjects have worked together a great deal and their data correlate well. One sub-ject, for example, has acted as agent in telepathic work for each of the other four, while some of them have reversed the arrangement with her and have themselves co-operated.

All five of these subjects have been Duke students, and all are good, normal, intelligent individuals, like the other ma-jor subjects, devoid of any marked peculiarity of personal-ity. Three are girls, and all five subjects are between 20 and 25 years of age, all in good health.

All five subjects have shown some definite inclination to-ward artistic interests. For one point, all of them are spe-cially interested in music, and all either play the piano or sing well. All are imaginative and have been at some time given to extensive daydreaming. All are quite sociable and friendly, though two are relatively reserved in expression. And, as almost of necessity follows, all five are more inter-ested in people than in things or causes.

All five of these subjects are what we may properly call religious in interest and ideals, but none is at all orthodox. All five also have had some 'intuitional' or hallucinatory or clairvoyant experience, though these vary widely. All three of the girls have had some sort of hallucination in childhood in which they saw apparitions, heard voices, heard steps or the like. But they do not regard these over-seriously.

The family histories of these subjects is of interest, on the point of similarity of background. In all cases there is reported a near relative with something parapsychological, if nothing more than 'intuitional' capacity. (In the popular sense, this usually means mildly clairvoyant.) One subject states that her aunt has had various clairvoyant experiences, another that her aunt (mother's sister) heard 'voices', while her mother had quite marked intuitional understanding of people. One of the boys states that his father and father's father possessed parapsychic ability, and the other boy related an incident that was regarded as typical, in which his mother showed clairvoyant or telepathic knowledge of a mishap that befell him.

All of the subjects are, I think, hypnotizable, though I have not gone far into that state with the two boys. Both, at least, made definite beginnings. One of the girls has done automatic writing and another has demonstrated other automatic phenomena.

These subjects are all of the kind that one can easily work with—they are highly co-operative; in part this may be because of genuine interest in the phenomena themselves. All of them have a major interest in psychology, the two graduates, Miss Sara Ownbey and Mr George Zirkle, being assistants in our Department. Miss May Frances Turner has about completed her work for graduation, and Miss June Bailey is an undergraduate. Mr T. Coleman Cooper is an undergraduate, formerly of Duke and now of Birmingham Southern.

In presenting the data in this chapter, I shall not give consideration to the question of fraud or deception, since that has been perhaps overdone in the earlier chapters. Not that all these results were obtained without any precautions— some of them had the best of conditions. But because it involves too much unnecessary duplication to describe conditions repeatedly, and because we are beyond the question of proof and are after the explanation and conditions. Besides these points, the very experimental conditions here are often in themselves incidentally the answer to the deception question, as well as contributive to knowledge of the process (*e.g.* long-distance E.S.P.) .

Altogether we have, from these five subjects alone, from less than a year's work with them, 26,950 trials, which have been very fruitful in scores as well as in general relationships. This is indicated by the fact that the average per 25 for the 26,950 trials, including all conditions, is 8·4 and the value of X, the 'anti-chance' ratio of deviation to p.e., is 81·9, higher than the whole 64,224 trials heretofore made. Combined with these we shall now have a total of 91,174 trials, with a combined X-value of 111·2. On this score figures can do no more.

I shall begin the 'carving' of the huge piece of work represented by these 26,950 trials by trimming off a portion that for our purposes is irrelevant. This consists of 2,625 trials in clairvoyance by Zirkle. These are really preliminary trials, since Zirkle has not developed, as yet, any measurable P.C. ability, although he is our best P.T. subject, so far. It was due to a slight misunderstanding that he and the assistant recorded this large item—before good evidence of his P.C. ability is discovered. And, once recorded, we cannot ignore it in the calculation of totals, averages, values of X, etc. But, for the comparisons we want to make in the processes we are working with, we may well exclude this block of results for the time being. This leaves 24,325 trials with a yield of successes totalling 8,499, an average of 8·7 per 25, and a value of $X = 86·4$. These may be compared with the figures of the last paragraph.

Of these 24,325 trials, 10,275 are P.T., 7,925 are made with the B.T. clairvoyant condition and the remaining 6,125 are D.T. clairvoyance. Their averages per 25 run as follows: P.T. 9·6, B.T. 8·9 and D.T. 7·1.

The data of this group of subjects may again be split apart in a direction that cuts across the tripartite division into P.T., B.T. and D.T. This is on the matter of witnessing. It is a matter of relative unimportance here, because, with the exception of one subject, the results are quite as good when witnessed as when not. The P.T. data are all witnessed, sometimes by the agent, when she was authorized as an assistant. Table XXVII will give the results on these points.

TABLE XXVII

*P.T., B.T., and D.T., witnessed and unwitnessed,
five major subjects*

Type of E.S.P.	Witnessed or Unwitnessed	Trials	Hits	Dev. and p.e.	X	Av. per 25
1. P.T.	Witnessed	10,275	3,937	1,883 ± 27·3	68·8	9·6
2. B.T.	Witnessed	1,750	596	246 ± 11·3	21·8	8·5
3. B.T.	Unwitnessed	6,175	2,220	985 ± 21·2	46·5	9·0
4. B.T. totals		7,925	2,816	1,231 ± 24·0	51·3	8·9
5. D.T.	Witnessed	1,725	406	61 ± 11·2	5·4	5·9
6. D.T.	Unwitnessed	4,400	1,340	460 ± 17·9	25·7	7·6
7. D.T. totals		6,125	1,746	521 ± 21·1	24·7	7·1
8. Total, P.T., B.T., D.T.	Witnessed	13,750	4,939	2,189 ± 31·6	69·3	9·0
9. Total, B.T., D.T.	Unwitnessed	10,575	3,560	1,445 ± 27·7	52·2	8·4
10. Grand total		24,325	8,499	3,634 ± 42·1 (By formula, 86·4)	86·4	8·7

It will be seen that both with the B.T. and the D.T. the witnessed data were lower in score, as shown in the last column. With the B.T. the difference is not great enough to be important (0·5). With the D.T. it is larger (1·7) and is entirely due here to one subject, Miss Ownbey, who does very good D.T. work unwitnessed, but drops with a witness present. Her later work has, however, shown that she is getting over this effect; her witnessed D.T. score has shown a value for X of 3·2, with the best results latest. This is evidently an exaggerated case of the phenomenon shown regularly by Pearce with visitors and reported in Table XIX, Chapter VII. Miss Weckesser also had the same effect of witnessing on her B.T.

The P.T. results bring the 'witnessed' up above the 'unwitnessed', if we include them. This immunity from the disturbing effect of witnesses, if we may so regard it, here in the higher P.T. results (which were all witnessed) is probably due to the fact of the participation of the witness in the agency of the experiments. It was noted by Lodge in his early experiments in telepathy that witnesses were not as disturbing if they participated, a matter possibly explainable on the grounds that a witness engaged co-operatively has his own attention engaged by his task, and consequently does not contribute so much to the percipient's self-consciousness and consequent inability to attend extra-sensorially.

Other points of interest in Table XXVII are the relatively similar averages per 25 of the B.T. and P.T. data, in spite of the fact that the phenomenal scoring of Zirkle in P.T. raised the average considerably. (And Zirkle has shown no B.T. ability as yet.) This is the largest group comparison we have yet made on P.T. and B.T. There are 10,275 trials in the one and 7,925 in the other, with averages per 25, respectively, of 9.6 and 8.9.

Another point of importance is the D.T. scoring and totals. This is the largest D.T. block of data yet offered and, while it is vastly significant mathematically, it is much below the B.T. It runs, however, at almost exactly the level that Pearce ran at, with about the same ratio to the B.T. scores. Yet these subjects did not know Pearce's averages, or even each other's and their own. Are we up against a physical barrier or a psychical or parapsychical limitation in D.T.?

It will be remembered that the subjects whose D.T. work has been reported earlier all showed a rate-of-scoring curve that fell to its lowest point somewhere in the 15 cards of the centre of the pack and rose again with approach to the top and bottom. (Cooper's work in D.T., done later, gave the same sort of U-curve.) But Miss Ownbey's data on the 3,350 trials at D.T., for which I have the detailed data in hand, show just the opposite type of curve. Miss Ownbey gets more hits in the centre 5 of the untouched pack than in any other 5. Next come the two adjacent 5's. Not only is this true of the totals but, when divided into the two main periods in which they were run, they show the same curve in the relation of the serial 5's in the pack. The details can be better presented in the later chapters (Chapters X, XII and XIV; for these data see Graphs 1 and 2) summarizing the 'curve data', but the gross results of totals by order of 5's in the pack are as follows: 210, 226, 248, 230, 211. Suffice it here merely to point out this contradiction of the thought that was already taking shape in our minds, that somehow there was regular difficulty experienced in the centre of the pack, possibly due to some physical obstruction. This hypothesis for the lower D.T. scores was inconsistent with Miss Ownbey's D.T. data.

And Miss Ownbey's results help to explain why the other D.T. scores are lower than the B.T. It has seemed probable that the difficulty of scoring in the centre of the pack held the total score for the run at its relatively low level. On this basis, those who score at a level of around 10 in 25 at B.T. would do little over 7 per 25 at D.T. Pearce is a good example of this. Now, Miss Ownbey gets better results in the interior and she scores the highest in D.T. work of all the subjects, once reaching 20 in 25 in one run and averaging 8.4 in 25 over a range of 3,275 trials. It would appear that D.T. scoring is as high as the B.T. for those portions of the pack which are favoured by the subject—the central 5 by Miss Ownbey, and the first and last 5's by others. What governs these curves—if not the expectation of the subject?

There is the further point to be added that the regularity of this D.T. curve of Miss Ownbey (for both subdivisions of her D.T. results) and its unexpectedness are further testimony to the genuineness of the data, for any who may have doubts on this point. That is, even had Miss Ownbey known what shape of curve to expect (which she did not), she would not likely have so regularly differed from what she would naturally suppose we might be expecting.

To provide a basis for further discussion and comparison, Table XXVIII offers all the data for each subject, under the different conditions, P.T., B.T. or D.T., and witnessed or not witnessed, merely stating number of trials and average per 25. I exclude again here the 2,625 practice trials on B.T. and D.T. by Zirkle, who has shown no ability in these phases of E.S.P. All the special experiments are included, however, regardless of their effect on the score.

A number of individual peculiarities appear in Table XXVIII, and others still escape this very general summary of the evidence. Miss Ownbey is, as mentioned above, our best D.T. subject if we take her unwitnessed records (as I am fully prepared to do for the help they may give us on comparison of methods), but she has done very little P.T., B.T. or witnessed D.T. work. Yet on all of these she has shown good promise of success. She has been so good an agent in P.T. work that her other work has been neglected.

TABLE XXVIII

All E.S.P. data from five major subjects, 1932–3

| Name of subject | B.T. | | | | D.T. | | | | P.T. | |
| | Witnessed | | Unwitnessed | | Witnessed | | Unwitnessed | | Witnessed | |
	Trials	Av. per 25	Trials	Av. per 25	Trials	Av. per 25	Trials	Av. per 25	Trials	Av. per 25
June Bailey	350	9·2	1,200	7·7	650	6·0	450	5·1	1,250	9·4
T. C. Cooper	350	8·7	1,550	8·5	—	—	—	—	2,950	8·1
Sara Ownbey	125	9·0	450	12·4	750	5·8	3,275	8·4	375	8·8
Frances Turner	925	8·1	2,975	9·3	325	5·8	675	5·5	675	9·1
George Zirkle	—		—		—		—		5,025	10·7
Totals	1,750	8·5	6,175	9·0	1,725	5·9	4,400	7·8	10,275	9·6

Zirkle is the best P.T. man by far, but he has not been able to develop B.T. or D.T., though he has tried a great deal. Cooper has not tried D.T. work as yet.[1] He was kept concentrated on B.T. and P.T. comparison work, to be reported later.

The other two subjects, Misses Bailey and Turner, are pretty well balanced between B.T. and P.T. and, though they are still low on D.T., they are able to do it with some success.

On the P.T., where all five may be compared, there is pretty general similarity, ranging only over 8·1 to 10·7 in the averages. And on B.T. the four who can score well do it about equally well, ranging over much the same averages as in the P.T. It will be of much interest indeed to see if, in

[1] Since the above was written Cooper has begun D.T. with some success.

the future, Zirkle can qualify on B.T.[1] Such results suggest some general level, a sort of *species level* for E.S.P., which level ranges from 8 to 11 approximately, under normally good conditions.

The B.T. and P.T. comparisons justify, I think, another rearrangement of these data in Table XXIX for the first four subjects, totalling and averaging the witnessed and unwitnessed data for the purpose. Note however, back in Table XXVIII, that the witnessed B.T., which are among the latest performed and should be the more comparable to P.T. because made during the period of P.T. experiments, are, in the main, strikingly similar to them. The widest difference between a subject's B.T. (witnessed) average and his P.T. is 1·0, and with 2 of the subjects the difference is only 0·2. This is very meaningful on the point of inter-relationship of the functions concerned in telepathy and clairvoyance. Could such a series be mere coincidence? But, because of the relatively small number of witnessed trials, we will include in Table XXIX also the unwitnessed, even though they widen the gap considerably.

TABLE XXIX

Comparison of B.T. and P.T. work of four major subjects

Name of subject	B.T. totals			P.T. totals		
	Trials	Hits	Av. per 25	Trials	Hits	Av. per 25
Miss Bailey	1,550	498	8·0	1,250	469	9·4
Mr Cooper	1,900	647	8·5	2,950	950	8·1
Miss Ownbey	700	313	11·2	375	131	8·7
Miss Turner	3,900	1,403	9·0	675	245	9·1
	8,050	2,861	8·9	5,250	1,795	8·5

This table brings out more comparable groups of data from the point of number of trials, and brings Miss Turner's data on B.T. and P.T. to an almost identical average,

---

[1] Later on he did in fact qualify very successfully, getting, in the 1,150 trials of the later series, a deviation of over 15 times the p.e., and an average of 8 per 25, which is only 0·8 below his P.T. average for the same period.

though we have widened differences between the results of Misses Bailey and Ownbey for the two conditions. But the totals of these four subjects for the two conditions come out most remarkably similar, 8.9 and 8.5. With only a difference of 0.4, we have no significant distinction between the two conditions for these subjects and the results. In a later chapter all the data on this point, from all subjects, will be mustered—with even greater coincidence resulting.

We had an opportunity to compare the daily fluctuations of one of these subjects, Mr Cooper, on both B.T. and P.T. They show, as did Mr Pearce's results under similar conditions, a very general agreement as to direction of change from day to day. With but two exceptions, both B.T. and P.T. rise and fall together. See Table XXX. In one of these cases, the P.T. dropped to chance because the laboratory was very hot (temperature around 100° F.) and the electric fan which was used on every other day of the series was not obtainable. (One is moved to remark that the once much talked-of 'involuntary whispering' had its one really superb opportunity on this occasion.) The B.T. of this day was done under the regular conditions. Due to this difference in conditions, I put the figures for this day, accordingly, in parenthesis. The reader can judge them as he prefers. In the other exception the case is a clear one for those who understand the workings of this mode of perception; the point is, there is no value to including, for comparative purposes, data not above chance average. On the day in question here, Cooper started off in his P.T. with only chance results for the first three runs, getting 6, 4, 4. Then after trying some special distance tests, not included in this table, he returned to plain P.T. and got 8 in 25. After another digression to other tests, he came back with 11, 11 in P.T. If we include the calls when he obviously did not show any E.S.P. ability, it makes an average per 25 of 7.3; but this defeats our purpose—to discover the daily level of P.T. and B.T. scoring, *when conditions are right for E.S.P. to function.* I feel, therefore, that most readers will approve my taking the above-chance scores 8, 11, 11 for the data for comparison for the P.T. of that day with the B.T. of that day. This is not a point of evidence for E.S.P. or the case would be different. I set the gross average 7·3 in parenthesis and the restricted average 10, without. Other days, too, show a low start-off; it is rather the rule. But all the others gave a quicker rise to good scoring; some special difficulty was present here.

TABLE XXX

Comparison of B.T. and P.T. in daily fluctuations of Cooper's data

No.	Date	Clairvoyance (B.T.)			Telepathy (P.T.)			Remarks
		Trials	Hits	Av. per 25	Trials	Hits	Av. per 25	
1	22 .vi. 33	100	25	6·3	225	72	8·0	
2	23. vi. 33	100	31	7·8	125	47	9·4	
3	24. vi. 33	(100)	(33)	(8·3)	(250)	(50)	(5·0)	See Text
4	25. vi. 33	100	28	7·0	200	64	8·0	
5	26. vi. 33	150	54	9·0	75	30	10·0	(150 : 44 : 7·3)
6	27. vi. 33	150	79	13·2	250	116	11·6	See Text
7	29. vi. 33	300	90	7·5	200	68	8·5	
8	30. vi. 33	250	97	9·7	150	86	14·3	
9	Totals	1,150	404	8·8	1,225	483	9·9	

Allowing the corrections made, we have here another good case of joint daily fluctuations in B.T. and P.T.—somewhat better, in fact, than Pearce's. Note the relative agreement of the average per 25 of the totals for B.T. and P.T., again differing by the small figure of 1·1.

I have not the data for a daily comparison of B.T. and P.T. on the other subjects, except for Zirkle, and his B.T. has not yet risen above chance average.

Turning from the point of comparison of natural scoring levels of the subjects to factors that influence these, we find that P.T., as well as B.T., is affected by sodium amytal, by caffeine, by illness (so far as we have data), and by sleepiness and general fatigue. The evidence on the last two points is merely incidental, but on the first two is experimental. It is not adequate on the last point, since in most cases the testimony of the subject to his fatigue and sleepiness came after the work was begun and he had already registered low scores. I accept these judgments, myself, since I follow the work and know the subjects very well, and can check up on such judgments to some extent, but I do not ask the reader to accept them. Yet the similarity of this condition of sleepiness to the effect of sodium amytal, and the similarity of results may help the reader to accept the fragmentary data on the point.

I have noted the disturbance to scoring of sleepiness and general fatigue on Linzmayer and Pearce on clairvoyance, and on telepathy between Miss Ownbey and Zirkle. Selecting only the data from the two last named where I am certain, myself, of the correctness of the judgment, I will make a small table (XXXI) showing the results taken before and after the period of sleepiness and fatigue in P.T. work, with Zirkle as percipient. On the first day reported on here, I myself saw Zirkle, and he told me, before beginning to work, that he had been up all night and had had only three hours of sleep in the morning. He said he did not especially want to sleep but was 'sort of groggy'. The second occasion reported was one on which both Zirkle and Miss Ownbey had returned late at night from a walk of about four miles into the country. We have the complication here that the agent, too, was tired. An equal number of the trials last preceding, and the same number of those next succeeding the period of sleepiness, are shown under general columns marked 'Before' and 'After'.

TABLE XXXI

Effect of fatigue and sleepiness on E.S.P. (P.T.)
Zirkle and Ownbey

Before				During				After			
Date (a.m.)	Trials	Hits	Av. per 25	Date (p.m.)	Trials	Hits	Av. per 25	Date (p.m.)	Trials	Hits	Av. per 25
17. vii.	125	70	14	18. vii.	125	36	7·2	19. vii.	125	43	8·6
25. vii.	50	32	16	25. vii.	50	11	5·5	26. vii.	50	27	13·5
Totals	175	102	14·6		175	47	6·7		175	70	10·0

These data are supported by the strong general 'clinical impression' I have that, on the whole, both P.C. and P.T.

work succeed best when the subject is least tired and sleepy. In this way the results from the effects of caffeine can best be harmonized and explained. This drug improves scoring when it falls off, and makes the subject more alert and integrated at the same time.

On the point of illness, too, the data are fragmentary and none too adequate, but they support the already mentioned observations made on Pearce. Miss Turner had a mild illness, a sort of general run-down condition, with a temperature rise that led the physician to suggest her staying in bed. She tried B.T. work under these conditions, but said she felt unable to do it well and, since the tentative trials were poor, she discontinued. She tried again several times, since she was rather bored, but did not get the feeling of success, and, since she did not get up to her usual good scoring level, she did not run for record and we thus lost the opportunity to measure the effect of illness. However, on her return to class, but before she was fully well, she was asked to try for record and made two runs of 25 in my presence, with results of 5 and 4. We stopped her because she did not like to score low and we thought the effect might be bad on the process. Miss Turner does not require an 'adjustment period' at the start; so this question is ruled out. On the last preceding occasion of my witnessing (also, the last preceding B.T. she had done) she had made 2 runs, yielding 10 and 8; and next before these, 5 runs averaging 10·2 in 25. We have no follow-up data, since the experiments were interrupted for two months thereafter. Her general B.T. average for 3,825 trials is 9·0. These fragments agree with Pearce's B.T. data on the point of illness. We have, too, some illness data with a similar bearing on the P.T. phase, obtained with Zirkle and with Miss Ownbey as agent. We can best state them, along with Miss Turner's few data, as a small table, XXXII. In this period of illness we have the complicating circumstance that both agent and percipient were indisposed. Further data, of course, will be required to discriminate between the relative effect upon the two. We offer these results for what they may mean as they are, with only the assurance that the percipient was ill for a time before the agent, and that the drop came at once with his indisposition. The illness was tonsilitis with Zirkle and a general cold with Miss Ownbey. It lasted approximately 9 days, affecting the results from July 12 to the 20th, inclusive.

The drop of Miss Turner was a drop of 9·9 less 4·5, or 5·4, and for Mr. Zirkle from an average of (from data before and after) 14·9 to one of 8·6 during the period of illness. This is a drop of 6·3 per 25, a highly significant value, and it leaves little question that, directly or indirectly, such illness is a condition very inhibitory to E.S.P.

TABLE XXXII
Illness and E.S.P., with Miss Turner and Mr Zirkle

Type	Subject	Before			
		Date	Trials	Hits	Av. per 25
B.T.	Miss Turner	8. i.–23. i.	175	69	9·9
P.T.	Mr Zirkle[1]	10. vii.–11. vii.	850	480	14·1
		During illness			
B.T.	Miss Turner	17. ii.	50	9	4·5
P.T.	Mr Zirkle[1]	12. vii.–20. vii.	2,100	722	8·6
		After			
B.T.	Miss Turner	—	—	—	—
P.T.	Mr Zirkle[1]	21. vii., 22. vii.	450	287	16·0

[1] Miss Ownbey as agent.

More striking still are the drug data obtained by Zirkle with Miss Ownbey as agent and observer. The experiments with caffeine on the telepathic phase here showed, as did those with the effect of caffeine upon clairvoyance with Pearce, that caffeine helped the subject to recover his normal E.S.P. scoring level when he was low, i.e., it helped to overcome disturbing (disintegrative) factors. But, as with P.C. work, we have no data on the P.T. with caffeine that shows that it enhances the actual E.S.P. function itself; it seems rather that it merely helps it to function better through counteracting the inhibiting elements, as seemed the case with the B.T. experiment. Again, like caffeine and B.T. with Pearce, the drug did not raise the P.T. score even to its highest level but rather to approximately the normal average level. Zirkle's level for his period of good health is 14.8 in 25 P.T., and the average per 25 with caffeine for 300 trials was 14.7. Now, Zirkle's highest score for a long series was 17.4 per 25 on an average, for 300 trials without drugs and all made in one day, as were the caffeine trials. So far as we understand the known psychological effects of caffeine on recognized processes, that is what we should expect; namely, a general integrative effect, overcoming dissociated states, but not directly strengthening a special ability or raising its specific efficiency. We were especially interested, therefore, in the results from giving caffeine to Zirkle some time after sodium amytal. This brings out sharply and experimentally the expected effects of both drugs on the general mental organization, thus relating E.S.P. all the more closely to the general functioning of mind.

It was planned with Miss Ownbey to give Zirkle sodium amytal and to take his scoring level one hour later, over a range of 300 trials. As a matter of fact, the level was also taken three hours after the drug treatment. Then, according to plan, with the subject in this very dissociated condition, he was treated with caffeine. The purpose was to put the general principle of the role of caffeine in known processes to test on this particular process (E.S.P.); and, in an anticipatory word, it worked quite as might have been expected for any cognitive function of mind.

In both the caffeine and amytal experiments 5-gr. capsules were used, both drugs being made up to look alike, and the subject was given no notion of the drug to be used for a given occasion and did not know what to expect from either one by way of effect on the P.T. ability. Miss Ownbey knew which drug was used but did not know what to expect in score effects.

After a level of 13.6 per 25 trials for the last preceding 250 trials over the day preceding and after 2 runs averaging 13·5 hits in 25 on the same day, a 5-gr. capsule of sodium amytal was taken by Zirkle (Pearce had taken 6-gr.; Linzmayer 15) and one hour later testing was resumed. By this time he was showing signs of sleepiness. He became very sleepy during the course of the experiment, which took about $1\frac{1}{2}$ to 2 hours. He wanted to lie down, felt a little dizzy on rising, occasionally wanted to pause, but seemed rationally clear when questioned and could walk in a straight line. If the experimenter left him alone a few minutes he dropped asleep.

The conditions of the experiments were these: the regular P.T. conditions were used, with the 5 symbols taken from the E.S.P. cards, and the telegraph key was used for signalling readiness by the agent. The agent chose a systematized scheme of variation from series to series and used no objective basis (cards, etc.), except the scoring record made of the calls of the percipient. These were checked for correctness as the call was recorded. The agent and percipient were in different rooms, out of sight of each other but with the door open, with an electric fan going (for comfort and 'covering noise' combined). The percipient sat or lay with eyes closed, back toward the agent's room. A distance of about 8 to 12 feet separated the two. The key tapping was monotonously uniform to my ear and judgment. All the data of the table, XXXIII, are from these conditions. In brief summary, the score average per 25 dropped from 13·6 for the preceding runs down to 7·8 for the series of 12 runs (300 trials); this is a drop of 5·8 and is very significant mathematically. Like those of Pearce (and his B.T. data) under the influence of the same drug and a similar amount, Zirkle's fluctuations are large, due, I think, to varying effort at 'pulling himself together' and its effect on attention. The run scores are as follows: 7, 8, 10, 4, 6, 10, 11, 10, 11, 8, 6, 3. Total 94. Average per 25, 7·8. It is interesting to see that Zirkle dropped from his average level (for period of good health) of 14·8 by a percentage roughly similar to what Pearce did on B.T. under the influence of the same drug;

namely, a drop of 47% from the upper score level as compared with 39% for Pearce.

Three hours after the drug was taken Zirkle was very, very sleepy indeed. Sensory perception, which had not been disturbed during the earlier runs, was now beginning to suffer slightly from illusion. A piece of chalk lying a few feet (3 to 6) away appeared to be another capsule. If a book was held close, he saw 'double', but he could still read without trouble and, with effort, walk straight. His recall of recent events was impaired. In this condition 12 runs of P.T., under the same conditions yielded only an average score per 25 of 6·2, with nothing higher than 9. These scores run as follows: 5, 5, 6, 9, 7, 4, 5, 5, 8, 7, 5, 8. Total 74; average per 25, 6·2. This is a drop of 8·6 from Zirkle's pre-drug level of 14·8.

Now, of course, was the superb opportunity to test the effect of caffeine's integrative influence upon this P.T. scoring. Would it work just as it does upon any complex mental ability or skill; *i.e.* would E.S.P. rise with the reachievement of self-control and capacity for attention? Our other data had suggested that it would—and it did! It rose from the level of 6·2 per 25, passed the older amytal level of 7·8 in 25, which had been reached one hour after taking the amytal, and attained the fairly respectable score average of 9·5 in 25. This was now 5 hours after the 5-gr. dose of sodium amytal and one hour after a 5-gr. dose of caffeine. The 300 trials yielded the following scores, varying rather widely: 10, 8, 4, 6, 13, 8, 13, 8, 11, 9, 13. Total 114, an average per 25 of 9·5. During this experiment Zirkle was still sleepy, but the effect of the caffeine was clearly noticeable in his general behaviour. He had become somewhat more alert and poised, but was by no means fully 'normal' yet. He seemed much as his score average of 9·5 indicated —approximately 'halfway normal'. Two to three hours later, however, he reported that he was fully recovered.

Still more data would have been interesting as the effect of the caffeine increased and Zirkle became much more alert; but he had already run 950 trials in one day and was leaving the next morning; and human endurance and patience ought not to be asked for more than this. Also, Miss Ownbey's work on this day alone deserves the highest comment. The agent's duty is often the more exhausting by far, as Lodge early pointed out.[1] And these data alone are highly significant, the conditions good for exploratory tests and suggestion ruled out by the disguise of the drugs. On these points of physiological changes also, then, the P.T. phase of E.S.P. responds in about the same degree and in the same way as the B.T., and falls and rises with the degree of disintegration of the nervous system. The summary of the drug experiments with Zirkle appears in Table XXXIII. In a final word, the results show that both the disintegrating and integrating drugs seriously affect the process of E.S.P. under P.T. conditions as much, in fact, as under B.T. The condition of the nervous system, then, is important in both. E.S.P. is pretty well indicated to be a nervous phenomenon, in both phases or conditions, P.T. and B.T., at least in its test demonstration.

TABLE XXXIII
Effect of caffeine and sodium amytal on P.T. scoring
Zirkle and Ownbey

Date	Conditions Drugs, etc.	Trials	Hits	Av. per 25	Remarks
	Total, with Zirkle well	1,300	767	14·8	Z's normal scoring level
23. vii.–24. vii.	Last 2 days before caffeine test	250	128	12·8	
24. vii.	5 gr. caffeine	300	176	14·7	Up to his average again
25. vii.–26. vii.	Normal; intervening period	250	136	13·6	
26. vii. (a.m.)	5 gr. sodium amytal	300	94	7·8	Very sleepy
26. vii. (p.m.)	3 hours after amytal	300	74	6·2	Extremely sleepy
26. vii. (p.m.)	5 hours after amytal; 5 gr. of caffeine	300	114	9·5	A significant change

[1] Lodge, Oliver J., D.Sc, 'An account of some experiments in thought transference', Proc. S.P.R. II, pp. 189–200, 1884.

One of the minor features of our pure telepathy work is the greater tendency to fatigue on the part of the agent than of the percipient, as it appeared at first. In working with Miss Bailey in a most remarkable series, from room to room, Miss Ownbey, the agent, reported headache and general fatigue. She reported fatigue more than once with other subjects as well, particularly with Mr. Zirkle, with whom she did the most of her P.T. work. The headache effect was stopped by hypnotic suggestion and, although she has served as agent in several thousand trials since, she no longer experiences this discomfort. But the fatigue effect was not included in the suggestion treatment and continued for a time. Then it declined with experience, until at length she was able to work without special fatigue and even to participate in the long series of 950 trials in one day. It seems probable that more strain goes with the stronger effort, combined with the greater uncertainty of success in the earlier trials, and that such strain, if prolonged, may cause headache perhaps and fatigue certainly. But it is doubtful if the calm, more experienced agent, who has grown into a confidence in her ability, need be especially fatigued or indisposed. I have earlier referred to Lodge's observation of this effect on the agent. I think the above explanation may be applicable to his case also.

There seems to be a great difference in the ability of the agents we have used. Our data are not conclusive on this point, because there are, as usual in this work, other factors to consider. The fact that a P.T. percipient does well with one and poorly with another agent may mean merely that the one personality is less disturbing and straining than the other; or more interesting or more suggestive and impressive; or perhaps there may be many different features involved. We know that even in B.T. work subjects have preferences as to whom they wish present and that scoring is much affected by such attitudes. (See Table XIX on effect of visitors, B.T., Pearce.) We should expect some such effect on P.T. also from the presence of different agents.

One point of fact, however, in this connection is that most subjects do better with certain agents than with others. For example, Zirkle did very well at once with Miss Ownbey, his fiancée; but he had been tried earlier by another friend, also an assistant in this work, with a very much smaller positive deviation from chance average. Pearce, it will be remembered, did his best P.T. with young lady agents. But we come in the P.T. work of Cooper, to a sharper comparison between the agency of two young ladies, Miss Margaret Parsons[1] and Miss Ownbey, in whom the factor of the social interest of the percipient is fairly equalized, but who differ in a very important way. Miss Ownbey has well demonstrated her E.S.P. ability in both the P.C. and P.T. phases. Miss Parsons has tried patiently and nobly, but has not yet scored very successfully.

We have a very similar situation with Miss Bailey's P.T. work, with Miss Beaven and Miss Ownbey as agents. Miss Beaven has not demonstrated marked E.S.P. ability as yet, while Miss Ownbey has. Miss Ownbey, Miss Bailey and Miss Turner, our three highest-scoring girls, are also our best agents. Can it be that the E.S.P. ability helps in the agency also? This remains to be better studied. Often the agent seems to perceive telepathically what the percipient 'wants to call next', but, in order to insure its being a one-way process, we adhere pretty closely to the policy of having the agent devise mentally a system of sequence of the images to be chosen and to alter the scheme every 5 calls. But the facts seem strongly to suggest that agents not only differ at their end of the function but also that it may be E.S.P. ability that makes a good agent. This is only suggested, however. The fact that Stuart, with his fair E.S.P. ability, did better in his early trance-telepathy work than did I, with almost no significant E.S.P. ability, is also in line. For a summary of the data on comparison of agents in the P.T. work of this chapter, see Table XXXIV.

[1] Miss Parsons has since become Mrs. L. C. Apgar.

TABLE XXXIV

Agents in P.T. work compared; the same percipients used

Percipient	Agent	Trials	Hits	Av. per 25	Remarks
Mr Cooper	Miss Parsons	850	220	6·5	Runs made on same days, with both
	Miss Ownbey	850	369	10·9	
Miss Bailey	Several agents	150	32	5·3	One of agents here, how- ever, was Pearce
	Miss Beaven	150	41	6·8	
	Miss Turner	50	20	10·0	
	Miss Ownbey	875	372	10·6	
Miss Turner	Several agents	100	22	5·5	
	Miss Ownbey	175	61	8·7	(Recently in distance P.T., this is 10·1)
	Miss Bailey	125	56	11·2	
Mr Zirkle	Mr Stuart	275	73	6·7	Stuart was running very low at the time
	Miss Ownbey	275	124	11·3	

The names in the heavier type represent agents who have been good subjects and the rest, with only exceptions noted, have not yet qualified. The name of Mr. Stuart is not in heavy type because he was, during the period in which these tests were made, running very low, close to chance average, on his other E.S.P. work. The total of the data taken with agents whose names are emphasized is 2,350, with an average per 25 yield of 10·7, whereas the remaining 1,525 yield an average per 25 of only 6·4. The very significant difference of 4·3 suggests that the agent is important and that E.S.P. capacity may be one of the important features.

But however much we may find (in the future) that E.S.P. ability may help in P.T. agency as well as on the side of perception, it is apparently not an equally reversible process. That is, the agent cannot turn percipient and receive from the former percipient with success equal to that of the original arrangement, so far as our results go. When Cooper tried to send back to Miss Parsons, after successfully 'receiving' from her for 800 trials, the score was not above chance average. When Zirkle and Miss Ownbey work, with Zirkle receiving, the normal average is 14·8, but with Miss Ownbey receiving it falls to 8·1. If we take, in order to have similar conditions, Zirkle's first 300 for comparison with Miss Ownbey's 300 trials with him as agent, we have 11·8 for him as percipient and 8·1 for her—still a significant difference, 3·7 for 15 runs. We have some data, however, to suggest that when we have agents and percipients equal in E.S.P. ability they can reverse the P.T. process without great difference. For example, with Miss Bailey as agent, Miss Turner got an average per 25 of 11·2 from 125 trials, and with the reverse arrangement for 50 trials, Miss Bailey got 10 per 25. Reversals between Miss Ownbey and Miss Turner differ in average per 25 by 2·1, but the number of trials are too small for significance. These interesting but inadequate results are summarized in Table XXXV.

Of the data in Table XXXV, those of Miss Ownbey and Mr. Zirkle alone are significant and they are clearly so. Those of Cooper are somewhat impressive because of the supporting fact that Miss Parsons shows as yet no clear E.S.P. ability. While it is dangerous to speculate on this table, it is safe, I think, to suggest that the differences between percipients are brought out here, while in the last preceding table the differences between agents were shown. The three girls in the last two items of the table (3 and 4) are very much on a par in E.S.P. ability and reversing makes very little difference. In Zirkle's case, he is our highest scorer on P.T. and the reversal with him brings a drop. With Cooper and Miss Parsons the contrast is even greater, since her E.S.P. ability is very low. Combining the data of the two tables, it appears: (1) that good E.S.P. ability in both agent and percipient means high scoring (as shown by Miss Own-

TABLE XXXV

*Comparison of P.T. results with reversed
direction of transference*

Condition Agent and percipient	Trials	Hits	Av. per 25	Remarks
1. Miss Parsons to Cooper	850	221	6·5	
Cooper to Miss Parsons	50	9	4·5	Too few trials
2. Miss Ownbey to Zirkle	300	141	11·8	
Zirkle to Miss Ownbey	300	97	8·1	Taking his first 300 trials
3. Miss Turner to Miss Ownbey	100	43	10·8	Too few data
Miss Ownbey to Miss Turner	175	61	8·7	In a recent distance test this is 10·1
4. Miss Turner to Miss Bailey	50	20	10·0	Too few data
Miss Bailey to Miss Turner	125	56	11·2	

bey as agent for all four percipients, who all have good
E.S.P. ability); (2) that good E.S.P. in a percipient, with low
E.S.P. capacity in the agent, means mediocre scoring
(Cooper with Miss Parsons as agent, 6.5; Miss Bailey with
Miss Beaven, 6.8; Zirkle with Stuart during his now period;
6.7; and others); (3) that with a percipient with low E.S.P.
ability and an agent with good E.S.P. ability the scoring will
be bad, or will be limited according to the ability of the percipient. (Miss Parsons as percipient, with no demonstrated
E.S.P., and Cooper as agent; and the lower scoring of Miss
Ownbey when she and Zirkle reversed, supports the point of
the E.S.P. capacity of the percipient being the more limiting
factor.)   These three situations have been illustrated and to
some extent demonstrated, though not adequately.   The
third situation is the weakest in data but it is strong in my
own conviction.   That is, there have been incidents that
support the point aside from the regular data.   Often someone helping as agent has playfully tried to obtain a reversal
of direction of the transfer of thought, perhaps for a few
trials or not for serious record; and the general impression
has thus grown up in my mind that, as the above data suggest, a good agent (as measured by his own general E.S.P.
record) cannot succeed in transferring thought to a 'percipient' who (as shown by the general evidence of the tests)
has shown no E.S.P. capacity or cannot go beyond the ability level shown.   In a word, the percipient seems to be the
more limiting factor but is in turn limited by agents who
are poor in E.S.P. capacity.   This hypothesis will be further
tested in future work.

In turning finally to telepathy-at-a-distance we come up
first against the question of the effect of the mental attitudes
of the percipient.   This is a question that concerns many of
the experiments and will be raised by many readers.   If the
percipient thinks a new experiment will not work, it probably will not.   If he suggests it and believes in it, it has then
a much better chance.   Such is the general impression I have
received, and for observations that support this I refer to
the effect of new techniques as summed up on one subject,

Mr Pearce, Table XX. Therefore, when we came to the drug experiments with Zirkle, it was decided to keep him ignorant of the drug taken and of its probable effect on his record. And when we were trying first to separate out a possible telepathic factor by looking at the cards for one series and not looking for the next, a screen was used to keep Pearce from knowing the condition used at a given time. And so on.

But it is difficult to test P.T. at a distance from the agent, and avoid the factors of suggestion and expectation, without practising deception. And it is hard for anyone to expect as good chances for success at a distance as in the same room. Most of our first 'distance P.T.' was handicapped, then, with an 'inhibiting idea' that it would not work as well. It certainly did not. As will be recalled from Pearce's data (Table XXIV), significant results were had with short distances of from 8 to 12 feet between agent and percipient; but with greater separation (20-30 feet) the score fell off and ran about chance average.

With Cooper too distance seemed to offer difficulty. He said he felt 'out of touch' with the agent. 300 trials made by him with Miss Ownbey as agent yielded only an average per 25 of 5.8—without mathematical significance. But Miss Bailey (who, incidentally, works in a semi-trance condition that is self-induced) was quite successful in overcoming the 'distance delusion', and in the short distance tried, 8 to 12 feet, and 30 feet, she held her scoring average up to par, obtaining in 475 trials an average per 25 of 9.1 at the shorter and 12.0 at the longer, with 150 trials. Both scores are above her general average.

Then Mr. Zirkle tried these shorter distances and after a time it seemed, as with Miss Bailey (and contrary to what a wave mechanics would lead us to expect), the farther away he got, the better he averaged. It was quite remarkably so, in fact. At the beginning, however, he got only a little above chance; he was at low ebb physically and was scoring then only from 7 to 9 in the same room with the agent. So we cannot evaluate the earliest 15 runs. They averaged only 4·8 per 25, and may have been due to a belief that he could not score at a distance, or due to illness, or both. At any rate, on July 21 he got well, raised his regular (same room) P.T. score from 7·4 (of the day before) to 15·0, and went into the next room and conquered the 'distance' obstruction at once by an average of 19 per 25 in 5 magnificent runs. He then invaded the next room away, adding still another wall between the agent and himself and reaching 28-30 feet distance, and made 5 runs, 125 calls with an average of 17 per 25. All the records were broken and on these data alone the significance went soaring to the heights of fullest satisfaction. And they continued. On the 22nd he called 50 across the table from the agent at an average per 25 of 10·5, 50 in the adjoining room (12 feet), average of 16·5 per 25, and 50 at 30 feet, 12 in 25. By the 26th, when he left the campus, we have for the period of restored health (which omits the first 15 runs and begins with August 21), at close range, 100 at an average of 12·8 per 25, 750 at 12 feet, with an average of 14·6 per 25; and, at the longer distance of 30 feet, separated by two walls, 250 trials with an average of 16·0 per 25. The only way in which we can suppose a law of inverse squares to apply here, as in wave mechanics, would be to suppose some very strong compensating factor to be present and to suppose the distance too small to be significant in the circumstances. With this in view, then, the next experiment is very much to the point.

Miss Turner and Miss Ownbey carried out, during the month of July, 1933, a long-distance experiment in pure telepathy, after the manner of the shorter distance tests. The distance was well over 250 miles, from Durham to Lake Junaluska, N.C. The principal exception to the regular procedure was that the time and rate of calling had to be arranged by correspondence. At first, 5-minute intervals were followed between calls and this was later reduced to 3 minutes. Both followed official time and worked by the arranged time intervals instead of the auditory signals used in the laboratory.

Mr Zirkle (left) doing pure telepathy seated two rooms away, 30 feet from, his back toward, Miss Ownbey (right), the agent, who signalled 'ready' with a telegraphic key. Thus he got 23 correct in 25, 85 in 100, and an average of 16 in 25 for 250 trials.

Miss Turner was a particularly good subject for this, since she has never shown the more usual drop with new techniques or conditions and with new witnesses. She has even boldly and successfully demonstrated her E.S.P. ability to one of her teachers who was openly sceptical. But her previous work had not prepared me for the shock of the first results of this 250-mile P.T. test. The first score was 19 hits in 25! Unquestionably significant alone, even if she never called another card. But the next 25 gave 16 correct, and the third again gave 16. These 75 calls alone yield 36 above the chance expectation of 15 and give an 'anti-chance' index of $(X =) 15.7$, which offers clinching satisfaction to the critical mind from that point of view. What of the other conditions? Miss Ownbey had turned her agent's record (made at the close of the 5-minute intervals) over to me and Miss Turner was expected to send her call records direct to me. She made an error and forwarded them for all three days to Miss Ownbey. Miss Ownbey, whose record I already had on my desk, brought the letters received from Miss Turner direct to me; and for the benefit of the reader, I will state that the recording was unmistakably in Miss Turner's own hand and ink, and no changes were evident. The notes that were written under the record were unmistakably those of Miss Turner. The point is, that if one of these excellent young ladies were to be suspected, both would have to be. Besides any motive to deceive me, difficult as it is to conceive it in these two, they would never aspire so absurdly high as to give me 19 in 25 on the first run!

Thereafter, the records came directly to me, from each one independently, but the scoring fell off seriously. It was, of course, a monotonous procedure sitting quietly for one hour and 15 minutes and not knowing how well the scoring is going until several days afterward. The whole list of scores ran as follows: 19, 16, 16, 7, 7, 8, 6, 2. At this point we stopped the experiment for a time, to await a recovery. The whole 200 trials average 10.1 per 25 and give a total positive gain over chance average that is 10.8 times the probable error. It shows that pure telepathy stands up under distance conditioning as no known physical process does. This average of 10·1 in 25 for 200 trials is higher than all Miss Turner's tests with Miss Ownbey right in the same room with her. Now, there were 275 trials made with only a table between Miss Ownbey as agent and Miss Turner as percipient and they yielded an average of only 7·7 in 25. Again we have, as with Miss Bailey and Mr Zirkle, *an appearance of improvement with distance in P.T. scoring*, rather than the decline expected by physical analogy. Miss Turner never ran under any other conditions such scores as the '19, 16, 16' which she got at once with 'P.T. at 250 miles'. There is an interesting suggestion in these facts. I hesitate to state it, for it is not in the least proved—purely hypothetic: that one who is at a considerable distance from the agent tends to relax those sensory processes commonly depended upon for perception and utilizes the process of extra-sensory perception the more; also, the rational judgment realizes its own uselessness and ceases to obstruct the E.S.P. function; the result is better abstraction and 'concentration'.

The 'distance' work on P.T. is summarized in Table XXXVI, in which will be given the records of the four out of the five subjects of this chapter who have worked under

TABLE XXXVI

Distance between agent (Miss Ownbey) and percipient,
in P.T.; 4 subjects

Item no.	Percipient	Same room		8-12 feet and wall between		28-30 feet 2 walls		250 miles	
		Trials	Av. per 25	Trials	Av. per 25	Trials	Av. per 25	Trials	Av. per 25
1	Cooper	1,800	9·2	300	5·8	—	—	—	—
2	Miss Bailey	275	11·4	450	9·7	150	12·0	—	—
3	Zirkle	950	14·0	750	14·6	250	16·0	—	—
4	Miss Turner	275	7·7	—	—	—	—	200	10·1
		3,300	10·6	1,500	11·4	400	14·5	200	10·1

this condition. First will be given their regular score average made with agent and percipient in the same room. Next will come separation by 8 to 12 feet, which means with a tile wall between the two subjects, with an open door in the wall but not directly between the subjects, so that vision was cut off. Third will come the 28-30 feet distance, with two tile walls between but each with an open door. Last will come the long-distance (250 miles) data of Miss Turner.

In all these data, with distance or without it, there was no chance for 'involuntary-whispering' (even if there were any!), since an electric fan was kept going practically all the time. And the percipients in these four cases do not look at the agent, even when in the same room. There is no sensory contact between the two, except for the methodical and uniform tapping of the telegraph key, and the calling aloud of the percipient. The agent is silent. And, of course, at the long distance all sensory contact is gone. The percipient does not know till the end of a run of 25 how many are right. The symbol thought of by the agent is not given objective record until after the call is made (thus excluding B.T.), or, in the long-distance work, after the time interval is about gone and the call has supposedly been made by the percipient. The data presented under the heading 'Same Room' are restricted to those obtained with the agents who worked on the distance tests also. This is done in order to afford a better basis of comparison, since results vary so much with different agents. We omit also the data of Zirkle during the period of illness. For these see Table XXXII.

The table shows the general increase in scores with distance, and this is more emphatically shown by totalling the distance P.T. data, as will be done in Table XXXVII, showing that in large numbers of trials distance makes a significant advance in scores. The difference of 1·2 in the average per 25 is of mathematically justified significance, being 5·8 times the p.e. for the difference. Two great points are affected by this fact: first, on the question of sensory perception (unconscious or fraudulent) it is very important indeed to find that the more the possibility of sense perception is excluded by walls and distance, the better the scores; and, second, on the question of the underlying physics of the phenomena, it is most baffling to present-day physical theorizing in terms of wave mechanics, since, instead of falling off rapidly with the square of the distance, as all radiation intensity is thought to do, it actually significantly increases with distance.

TABLE XXXVII

P.T. totals, general, and for distance comparisons; five subjects

Item no.	Conditions	Trials	Hits	Dev. and p.e.		Value of X	Av. per 25
1	All P.T. data, 5 major subjects	10,275	3,937	+1,882	±27·3	68·8	9·6
2	All P.T., same room, Miss Ownbey as agent;[1] fan going, no vision	3,300	1,401	741	15·5	47·8	10·6
3	All distance P.T., 8 ft. to 250 miles. Wall between, fan going; Miss Ownbey as agent	2,100	995	575	12·4	46·4	11·8

The P.T. totals of these five subjects have been given already in Table XXVII but are more fully presented here as a background for completeness.

With these results our chapter closes, but the work goes on. One wishes at most points to go on to larger figures and for more variations, but with 90,000 trials there is some justice in a pause for discussion. Truth, however, is not a matter purely of huge figures, and we must often be more attentive to small but meaningful series than to those numbering in thousands.

I feel, however, that the task of interpretation of these data is not one for the weeks spent in the writing of this report, but one rather for years of thinking about them and discussing them. So that, however they are interpreted now, I shall steadfastly refuse to defend the interpretation

[1] Zirkle's period of illness, of course, excepted. It is included in item no. 1.

and shall hold it as necessarily tentative. I hope that readers will, in the main, do the same.

Here again we have to add a final note on current progress achieved during the writing-up period. Miss Turner and Miss Ownbey resumed their distance P.T. work after a short rest and at 300 miles distance this time, but could not get back to good scoring. After four runs at chance average they discontinued again for a time. Miss Ownbey was in an unusual situation; she was expecting soon to be married and, for lack, perhaps, of a better theory, we suppose it may have been hard for her to give her fullest attention to the role of E.S.P. agent in such circumstances. This is, of course, only a conjecture. Miss Turner stated that she could not get back the feeling of *rapport*.

At the same time a distance P.C. test was made with Miss Turner, Miss Ownbey handling the cards for her. Miss Ownbey would place the card, without observing its figure, on a book in the center of a table in her home in Asheville, N.C., with which Miss Turner was familiar, and Miss Turner, in Wilson, N.C., would call the cards at the intervals arranged for, every 3 minutes. These began low, 4 per 25 for the first two runs. Then she rose to 7, 8, 7 in the next three, when the experiment was interrupted for a time. (But see the Pearce distance P.C. results, which began about the same time, addendum to Chapter VII.)

Cooper and Miss Ownbey, too, were at this time engaged in a distance P.T. experiment over seven or eight miles of extent, but it did not rise above the chance level, either, before it was interrupted. There were seven runs at an average of only 4.4. Cooper did not expect it to succeed, since at a distance he loses his feeling of *rapport*.

Also at the same time Miss Ownbey and Zirkle tried distance P.T. at 165 miles, but got little above *np* or chance average, 5.5 in 25 for the ten runs tried. This, too, may be interpretable in the same way as suggested for the Turner-Ownbey failure. But, actually, we do not know, in so complex a situation, all that might be concerned. Zirkle, too, felt out of *rapport* and wrote his impression on his records before he knew of the low scores he was making.

And, in some respects, it is more reassuring to have such failures following such striking successes than to have uniform success. First, because it is essential that we have variation of phenomena to reveal to us the laws of nature. And, second, the sceptic can get some degree of reassurance on the ground that at this point when we expected good results to come in, as they had done before under the same conditions, they failed us flatly, although any practice of deception was as fully available as before. Nor was it because we changed conditions essentially, except as the subjects themselves change from time to time. There were, of course, three experiments being conducted with one agent and, as mentioned before, she had other things on her mind. Naturally we expect strain to interfere with perception; and good agency has been shown above to be required for good P.T. perception. In any event, Miss Ownbey's long and splendid record as agent can take a lot of failures without appreciable suffering. And Miss Turner's brilliant series of P.T. at 250 miles cannot be statistically impaired by a score of such failures.

PART III

Explanation and Discussion

CHAPTER IX

Elimination of Negative Hypotheses

T his chapter will be largely a summary of the special evidence bearing upon the different hypotheses that have been offered for the explanation of such phenomena as we have obtained. I will take up the principal hypotheses, one at a time, with a summarized regrouping of the evidence that bears particularly on the evaluation of the given hypothesis. The detailed conditions will mostly be omitted, since they have been given in Part II, along with the presentation of the results. These main hypotheses have been referred to occasionally in Part II, in passing. Doubtless, most readers will by this time already be convinced of their inapplicability. In such case, this chapter may be omitted and the thread taken up at Chapter x.

(a) The Hypothesis of Chance

Logically, the first alternative suggestion that is evoked to explain unusual results such as these high scores in card guessing is that they 'just happened'. That is, that no special principle of causation is responsible; rather, that a number of unimportant circumstances contributed the peculiar results. This general absence of a special causal principle we can call the Chance Hypothesis.

According to the Chance Hypothesis, we should be as likely to go below chance average, if we ran 90,000 more trials, as we should be to go above. All the positive deviation we have accumulated has just been one grand, persistent accident, stretching through three years of varied conditions and over a wide range of subjects. It has actually been suggested to me by a colleague urging this hypothesis that I shall someday find my results swinging as far in a negative deviation as they have already in the positive. What, then, can we say to this?

First, there is the mathematical evaluative principle of probability, by which we may be sure of the odds against an event occurring by chance alone. Since this principle is used throughout Part II, and is explained at the end of Chapter II, it is unnecessary to go into its explanation here. It is only necessary to repeat that general practice among statisticians relies upon a deviation of four times the probable error (of the mean expectation, np) for the minimum limit of significance to reveal the operation of a general factor that is something more than mere accident or chance. This is arbitrary (but one might require 3 or 5 as his minimum value for X [*i.e.*, $X = D$/p.e.] if he feels it is warranted). With $X = 4$, the odds against the Chance Hypothesis are 142 to 1; but with $X = 5$, the odds advance to 1,300 to 1. If $X = 6$, we have the Chance Hypothesis at a disadvantage of 20,000 to 1. And as X increases to 10, the odds against chance are enormously increased, approximately 10,000,000,000 to 1. Note the tremendous jumps of these odds with every unit of the value of X. What 'chance', then, has the Chance Hypothesis, when from chapter to chapter in Part II the value of X rises by leaps and bounds to a grand level of 111·2 and is still going up daily? The relative certainty herein established for the Extra-Sensory Perception principle thus goes far beyond the highest standards and requirements we have for any phase of inquiry.

If anyone wishes to test the mathematical value for probability, it is easy to do. I have, myself, conducted 4,000 'chance' trials, by first making and recording the calls, and later shuffling the cards and checking them against the recorded calls. This eliminated clairvoyance; I did not even try to think of any particular pack of cards. Chance average of 4,000 trials is 800. I got 801. For the last 1,000 of these I took the scores made by Pearce, who was then averaging around 10 hits per 25 trials; I took the same packs of cards he had been using (about 12 in number), cut them once each time and checked them against the record. Chance expectation was, of course, 200 for 1,000 trials and Pearce had almost doubled this, getting 386 correct. My 'chance' control series, however, gave only 204 or a deviation of less than 0·5 of the probable error. Of course, the mathematical theory has been tested many times and it would be a waste of time to go further into testing it for our purpose. Also, the minimal value of 4 for significance in X seems, according to this brief testing, amply adequate and relatively conservative.

Most people are more impressed by a spectacular series of successive hits than by lower but cumulative scoring. Pearce's scoring 25 straight under clairvoyant conditions, in my presence, and Zirkle's 26 straight hits in pure telepathy with my assistant, Miss Ownbey, are the best instances of these. Other subjects have approached these. Linzmayer scored 21 in 25 with clairvoyance, in my presence; Miss Ownbey herself, unwitnessed, scored 23, pure clairvoyance. Miss Turner's score of 19 in distance P.T. work stands out because of the 250 miles between her and the agent. Miss Bailey scored 19 in P.T. in the same room with the agent, as did also Cooper. The odds against getting one series of 25 straight hits by mere chance would be 5^{25} which is nearly 300 quadrillions—just one score of 25! A small part of our 90,000 trials.

(b) Fraud Hypothesis

Once we are certain that we are not dealing with a mere accidental deviation—that the Chance Hypothesis has been adequately ruled out mathematically and by empirical controls—we want to question the human reliability in the case. Are we dealing with real facts of actual occurrence or are they fictitious? It is a question, first, of the honesty and sincerity of the observers and the subjects, and, second, of the competence of the former.

One really ought to begin with one's self, though I doubt if my own sincerity will seriously be questioned; an academic person has seldom, if ever, been found to work a deliberate hoax involving hard work and long hours for several years. Yet it is a possibility. Here, however, we have a whole set of persons involved: several assistants, who are responsible graduate assistants in our Department of Psychology. Four of these have done significant (*i.e.* X is above 4) E.S.P. work themselves and there have been other subjects who under observation have done significant work. There are in all eight major subjects whose work would individually constitute magnificent independent proof of E.S.P., so far as value of X goes. There are many minor subjects, too, whose work stands on its own merit, individually. I can think easily of six such, whose X value has been computed separately. There are, then, in addition, my colleagues and friends who have witnessed the subjects at work. Some of these, those who have seen Pearce work, are listed in Table XIX in Chapter VII. Among these seven witnesses are three psychologists, an education official and a professional magician. The very magnitude of the system of persons involved, whose names are herein published, must discourage any attempt at a charge of sheer dishonesty. Perhaps I may, for brevity's sake, refer the possible doubting reader to Dr McDougall or Dr Prince (both of whom have known me now for many years) concerning such a point.

All the major subjects, themselves, have been witnessed to some extent and most of them almost entirely. Much of this witnessing has been done by trusted graduate assistants, young research students who are themselves going in for a psychological career and are fully responsible. The very division of this responsibility offers in itself a more complex obstacle to the 'Fraud Hypothesis'. Each one witnessed results of ample significance to prove E.S.P. on their own merit. Those subjects who have not been wholly witnessed throughout have in many cases shown better results when witnessed than when unwitnessed (see Table XXVIII, for one illustration; Stuart is another instance). And finally, on the point of witnessing of subjects, there are several long and very significant series of tests by major subjects *doubly* witnessed, *i.e.* with two of us present. See, for example, Table XIX, columns headed B and C. Note that column C totals with a deviation over 23 times the p.e.—doubly witnessed figures. The honesty of the subjects does not matter under such conditions. But, in my judgment of them, these subjects are all splendidly sincere and reliable.

No one can, I think, long hold to the 'Fraud Hypothesis' after reading the excellent results obtained, (1) with P.T. at a distance[1] (Tables XXXVII and XXXVIII), (2) under the D.T. conditions, witnessed, and with no sensory contact with the individual cards (Item 6, Table XVII) and (3) with the screen data (Item 5, XVII), no matter how doubtful of the subjects' honesty one may be. The Fraud Hypothesis, then, may be abandoned also. The possibilities for the unconscious following of cues or marks on the cards, though equally well excluded by these results, will be considered separately and more fully under (c).

(c) Hypothesis of Incompetence

In view of the simple technique used and the relatively simple computations required, it can hardly be seriously thought that the results herein reported are the consequence of errors made by the observers. Moreover, on this point, Mr Pratt and I together witnessed several hundred of Mr Pearce's best scores. Dr Zener and I together witnessed 300 trials with Pearce, observing all points of the procedure together and using new cards. The deviation of the results is 9·4 times the p.e. for these 300 trials. None of the various observers have been able to point to any adequate weakness or combination of weaknesses in the procedure that could, in their judgment, explain the results. Some suggestions have been made for further improving the technique but no adequate loophole discovered. Again, the independent recording of the able assistants and myself is a check, to a certain extent, upon the competence and reliability of us all.

Moreover, the early results, obtained when we were all less experienced, were among the very poorest. With im-

[1]And to this we can now add the excellent distance P.C. results of Pearce, mentioned at the close of Chapter III and VII.

provement in technique and judgment, the results have risen in value. This does not look like incompetence. Furthermore, the natural outlines of the data, the curves, the fluctuations with physiological conditions, the effects of the presence of strange witnesses, of changes, of illness, all show a lawfulness that gets us considerably beyond this 'Hypothesis of Haphazard Observation'. It is true, much of this work was of a tentative, exploratory character and lacked standardization. It is also probable that some errors have been made in recording, totalling and computing the values. If so, such errors are at most of trifling consequence. The general ground has been covered too often and by too many individuals for serious error that would vitiate an important conclusion. So the Hypothesis of Incompetence will, I think, find few adherents and no justification.

(d) *Unconscious Sensory Perception*

There is left, then, when we safely pass the above mentioned hypotheses, that of Unconscious Sensory Perception. That is, assuming that the investigator is honest and competent enough to pass muster, and that the subject is guarded carefully enough to prevent outright dishonesty on his part (if it should exist), might there not be sensory indices such as marks on the back of the card, peculiarities on the edge of the card, unconscious whispering from agent to perceiver in P.T. work and the like? This is unconscious sensory perception, since, if the subject is honest and is conscious, he would not presumably do this, knowing he was deceiving. But the conditions for prevention of deception, conscious and unconscious, are just about the same and the two may be discussed together.

Beginning with Linzmayer, there were 120 trials made with combined P.C. and P.T. conditions (*i.e.*, I held a card and looked at it also), with screened card, subject's face turned away and a motor going to cover possible unconscious whispering. Results gave a deviation 11.2 times the p.e. With pure clairvoyance in 105 trials, excluding sensory perception by screening with 55 and by using new cards with 50, the deviation is, alone, 7 times the p.e.

Turning now to Pearce, we find first that the new card data, totalling 1,675 trials, yielded a positive deviation of 291 ($\pm$11) and X = 26. These averaged 9·3 in 25. The trials included the 1st, 2nd and 3rd runs with the new cards. The first runs averaged as high as the 3rd. During these runs Pearce did not look at the cards before he called them, as a rule. He would glance at the pack now and then, however, absentmindedly. He called each card before lifting it off. There had been no chance for him to learn any indication marks on the backs of the cards, since he never saw them before the period of experimentation, and during that time he did not see the face and back of a card consecutively.

The 600 trials made with a screen between the cards and the subject, Pearce, are also highly significant, both the B.T. and the 300 with the possible telepathic factor included. The significance indices (X) are, respectively, 8·3 and 11·9.

The D.T. data, obtained with nothing but the edges of the cards visible, except the top card, afford good exclusion of sensory perception. Most of the time Pearce did not even look at the pack after starting the calling. But, even when he did, apparently uniform edges of the cards offered no clue to their identity. Often they were new cards, and never were they so old that differences in battered edges could be detected and associated with the face. Moreover, there was no chance to learn the connection. The calls were made rapidly (25 in 1 to 2 minutes) and the check-up likewise (1 minute). There was a different pack used for each run, as a rule, with perhaps 10 to 20 packs lying about on the table in my laboratory. And, again, I repeat, Pearce's favourite posture for D.T. was with eyes closed, sometimes hand on his eyes or forehead, as if in deep abstraction. The 1,625 D.T. trials yielded a positive deviation 14 times the p.e. (see Table XVIII).

Combining these data and in view of their significance, what sensory perception is possible? No one present at the tests, or absent, has been able to suggest a possibility. Did this young minister sneak into my laboratory and 'thumb-nail' the edges of the cards for the D.T. work? Apart from the fact of the other data (screen and new cards, etc.), and the not unimportant facts that my laboratory was kept locked and that Pearce did not usually look at the pack during D.T., there is the simple obstacle that I, too, can see such marks and have looked for them frequently during the thousands of hours I have spent in this work. I have never discovered marks that might have been purposely made, except once, on the backs of some of one old pack of cards, and these were not consistent. They may well have been nervously and absentmindedly thumbnailed by an idle observer. In one lot of cards, also, Stuart showed me that the rectangles were on slightly broader cards than were the other figures. Thereafter we had the cards cut better and more evenly.

On the telepathic side there are the distance studies, which get well beyond the range of sensory perception of the unconscious order. However, in all our later and better P.T. work done in one room we kept an electric fan going. The noise of this motor is enough to 'drown' any supposed unconscious whispering. Also, in the excellent P.T. work of Miss Turner, Miss Bailey, Cooper and Zirkle the percipients did not look at the agent. There was, then, no sensory contact between the two, except for the uniform tapping of a telegraph key, giving the signal for each call to be made. In the distance work, the distance was simply added to these other conditions, and a tile wall or two interposed along with distance. Sensory perception is simply eliminated from the case. And, as a climax, there is the long-distance telepathy of Miss Turner, over 250 miles away from the agent, Miss Ownbey, and the already very successful distance P.C. work of Pearce from one building to another on the campus. For the details of these various P.T. scores and totals under the various conditions, consult Table XXXVII, in Chapter VIII. The results are all splendidly rich in significance. In fact, the anti-chance index, X, for the distance P.T. data alone on Misses Bailey and Turner, and for Cooper and Zirkle is 46, an enormous value.

There is, I think, no point in elaborating further on the Sensory Perception Hypothesis. There can hardly be any just doubt of its successful elimination. And when we recall that 7 of the 8 major subjects do both P.C. and P.T. work, successfully, under a wide range of conditions, the Sensory Perception Hypothesis would have to be stretched beyond all reason to account for the facts. With the P.C. there are no sounds, with the P.T. no objective stimulus such as a card. The common supposition would involve vision for the P.C. and hearing for the P.T., and these senses we have laboured to eliminate. We shall, then, leave this hypothesis as one against which the facts would seem to be quite conclusive.

(e) Hypothesis of Rational Inference

What are the possibilities for rational inference? That is, how successfully can the subject determine by reasoning what card is on top of a given pack or at any other point in it? It is almost obvious that in a shuffled and cut pack of cards, containing 5 each of 5 suits, no logic known can determine the distribution. And, in our experience, the effort to use logic only interferes with success in E.S.P.

When the cards are called and checked in 5's, as was often done, there might seem to be a chance for the subject to remember to some advantage in the last 5 calls the number of various circles, rectangles, etc., already called. But our good subjects did not depend on inference and did not attempt to use it. If this had been a factor, one would expect the last 5 calls in the B.T.-by-5's to be relatively higher than the B.T.-by-25's (i.e., where all were called before checking up). This is not the case. In fact, the opposite is true. While Pearce comes in heavily in all P.C. work on the last 5 calls, he gets a much higher relative score on the last 5 of the B.T. 25. He does also in the D.T. (which is also run straight through by 25's). So we may see that this seemingly possible slight weakness is not a measurably actual one. We may, then, discard the Hypothesis of Rational Inference from the P.C. end—as a matter of fact, only a small portion (2850 trials) of the 75,000 or more P.C. trials were run as B.T. 5, and then, mostly, after each five the cards would be returned to the pack and reshuffled for the next five calls.

But, turning to the P.T. phase, we have a more difficult problem. In order to get free from possible clairvoyance, we avoid the use of cards or objective record of any kind, except that made after the call is given. The agent chooses, without objective aid, what symbols to visualize in imagination. One may well ask, then, if it is not possible that two persons, agent and percipient, may naturally and accidentally fall into the same routine order? 'Circle, plus, rectangle, star, waves', for instance, as seems to come most easily to some people. Or, what would be equally antagonistic to the E.S.P. hypothesis, the percipient may try to infer what order the agent would be likely to follow, if the order is followed that comes most easily to her.

We decided that the best way to avoid trouble on this score was to have the agent choose not just one figure at a time, but a series of 5. The order of the five would be determined upon and would be followed out, concentrating imaginal attention upon each one as its turn came. After these five were used, another five would be mentally selected, usually some variation of the first five. The same five symbols as are used on the E.S.P. cards are used throughout the P.T. work. The degree of repetition and variation is measured roughly by the range one gets from the average pack, and the percipient is told to expect that. Thus a system is followed by the agent, yet a system that varies continually, and thus avoids stereotyped order that might be inferred or fallen into by accident. A study of the agents' records shows no detectable order, except the orderly avoidance of order. The percipient was not told by the agent of his success until the end of the run of 25. Thus he had no basis for inference as he went. And here, too, we may dismiss the Hypothesis of Rational Inference. At its best, no one could suppose it capable of explaining the brilliant long runs, the 25 straight successes, under both P.C. and P.T. conditions.

The hypotheses discussed here are the main ones that conflict or compete with the E.S.P. hypothesis. They have been, one by one, eliminated and, since they have no special strength in combination, we may conclude that E.S.P. stands without a serious opposing hypothesis. The evidence for the elimination of these opposing hypotheses was such that it eliminated each one completely, not leaving a partial support for any one of them. On this ground, too, then, we may omit discussion of combinations of the opposing hypotheses. For those, then, who can accept proof before explanation is arrived at (*i.e.,* for the scientifically mature) E.S.P. is a natural fact and principle, puzzling as its explanation may be. We can turn now to the facts that tend to throw light upon its nature and functioning.

CHAPTER X

Physical Conditions in Functioning of E.S.P.

If one is reasonably sure that he is dealing with a process of reality that is not explainable by the commoner hypotheses of chance, fraud or error, he naturally must seek the explanation in some newer direction. It may be that the route to explanation will lead in a roundabout way to old and known principles, as is the more common type of scientific advance, *i.e.*, explaining the new in terms of the old. On the other hand, it may be that quite new principles of reality will have to be found before these new phenomena can be explained. In any case one must be guided by the new facts, of course, and not by the present limits of knowledge. Some of these new facts have already appeared and are still appearing in these data, and many more will have to be sought through longer periods of study.

The facts of interest in the explanation of E.S.P. may roughly be grouped as: physical, physiological, psychological, 'psychical' (parapsychological) and, more generally, biological. On some of these I have but few facts to offer, but it is better, even so, thus to keep them clearly separate. Because of their relative simplicity I will first discuss the physical aspects.

It is so customary to think of physics as the best developed of the natural sciences that one is prone to use it as an ideal and standard background for his psychological thinking. It is difficult, therefore, to think of physics as probably very far from complete in its grasp of world processes. Yet that is the very point that is indicated or strongly suggested by the facts of this chapter. What are the facts and the logic behind such a statement?

By 'physical', here, is meant the 'demonstrably energetic' (though not necessarily demonstrable on a particular instrument of measurement); and by 'energetic', that which 'does work' or 'effects changes'. Again, the changes need not yet have been measured in ergs or in any other official unit. If they systematically and demonstrably lead up to the vocal behaviour producing given, experimentally selected sound-vibration patterns we call words, such as 'circle, rectangle, star, etc.', in a prearranged order, we infer, as is done in all physics, a chain of energetic causation extending back through the prior history of the event to any arbitrary point one may choose. This causal capacity to 'do work' (to effect changes) is 'physical' in the professional use of the term, even though the profession has as yet no theory of the nature of the particular kind of energy process at certain points in the causal chain.

Of first importance, perhaps, are the facts pointing to the absence of any yet known energy principle in E.S.P. All the senses in sensory perception function by the interception of some appropriate form of energy by the sense organ concerned—light rays, molecular vibration, chemical energy, etc. This interception of energy by the sensory endings is a necessary link between the nervous system and the outer world, for all perception occurring through sensation. The energetic causation involved is seen clearly when one looks at the face of a card and perceives it to be a 'circle'. Between the card and the eye there have been light-energy connections. Human experience and science expect, therefore, some energetic causal connection between the card and the act of perception. When, in E.S.P., the subject perceives the card, what energy is involved? Sound waves are barred out; it cannot be pressure or contact; the chemical energies are inapplicable. Visible light energy is excluded by the screen, by the D.T. conditions, by distance and even by the B.T. condition. No light gets in to the face of the card and the cards are of heavy opaque cardboard, somewhat opaque even to X-rays. Of the possible forms of energy known only extremely short rays would be capable of penetrating such cardboard, especially in D.T., when they are 25 cards deep.

The Radiation Theory

The only hypothesis that modern physical theory could at present offer, so far as I can judge, would be a wave theory, a radiation of extremely short and very penetrative waves. The radiation theory is an old one and has been frequently discussed in connection with telepathy and clairvoyance, particularly with the former. Even the mediumistic jargon often includes 'getting into the vibration'. This hypothesis was set forth by William Crookes and may possibly have antedated him. (See Chapter II.) Brain waves were supposed to be emitted by the agent and intercepted by the brain of the percipient. But, to cover our phenomena of P.C. and P.T., both in the same subjects, in like degree, roughly speaking, there would have to be rays originating not only in the agent's brain but in the cards used in P.C. work as well; either that, or else originating outside them and selectively absorbed by them.

Now, the cardboard is slightly opaque to X-rays but the ink-figures on it are not. An X-ray photograph of the card shows only a dim outline of the card after a 10-second exposure. When a pack of the cards used is photographed with X-rays, it shows only a clearer rectangle. There is no difference made by the figures printed on the cards—no differential absorption. If these rays are not obstructed by the ink figures, it is surely not to be expected that shorter ones would be. And if longer waves were in question, the cardboard would interfere. And even if these difficulties were not in the way and there were a suitable ray penetrating the pack of cards, giving differential absorption on every card, the impression given on a receptive plate or organ would be one big blur in the centre of the card. For the effect would presumably be additive, and one figure indistinguishable from another on the analogy of sensory perception and mechanical reception. So I see no way to use the radiation theory unless the ink figures themselves give off the special radiation, and that its waves are short enough to penetrate cardboard even when piled up 25 cards deep and about ¾ inch thick.

Such radiation, supposed, then, to come from the ink-figures on the cards, would have to be (1) continuously emitted (old cards, a year old, are as good as new,) (2) would have to penetrate 25 cards with undiminished force, (3) would have to be incapable of affecting an X-ray sensitive plate after ½ hour exposure (actually tested), and (4) would have to be as detectable at 250 yards as at one yard. This takes it out of the range of present physical knowledge. And when it is recalled that such radiation, in order to make possible the D.T. results, would have to permit of 25 figures being distinguishable in a pack, at one time—that is, with continuous radiation striking the receptive organ (perhaps the brain)—the discrimination between the 25 figures on the cards in the pack would presumably have to be based upon relative intensity. But the cards themselves are stamped with rubber stamps with varying pressure and ink supply, and individual differences are so large that this could not be relied upon. There would be a situation too baffling even for sense perception, which is manifestly more certain and dependable. Suppose one were to try to distinguish visually 25 luminous figures set one behind the other, all 25 in ¾ inch space, when he was seated from 2 to 5 feet away from them. The impression would be much like the differential absorption case pictured above in which an incoming ray was assumed, one that was more absorbed by the ink-figure than by the cards. One great unanalysable splotch! Furthermore, in the D.T. work the card pack may be perceived from any angle: from above, from the side, or from an intermediate angle. Whether the supposed rays came from the figures or came from without, the angle would be important on any radiation theory—

as much in fact as it is to a photographer or a reader. But, actually, the angle is not seriously regarded by the percipient.

On these many scores the facts are against the Radiation Hypothesis and there are none at all to favour it, except that it is familiar.

Now, if we are dealing with the same general function in P.C. and P.T. work as the evidence (see Chapter XIII) would seem to indicate, we have to suppose either that the human nervous system radiates 'thought-waves' or that it selectively absorbs some outside radiation. The former seems to be the only one of the two worthy of attention. The general electrodynamics of the nerve cell is not well known but it has been likened to a small dynamo. And the trend of neural physiology is strongly toward more electromagnetic interpretation of nerve functions. To suppose some electric radiation here would not be a large leap at all. But what are the requirements for this?

First, for an adequate E.S.P. hypothesis we must have something that can hypothetically cover both the P.C. and the P.T. conditions. The radiation coming from a card or coming from a brain probably will need to be quite similar in view of the many facts that tie the P.C. and P.T. processes up together. It is difficult, as already stated, in physical theorizing to think of wave emanations coming from a brain and an ink-figure. In doing this electro-physiology cannot help us, for we have to go down to a level of the card and ink, since they serve quite as well as the brain (or 'thinking organ') as a source of E.S.P. stimulation.

But assuming, even, that the two sources have different wave characteristics and dealing alone with the wave features under P.T. conditions, the radiation hypothesis is rendered pretty thoroughly inapplicable by the distance data. All radiant energy declines in intensity with the square of the distance from the source. We should then find that, other things being equal, distance would bring about a sharp decline in P.T. scoring. Turning to Tables XXXVI and XXXVII in Chapter VIII, we see that this is not the case with P.T. In fact, it is just the opposite, distance P.T. giving higher scores than did P.T. in the same room with the agent. In view of the large number of trials, 3,300 in the same room and 2,100 with some distance, the difference in average scores per 25 of 1·2 is quite significant, being 5·8 times the probable error for the difference. Most of the distances are short, 30 feet and under; but even a distance of 8 to 30 feet is a prodigious distance for the detection of patterns in short-wave radiation that will penetrate flesh, tiled walls, heavy doors, etc. Declining with the square of the distance would give great fall in intensity. But when we extend the distance to over 250 miles, and have Miss Turner jump from her 'close-up' average of 7·7 in 25 to 19 hits in 25 at the long distance in the first run, any radiation hypothesis depending on the inverse square law can hardly be regarded as plausible, in my judgment. And if it be a radiation hypothesis without the inverse square law, what would it be?

Shall Hertzian or 'radio' waves of short cycle be considered? They are at once thrown out by the distance data. One needs only to remember the tremendous difference in radio reception between being within a mile of a powerful broadcasting station and being over 250 miles away. In Miss Turner's case that is reversed. And the data are independent. Even though she never gets so high again, the point is amply established, unless the standard mathematics for the evaluation of such data is in grievous error; for her first 75 trials gave a gain over chance average that is 15·7 times the probable error. And when one reflects upon the high intensities required for radiation from the agent's mind in order to reach out over 250 miles, allowing for a decline proportional to the square of the distance—even if the results were to grade down with distance—the agent would have to be an incredibly powerful broadcasting station.

In view of the E.S.P. at a distance and the D.T. work there is little chance for a radiation theory, along lines of present physical theory, intellectually delightful though it would be to bring these results into more easy explanation and acceptance by finding such a connection between new facts and old laws. There are general considerations, too, that are against the radiation theory. One of these is the problem of explaining orientation and focussing on radiational lines. I refer now not to the problem of localizing a card in the middle of the pack by E.S.P. but of keeping the right pack in mind. I have, for instance, worked with Pearce with the table literally covered with cards, with sixteen packs and some odds and ends strewn about. I pick up one pack and start him at calling it B.T. or D.T. Now, if all the figures on all the cards are broadcasting more messages, there are perhaps 75 to 100 vibrating 'circle', 'circle', 'circle', while simultaneously (mark!) are 400 others discordantly chiming in with 'wavy lines', 'star' and the rest. If we use a wave hypothesis, we have to play it throughout, and on this problem of localization or focussing, it seems preferable to wait rather than accept the confusion attending the wave hypothesis that makes every figure a broadcasting unit. In P.T. it is even worse! What percipient could, even if he were a 'sort of radio receiving set', possibly distinguish his agent's messages in spite of the fact that there are many millions of other 'stations' sending in the same cycle? Or can we suppose that every mind, if not every card, has its own cycle? This is probably implied in the medium's remark that she is 'trying to get into your vibration'. But what a range would be required for the race and what a task 'receiving' would be! A few dozen stations are a trial to keep from overlapping; what about the millions, with no Federal supervision! It is just one more little point of difficulty for a Radiation Hypothesis.

The hardest fact for the Radiation Hypothesis to face is that in Pearce-Pratt distance P.C. series not only does Pearce select the right card from 25 lying on the table 100 to 250 yards away, with hundreds of similar cards (radiating?) in adjoining rooms even nearer the percipient than the one to be called, but the cards to be called all lie flat on the table. That means that a radiation picture would show only a straight line, alike for a circle, a star or any of the card figures. I can see no hope for a radiation theory of E.S.P.

And now we turn to the point of the need for a larger concept of physics, if physics is to follow the phenomena of the energetic world. In these tests from Durham to Lake Junaluska, Miss Ownbey regulated—controlled to a degree—the organism of Miss Turner, guiding her to make a certain set of marks. Had this been done by wireless telegraphy, we should not think of it as anything but physical. It is a physical axiom obviously deductible from the Law of the Conservation of Energy that energetic processes cannot be guided or regulated, except by the expenditure of energy; however little it may require, it takes energy to change the direction of energy. Hence, we may say, it is a clear-cut problem for physics to explain through what energetic means Miss Ownbey changed the organism of Miss Turner from its 'chance' or unregulated behaviour to that designed by Miss Ownbey in Durham. What is the connecting energetic link between these cards and the E.S.P. subject's energetic responses? If he sees the card faces, we say it is light energy that connects. If he does not, cannot, see the faces—if all known sensory reception of energy is excluded —what energetic link is still there, for nothing yet known can guide his energy system but energy itself? That is, if anything were known that *could* change one's responses that was not one of the known energies, it would promptly be declared another kind of energy, because it 'does work' and 'effects change'. This would have to be done to save the coherence, unity and comprehensibility of our basic physics. At this point we are, then, it seems, faced with the need of another order of energy, not radiant.

If this seems especially bold as a conclusion, it is quickly, I think, reduced to modesty by the reminder that all conscious process is in pretty much the same need, though possibly this comes closer to the range of present working theories. Yet whatever is found out in either field, in E.S.P. or mind in general, as to ultimate energetic nature, will probably help us to understand the other. It seems quite possible that the long untouched mystery of the physics of conscious process may yet be first peeped into from the odd corners of these more bizarre mental phenomena. Pierre Janet has very well said: "Attention is first drawn to a particular force by its exceptional manifestation."

As an appendix to this chapter, it seems worth while to give some data on D.T. curves that looked for a time very much as if we were to have an interesting physical law revealed in them. The facts that this first appearance was misleading and that the results are more psychologically interpretable as 'effects of anticipation' do not rob the point of interest. The negative effect is itself of value.

The D.T. data of Pearce, Stuart, Cooper and Linzmayer had all strongly favoured the hypothesis that it was 'physically' harder to get at the centre of the solid pack. Their data showed more hits by percentage in the first five cards of the pack and in the last five at the bottom, with the lowest rate of scoring in the central fifteen. This fact, combined with the fact that their D.T. scores were, on the whole, lower than B.T. scores (cards taken off the pack as called), made it appear that there was some difficulty in penetration (or in radiation) as the centre was approached. Of course, there is no known basis for such a principle. On any kind of radiation theory it would not be that way. The deeper down the card, presumably the more difficult, if there were any difference at all. But in an unknown field it is well to regard ever poor hypotheses. On the other hand, it seemed somewhat probable that mere convenience in keeping the order straight might be a determining factor, perhaps. On this hypothesis, the percipient might be abler to keep the two ends of the series of 25 calls more correctly in order, because he could work in from either end as a guide point. In the centre he was farthest away from the easier measuring points and migth be more easily lost. Also he might merely expect this to be true and he might not try so hard in calling the central 15. There were, then, one physical and two psychological hypotheses.

But Miss Ownbey put an end to the physical speculation on this point by giving us a D.T. curve that goes very definitely in the opposite direction. Her scoring is highest for the central five and lowest for the top and bottom fives. The curve obtained by plotting scoring against order of fives down through the pack in D.T. gives an inverted U-shaped curve even more regular than the upright U curve given by the four others. This work was done by Miss Ownbey without, of course, any notion of how the other work came out and free from any knowledge of my interest in the curves produced. The importance of these curves to psychological relations will be taken up in Chapter XII; it is

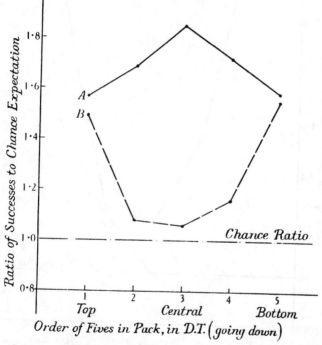

Graph No. 1. This shows the success in scoring in D.T. as distributed over the average run (of 25), indicated for each 5 cards down through the pack. Curve A represents 3,350 trials in D.T. by Miss Ownbey. Curve B represents 4,225 trials in D.T. by Pearce, Stuart, Cooper and Linzmayer.

clear that no conclusion could be drawn favourable to a difference in penetrability with position of the card on the pack. Rather does the evidence add strength to the non-radiation side of the theorizing on the nature of E.S.P. It will be recalled that we found there were no radiation effects from the cards on the sensitive plate and no differential absorption by them with X-rays. Now we go right

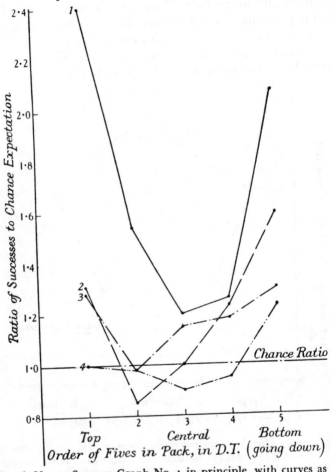

Graph No. 2. Same as Graph No. 1 in principle, with curves as follows: Curve 1 represents 1,500 trials by Pearce; Curve 2, 1,200 by Cooper; Curve 3, 1,000 by Linzmayer; Curve 4, 1,000 by Stuart.

to the sensitive organisms themselves, the only system receptive to the causal energetic principle involved in E.S.P. And these sensitives in one case get more in the first five, in others most in the last five at the bottom; in the one case of Miss Ownbey, most in the central five. These differences are striking evidence of the physical non-essentiality of position in the pack, quite as the long-distance P.T. and P.C. evidence the non-essentiality of position in space in general.

Logically, then, must we not say that, if space is not important or essential in these processes, its absence of function means, for these functions, non-existence, since it is 'function' that makes 'existence'? If so, then, E.S.P. is a spaceless function and its relationships must be sought in terms of such a physics. Of course, such hypotheses must be regarded conservatively but the facts seem to compel us rather in that direction.

The D.T. curves under discussion may be seen in Graph No. 1. Curve B is that obtained by combining the scores for the D.T. work of Pearce, Cooper, Linzmayer and Stuart, and taking the joint results in scoring for each five cards down through the pack, giving the scores in 5 divisions. These are then divided by the mean chance expectation (np) to put all on a relative basis, and plotted as the ratio of success to mean chance expectation for each 5 cards in the pack (of 25). The curve is a pretty fair U-shape. Curve A is the expression of Miss Ownbey's D.T. work given in the same way. Her curve is obviously of the opposite type. This curve is typical for her, as is shown by the fact that, if her work is divided and plotted, it gives two curves of this form, almost identical. The individuals whose results are drawn up in Curve A do not all have the same rate of scoring. They differ quite widely. Also they have different low points. But they all agree in being higher in the top and bottom fives, and lowest in the middle fifteen. Graph No. 2 will show their individual curves.

CHAPTER XI

Some Physiological Conditions Affecting E.S.P.

If it is correct to assume some energetic causal relationship between the percipient and the agent or card, as, I think, our scientific logic requires, then the percipient is somehow intercepting energy of some kind in E.S.P., clear as we may feel that E.S.P. is not simply a phenomenon of short-wave transmission. But what is the receptor system by which this is done? Is it an organ of the body or a nonmaterial system? Is the nervous system definitely involved in the primary act of reception? Is E.S.P. a function of the integrated organism or a passive reception depending upon dissociation? Does it require physical orientation (*i.e.,* any turning toward) of any sort? Is the reception system given or developed? Can it be injured or destroyed? These are some of the questions one wishes to have answered in terms that are physiological in some measure. The work so far has not gone far to answer them, but it does offer something.

There is nothing to indicate that any special organ of the body is involved in E.S.P. in the mere reception. There may be, of course, since there is no way as yet of telling in a conclusive way. But the circumstances are against it. First, no subject has ever had any definite feeling of getting reception localized in any special organ or tissue of his body. The process has been as unlocalizable as mind itself. Sensory reception is, of course, easily localizable in the sense organs. Second, there seems to be such a variety of angles and directions, as well as distances, which the recipient may take with respect to the source (agent or card) that it is quite clear no special orientation is of importance. It may seem to be so to the subject at first. He may feel that he can do best with the card in a certain place but we are now certain that such inhibiting notions are grounded only in his own misconceptions. They may continue to inhibit as long as he actively expects them to, and then cease. (Nothing may be treated with more scepticism than the subject's explanations of limitations; yet they are, as effective factors, to be taken seriously, however delusional they may be.) Stuart after a time found he could work as well with the cards behind his back. Linzmayer has worked well at nearly all angles— with the card behind him, beside him, in front, on his stomach, forehead, etc. Others, too, have had varied conditions with no important difference in results. There is no evidence whatever for a reception centre recognizably more sensitive than any other part of the organism, and the facts just given are against it. This extra-sensory reception of energy would seem to be a general, rather than a local, function. Is, then, the organism as a whole involved?

One conclusion that seems fairly clear is that E.S.P. depends upon the higher functions of the nervous system. It requires a degree of control by the higher functions that permits a certain amount of 'concentration'; *i.e.*, attention to one thing and exclusion of others. This depends upon a certain degree of integration of the nervous system. Dissociative drugs,[1] sleepiness and certain illnesses work to lower this integration and self-control; whereas drugs that antagonize dissociative drugs help to recover normal control. And in our results the data show plainly that dissociative factors likewise lower E.S.P. ability, while counteractive factors help to restore it.[2]

[1] I am drawing the general principles stated here largely from Prof. McDougall's discussion of 'Fatigue, Drugs, and Sleep', Chapter III of *Outline of Abnormal Psychology*, Scribners, 1926, and from his earlier work on the mutual antagonism of certain drugs in their influence on certain mental processes.

[2] Brugmanns' results of increased 'telepathy' with 30 gms. of alcohol (see Chapter II) are not contradictory. So small an amount would not for many individuals be noticeably dissociative. In small amounts this drug gives the effects of stimulation through the removal of inhibition and the vasomotor changes. But a certain dulling of sensory acuity would probably add to ease of abstraction, too. These considerations are adequate to account for Brugmanns' results.

The effect of sodium amytal has been rather strikingly destructive to E.S.P. in all three experiments, with Linzmayer and Pearce in P.C., and with Zirkle in P.T. The results are significant beyond question. (See Table XXXVIII.)

TABLE XXXVIII

Summary of data from sodium-amytal experiments

Name of percipient	Condition	Before and after		During drug treatment		Drop in av. per 25
		Trials	Av. per 25	Trials	Av. per 25	
Linzmayer	P.C.	960	6·8	275	5·1	1·7
Pearce	P.C.	2,250	9·7	325	6·1	3·6
Zirkle	P.T.	1,300	14·7	600	7·0	7·7

There was here no serious interference with perceptual capacity itself, since sensory perception was clearly possible. In all the common mental processes, especially with Pearce and Zirkle, there was no serious impairment. In ordinary conversation, attention was not lacking. Rational responses were made to questions. In all the external features of the experiment, there was no marked difficulty. Only the higher and more complex features of nervous organization were altered. Does it mean, therefore, that E.S.P. involves a higher and more complex nervous process? I think it does suggest just that; though there may be a relatively simpler and lower phase to the actual reception itself. Perception, however, in requiring a recognition of the reception phase, may involve the higher organization. Yet I think it is fully possible also, and a little more probable, that we are dealing with a phenomenon of the super-organization of the brain process system, one that in itself may function only at a certain level of organization, yet not involve specialized structure necessarily. This cannot be decided now, however, and is not of importance here.

Sleepiness, whether from fatigue or from sodium amytal, has the same effect of lowering the scoring. With Zirkle, too, in P.T. the effect of caffeine was equally striking. The first treatment brought his average up from 12·8 to 14·7 in

300 trials. The latter average is approximately his average under normal conditions of health, rest, etc. But the best test for caffeine came 5 hours after taking the sodium amytal. Under the influence of the amytal he had dropped to an average of 6·2 in the last 300 trials. One hour[1] after the 5-gr. dose of caffeine, he rose to an average of 9·5, which is a rise of 3·3, a marked and significant advance.

It is, then, only with the best functioning of the higher processes of the mind that E.S.P. of either type succeeds well. It is, in this, like creative thinking and higher mental skills. The composer, the inventor, the poet, the reflective scientist needs this condition for his constructive work. He requires the highest integration of the nervous system for his best creation. He may, then, like some of these subjects in E.S.P., go off into abstraction from the surroundings, amounting almost to a trance. But this is an intensification of attention in one direction by withdrawal from others. It is 'concentration'.

TABLE XXXIX
Effect of illness on E.S.P.

Name of subject		Before and after illness		During illness		Drop in av. per 25	Conditions
		Trials	Av. per 25	Trials	Av. per 25		
1. Linzmayer	P.T., B.T.	700	6·6	350	4·3	2·3	Cold with headache. 'Before' and 'after' are of equal numbers
2. Pearce	B.T.	700	10·0	350	7·0	3·0	Tonsilitis
3. Miss Turner	B.T.	175	9·9	50	4·5	5·4	Fever following flu. No data 'after'
4. Zirkle	P.T.	1,300	14·8	2,100	8·6	6·2	Cold

Not that E.S.P. is comparable in other respects to higher creative mental work. It is not, as we shall see in the next

[1] After discusing these results with Prof. McDougall in the light of his researches on drug antagonisms, I see that one hour was not long enough after the drug ingestion for the maximum effect. In fact, the subjective report of Zirkle confirmed this point. He was more alert several hours later. Prof. McDougall found five hours after ingestion to be the time of greatest effect for caffeine.

two chapters. But it does require, as they do, the highest integration of the nervous system. The data on illness support this view, though it is amply established, I think, anyhow. The data given in Table XXXIX are to this point. The illnesses in the four cases were tonsilitis, colds or flu, all very dissociative and depressing to most people, and destructive to higher mental functioning.

There is another important bearing of the data reviewed here on the connection between integration and E.S.P. It appears to favour the point of the agency of the percipient himself in the process and to count against the theories of passive percipience which we shall take up later on—for example, the 'spirit' hypothesis, which has been suggested to explain telepathy and clairvoyance. My point is that if a dream state, with a light sleep, had been found favourable to E.S.P., we might have a favouring circumstance for the theories of outside agencies. But since alertness is favourable, and drowsiness is unfavourable, we must interpret this as negative to the hypotheses which suppose outside agencies. It will be recalled that many of the reported spontaneous parapsychological experiences (of apparitions, voices, premonitions, etc.) come during sleep, as veridical dreams, or during a time when sleep is expected. The dissociation is then such that, according to our results, E.S.P. would not be expected to succeed well, if at all. All such spontaneous phenomena do, of course, as a rule, take on the appearance of being activated by an outside agency, while in no case of this E.S.P. work of ours is there any suggestion of that. I think, then, that the facts reported here of the relations between dissociated conditions and E.S.P. ability favour pretty strongly that hypothesis which stresses the active agency of the percipient subject himself, for the conditions of these experiments, rather than of the superior order of agencies sometimes proposed. This would hypothetically separate this experimental work from the spontaneous occurrences. If correct, this is the most important point in the physiological data.

It has already been pointed out that, when sufficient

amytal has been administered to prevent or nearly prevent E.S.P., sensory perception is still possible. Such a ranking in stability and complexity suggests that the sensory antedates the extra-sensory in the evolutionary development of mental processes. This is counter to some of the speculative hypotheses which attribute telepathy to the amoeba, the ant and other lower animals, as a pre-sensory and a pre-language mode of communication. There has been no favouring fact for this hypothesis, to my knowledge, except the mere convenience of closing two gaps in our knowledge by one theory. Telepathy or clairvoyance in birds, if any exists, as is believed by many from the general facts of homing, migrations and simultaneous group responses (and I am not convinced), or in dogs and horses, of which instances have been reported in the scientific literature,[1] is a quite different matter. For here we have sensory perception already developed to a very high degree. I venture to suggest, therefore (and *merely* to suggest), that sensory may be evolutionarily prior to extra-sensory perception. I propose this because nervous dissociation more quickly affects the extra-sensory capacity, and that, in general, this would mean greater specialization and complexity, as well as less stability and basic biological survival value.

The general effect of the physiological observations of the effect of fatigue, of amytal, caffeine, illness and sleepiness has been to 'naturalize' fully the whole function of E.S.P., making it as clearly natural a process as any other physiological phenomenon. For in these drug tests we have been arbitrarily controlling the phenomenon in question, lowering and raising it at will, according to an already established principle of the effect of the drugs on the nervous system, and assuming that E.S.P. is a phenomenon of that system. The assumption has been borne out very satisfactorily in every test, and we may now without hesitation invite the attention of physiologists to another mode of energy reception and to another function of the nervous system.

But does the fact of the causal connection established be-

[1] See Chapter II.

tween cards and percipient or between agent and percipient, apparently involving a work-producing or energetic sequence, necessitate our calling the process 'sensation' and designating the unknown receptive system a 'sense', as Frederic Myers and Charles Richet have done (in Myers' case by implication in his proposed term telaesthesia for clairvoyant perception and in Richet's case by definite statement; see his book, *Notre Sixième Sens*, Paris, 1928)? I think not, indeed. None of the features of E.S.P. have indicated or suggested sensation or sense organs. First, the E.S.P. experience seems rather to be that of a more complex level, one that is readily broken up by sodium amytal and fatigue while the senses are still functioning. Second, the experience of the percipient is one of cognition or 'knowing', not a 'sensing' in the strict psychological meaning of the word. That is, he knows but cannot tell 'how he knows'; there is no analysis possible apparently, as there is for sensory perception. Third, there is no consciousness of localization of the basis of the cognition, as is possible in sensory perception. Fourth, and objectively, there seems to be no special orientation required for success. Fifth, as shown in the last chapter, there is the further basic difference also that the known energy forms seemed inadequate as a physical basis for E.S.P., yet they are the known basis of all known sensory perception. This is at least a very great difference between them, if not a conclusive one.

It is a given fact, obvious in the experience of the percipient, that there is cognition. And cognition of an object outside of the organism would be perception. Further discoveries may reveal something comparable to sense structures and functions, but thus far they have not. Instead, the facts of the last paragraph above lead us strongly toward the opposite conclusion, that this mode of perception is above and outside the sensory sphere, and is likely to be more of a total response, undifferentiable and unanalysable—a reception on the complex level of knowing. Hence I call it 'Extra-Sensory Perception'. But to avoid spending my time in disputing a mere name, I agree to mean by this merely

'Perception by a means or way that is outside the now recognized sensory modes'.

The expression 'Supersensuous Perception' has been used by certain English writers on the subject and, personally, I think 'super' probably indicates hypothetically the right relation E.S.P. has with the sensory mode; but it is an unnecessary additional hypothesis; also 'super' often simply means 'highly' or 'overly,' as in 'supersensitive', and this would be ambiguous; and, finally, it suggests to some the undesirable connotation of 'supernatural'.

It is probable that someone has already used the expression 'Extra-Sensory Perception';[1] and I should like to regard its use here as a choice rather than an attempted innovation. Mr Harvey L. Frick entitled his M.A. thesis submitted to this Department in 1931 'Extra-Sensory Cognition'. But this is not specific enough; rational and mnemonic cognition would also be 'extra-sensory'. Perception is cognition of outer objects or relations, and is, therefore, the proper word here. Extra-Sensory, then, limits it in the necessary way.

[1] It was later discovered that Sir Richard Burton, as early as 1870, used an expression almost identical; his term was "extrasensuous perception."

CHAPTER XII

The Psychological Conditions and Bearings of the Results

In the more restricted psychological field there has arisen as yet no special hypothesis for the explanation of the E.S.P. type of phenomena, excepting those already dealt with under other headings: hyperaesthesia of the known senses, with involuntary whispering (for telepathy) and unconscious reliance upon faint visual indications in the card-calling clairvoyance, were discussed in Chapter IX and were shown to be excluded by the conditions; and the cryptaesthesia or 'sixth sense' hypothesis was considered in the last chapter, and was shown to be opposed by a number of damaging facts and to be supported by none. These hypotheses are all psychological in part; but the first are primarily methodological and the last physiological in bearing. I find no other definitely psychological suggestion as to the nature of E.S.P. presented in the literature. However, in the course of this chapter there will be developed some more purely psychological suggestions taking the form of a partially explanatory hypothesis. But the main content of the chapter will consist of the general mental conditions associated with E.S.P. and their interpretation. Upon such facts must depend whatever advance in the understanding of E.S.P. will ultimately be made.

The most important mental condition associated with success in E.S.P. is one that the popular mind has long recognized in such connections, though it needs some technical refinement for the purpose here in mind; I refer to 'concentration'. It is not a technical term in psychology, to my knowledge, but it refers to a mental condition that most people fairly well understand and agree upon. Obviously, concentration of attention is implied, and, if one is trying to perceive by a non-sensory mode, concentration of attention would mean withdrawing attention from the sensory fields and directing it into another route. Hence we should have relaxation of all sensory functions and abstraction from all sense stimuli. This would necessarily accompany the concentration of attention upon a special extra-sensory function.

Attention directed into extra-sensory routes would not be so readily observable as sensorially guided attention. The straining of the eye, the listening attitude and the like would be wanting; but we must not be deceived by this appearance of passivity. We find it unmistakably present, as logically it should be for any cognitive process. The evidence of abstraction is itself confirmatory of attention, since abstraction from sensory stimuli is an evidence of at least some form of non-sensory attention. Let us, then, consider first the facts of abstraction in E.S.P.

Several subjects have described their E.S.P. experience as involving a state of 'detachment', 'abstraction', 'relaxation' and the like. And it is rather apparent to the objective observer in many of them. Miss Bailey practically goes into light trance with eyes cloesd. Pearce seems to me to approximate light trance after he works steadily for some time. In fact, his eyes almost close and the pupils turn somewhat upward. Cooper, Zirkle and Miss Turner close their eyes when they do not have to keep them open. This was not required of them. Both Linzmayer and Pearce like to look off with a 'far-away look' much of the time. The former especially was given to staring out of the window. He preferred this to closing his eyes, saying that the images were uncontrolled with the eyes closed. The fact that Miss Ownbey perceives the figures on the backs of the cards and on the wall, by hallucination, suggests that she, too, has achieved relatively good abstraction from sensory disturbances. (She, like Miss Bailey, has the ability to go readily into trance by her own volition.)[1]

[1] In *Mental Radio,* already referred to, Mrs Sinclair, the percipient, describes very fully her introspections and her views as to the way 'telepathy' occurs. She emphasizes relaxation of body and 'blankness'

In addition to the positive evidence of abstraction from the surroundings in doing good E.S.P. work, there are on the negative side the still more convincing facts of distraction and its damaging influence upon this mode of perception. These will need only to be mentioned here, since the details have been given before. There is, for example, the temporary, but decided distraction effect of visitors upon the percipient, observed in the case of Pearce (see Table XIX, Chapter VII); Miss Ownbey, Linzmayer and Miss Weckesser show somewhat the same effect. (Tischner's Mr H. and Prof. G. Murray were affected similarly.) Likewise, any change in procedure is likely to disturb Pearce's scoring rate. Others, too, are somewhat affected but in most instances these disturbances are only temporary, lasting merely until adaptation is adequate to permit good abstraction. We have had also various minor instances of other types of distraction, as, for instance, the appearance on the scene of a girl with whom the percipient was emotionally involved in an unsettled way and degree; and, in another case, a disturbing telephone call came for the percipient and so agitated him that he said he was sure he would fail to score. He got only 3 in 25 immediately, but the score rose, as he recovered his poise, to his usual level of approximately 8 in 25. This detrimental effect of distracting factors only emphasizes the more strongly the importance of abstraction in E.S.P., and of the advanced degree of abstraction required.[2] We get the im-

of mind as requirements; these constitute the negative or abstraction phase of the 'concentration' required. Later she mentioned the need for 'training in the art of concentration' and thus adds the positive effort phase. She, like Osty, Tischner, Myers, etc., attributes the positive activity of this mode of perception to the subconscious level of mind. Mrs Sinclair has also many excellent practical suggestions for the prospective E.S.P. subject.

[2] I would predict that with most E.S.P. subjects initial failure would be highly probable if they were to be taken before a committee; failure would be practically certain if the committee were made up of impressive people, or if its members did anything to excite or distract the subject. To impose even little precautions at the start is hazardous. Placing a small screen over the cards, at which Pearce seldom looked anyway, stopped his E.S.P. for a time—until adjustment took place.

pression that E.S.P. is a most delicate function, most easily disturbed and inhibited by the more common and more stable processes. (One is reminded of Prof. Gilbert Murray's comment on his own E.S.P. experiments with himself as percipient, 'The least disturbing of our customary method, change of time or place, presence of strangers, controversy or especially noise is apt to make thinks go wrong'.)

When we turn from the abstraction phase of the 'concentration' process to attention itself, we find really the continuation of the abstraction picture itself: the necessity of abstraction from other activation. First, again, is the subjective testimony of the percipients themselves. They agree pretty well that a state of alertness and freshness is best for good E.S.P. work. And this is certainly my own conclusion from three years of observation; it is, also, well supported by the results obtained from the drug caffeine. This drug is recognized as counteracting the effect of fatigue or drowsiness, and making the individual more alert. We have found that it raises the scoring level of the percipient if he has been running below his usual level. Alertness of attention would seem to have been improved here, necessarily, and it is likely the connection is causal. (Osty[1] thinks the use of the 'object of fixation' in 'psychometric' E.S.P. aids in attention. It is regarded by many as a focus for concentration.) In watching the subjects work and in getting their subjective observations from day to day, I have opportunity to form 'clinical impressions' that are possibly of some value in interpretation. One such impression is that attention is closely correlated with success and that it varies widely without the subject's realizing it himself, very often since it is not an overtly registered attention that is concerned. The subject may think he is giving himself fully to the task but, if some stimulating (but not distracting) factor comes into the situation, the score may rise at once. On the day of Pearce's scoring 25 straight successes, he did not want to work but consented to "run a few." He began rather indifferently and

[1] *Supernormal Faculties in Man*, pp. 124, 161, etc. Dutton, New York, 1923.

got no hits in the first 5. I urged him to try harder and he got 3 in the next 5. Then I challenged him vigorously, albeit goodhumouredly, urging him more strongly than I have ever done before or since, and he got 25 consecutive hits. The very strain he showed at the end was evidence of strong effort to concentrate attention. He said, 'You'll never get me to do that again!' He could not describe his feeling further, however. (And, to avoid developing self-consciousness, I do not push introspective exploration.)

On the negative side, the role of attention, and effort which is expressed as attention, is likewise well supported. Sleepiness and fatigue, the states opposite to good attention, are demonstrably poor conditions for E.S.P. Worst of all is the artificial sleepiness induced by the dissociative drug sodium amytal. With the subjects under the influence of this drug, there was noticeable difficulty in the capacity to give attention, as evidenced in the appearance of struggle with the task. Pearce got up and washed his face in cold water, he struggled with himself, trying to fight off sleepiness and maintain better attention. Zirkle succeeded in doing this to a great degree when we gave him caffeine and then raised his score level at once from 6.2 to 9.5, making another strong case for the role of attention. This does not exhaust the evidence for the causal function of attention but there is no need to elaborate further. Attention, as the expression of effort, which is in turn guided by interest is, I think, essential in E.S.P., as in any other mode of cognition. It is probably required even to a greater degree, judging by the apparent delicateness and instability of the functioning E.S.P.

The connection of interest with E.S.P. is clear, then, also, for those who recognize attention as a function of interest. We can see, then, logical ground for the general belief that strong personal attachment seems to enhance parapsychical relations between two individuals. It is noteworthy in this connection that the best P.T. work we have—best by a good margin—was done by Zirkle with Miss Ownbey, his fiancée, as agent. Their deep personal attachment and mutual understanding would most probably facilitate parapsychic *rap-*

port. Personal interest strengthens the effort to establish contact and this means stronger attention. If attention is not divided by self-consciousness or self-doubt, and does not partially escape over the sensory routes, then the additional personal interest is drawn into supporting the attention given through E.S.P. If there is this strong effect of motivation upon the attention link and this is so very influential, in turn, with the scoring level, it is very easy to see how Linzmayer might have got his below-chance scoring when I pushed him into working very much against his will, with a definite view to testing whether he would go below significantly (see Table XI, Chapter v). Given his unconscious negativism, he would have unconsciously opposed the work he was forced into and, without realizing it, he probably responded negatively—actually purposely calling the cards wrongly. Voluntarily and consciously, Pearce and Stuart have called consistently below chance, showing that E.S.P. can be directed by volitional preference in just the way suggested to explain Linzmayer's lowered score test. Guidance and strengthening of attention through changes in interest are the points here involved.

If this picture is correct as drawn, then, if interest should decline, as it might well do in any such task, proper attention and abstraction could not be attained, and the scores would drop to chance. Now, after Stuart spent a year of monotonous work at B.T., alone, without the stimulation even of an observer's presence, and without any special recognition or encouragement (I regret now to have to confess), he reported to me that his scoring had fallen off badly! I asked him (the 'leading' question) whether he had not become a bit tired of it. He confessed that perhaps he had. When I discovered later the amount of work he had done I felt pretty certain he must have grown weary and less interested in the work. And his scoring rate had declined from the first 500 trials on. In these 500, he had averaged 9 in 25, but for the first 1,500 of the total of 7,500, he dropped to 7.1 in 25. The average per 25 for the 5 serial groups of 1,500 trials each are as follows: 7.1, 6.1, 5.7, 5.9, 5.4. The curve of decline is shown in Graph No. 7, A, in Chapter XIV. I am fairly well convinced that it is a curve of 'decline of interest', especially by the facts of the sequel. After a few months of 'rest' for him, and after I had discovered the excellence of his results, and given him proper recognition for his huge undertaking and accomplishment, I urged him to try again. Certainly he must have been more interested at this point. At any rate, the scoring came back to 7·3 for the first 400 trials, and then declined again during 2,000 trials and declined by 400's as follows: 7·3, 7·3, 7·2, 6·9, 6·0 After discussing this work with him I became more certain of the decline-of-interest explanation. This work was done by Stuart at his home and was reported by correspondence. The latter part of it was carried on under somewhat depressing and discouraging circumstances, likely to contribute to a decline of interest.

Related to the curves described above as probably decline-of-interest curves and giving some support to the view, are the 'curves of operation', better described perhaps as attention curves. Just as we should expect interest, and consequently attention, to decline in certain circumstances, so may we also expect greater attention to be given to some calls in the runs of 5 or 25 than to others. With most subjects the first call might be expected to be emphasized by greater effort and perhaps next in rank would come the last call of the run. It would be less likely if the middle call or another in the interior would be especially emphasized. What do we find actually (among such of the data as have been combed over for such internal relationships)? Linzmayer gets the first card correct more often than any other, except when forced into low scoring, when he got it incorrect more than any other. Pearce, Cooper, Stuart and Linzmayer, in their D.T. work, and Pearce in his B.T.-25 (*i.e.*, run in 25's) all favour the two ends of the run and slight the centre. (See Chapter X with Graphs Nos. 1 and 2.) Miss Ownbey in her D.T. does just the opposite, scoring highest in the centre of the pack, and lower toward the top and the bottom. Most striking of the operation curves, however, is

Pearce's B.T.-5 curve. These are run and checked by 5's, and they show a rate-of-scoring curve over the whole 25 of the pack that consists of 5 similar units, one for each 5-card run. That is, there is shown a typical rate of scoring for 5-card runs that is strikingly regular for the whole 25. Invariably the 2nd call is the highest and the order of the others is quite regular also. See Graphs Nos. 3 and 4 that follow. In Graph No. 3, the number of successes divided by the chance expectation is plotted against the order of the call in the runs through the pack of 25. The curve is broken after each 5 calls to remind the reader that the calls were made in these short runs of 5 each. Each run of 5 is thus a check on the others. In the case of Graph 4, these 5 runs of 5 each in the pack are summated, keeping the serial order intact, as if all had been merely 5-card runs. First calls are totalled, 2nd calls, 3rd, etc. The curve of these total hits divided by chance expectation (np) is plotted likewise against the order of the call in the run. This gives the complete summarizing curve for the 2,250 trials.

The unquestionable order shown by these curves reveals a factor that has become habitual for Pearce, varying regularly from call to call, giving the same general pattern with each cross-section group of 5 calls. What factor varies thus regularly, habitually? We would not expect ability to vary; cognitive and perceptual abilities are not known to vary thus. We look rather to the conative side, to variation in effort, again in the form of attention, since this is a factor we would naturally expect to find varying. Why attention should vary in just this pattern cannot be said. Some rhythm of the mind, some odd habit, perhaps originating in counting habits, or some earlier experience with the number 5 may be responsible. More force of conation is put into call No. 2 than in the others. And, as Dr McDougall would say, more striving in perception would mean increased attention. These are, then, curves of attention pattern peculiar to this percipient for these conditions.

Under other conditions the attention pattern changes. For instance, with D.T. there is the U curve given by the run of 25 as a whole but with no rhythmic order by 5's such as is shown in Graph No. 3. Here the 'attention' decreases from the first call to the middle of the run and increases from there to the end. On the last calls of 40 of Pearce's D.T. runs studied, he got 33 of the 40 correct. He likewise increases effort in concentration toward both ends of the run in his B.T.-25. Of 60 runs studied under this heading, he got 52 of the last calls correct. In fact, through the whole series he drops in the interior of the run but rises at both

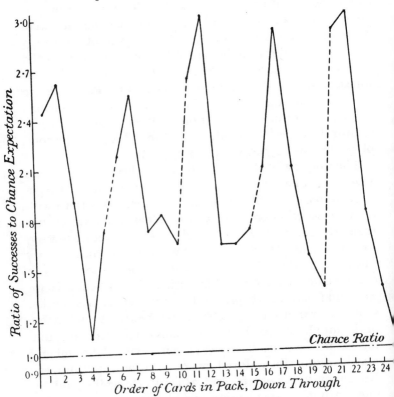

Graph No. 3 Pearce's operation curve in his first 1,375 trials at B.T.-5, showing distribution of success over the average run of 25, plotted to show relative success for each call. The broken line shows the points at which checking-up was done (after 5 calls). Note the rhythmic character of the curve, taken by 5's of abscissae.

ends, much more in the last 5, as was the case in his D.T. Some of these totals may be of interest in addition to the curves and will be given in Table XL below. For comparison, the results will be stated in total hits over the series per 5 trials in cross-section of the whole run of 25. This will give five columns of results and they together will show in steps of 5 calls the success of the subject in general over the

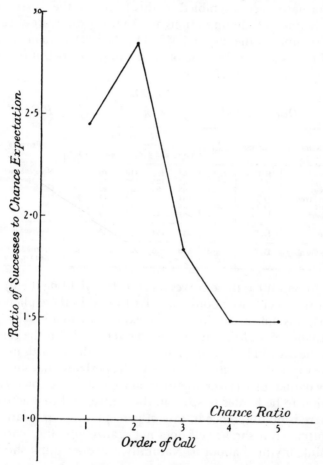

Graph No. 4. Same as No. 3, but showing distribution of success over Pearce's average run of 5 calls; this represents an average of the five curve parts of Graph No. 3.

run of 25 trials for the pack. We can compare Pearce on B.T.-25, B.T.-5 and D.T. Note that on B.T.-5 he runs rather evenly by 5's, though within each 5, as Graph No. 3 has shown, there are wide variations on a regular pattern. But on B.T.-25, while there is not such rhythm by 5's, the results would give a general U-shaped curve, a bit W-shaped. But in D.T. his curved is markedly U-shaped. Only the D.T. data have been assembled in this form for the other subjects, due to time limitations and to the greater pressure of other lines of the inquiry. Miss Ownbey's D.T. data are set off by themselves because of their unique distribution and the large number of trials.

TABLE XL

Distribution of scoring rate, over the run of 25, P.C.

Name	Condition	No. of trials	No. of hits					Remarks
			1st 5	2nd 5	3rd 5	4th 5	5th 5	
Pearce	B.T.-5	1,375	108	109	118	110	112	Note evenness
Pearce	B.T.-25	1,500	145	122	133	128	159	U-shaped curve
Pearce	D.T.	1,025	98	63	49	52	85	Do. See Gr. No. 2
Linzmayer	D.T.	1,000	51	39	46	47	52	Do.
Stuart	D.T.	1,000	40	39	36	38	49	Do.
Cooper[1]	D.T.	1,200	63	41	48	59	76	Do.
Total	D.T.	4,225	252	182	179	196	262	Do. See Gr. No. 1
Miss Ownbey	D.T.	3,350	210	226	248	230	211	Inverted U curve. See Gr. No. 1

Important as these curves (*i.e.* the data yielding them) are for their evidence of order and lawfulness in these phenomena, it is difficult at this stage to explain them all. Why, for instance, does Miss Ownbey get better results in the centre of the pack in D.T. work than she does with the cards nearer the top and bottom? It is conceivable, perhaps, that she may try harder, give closer attention, as a consequence of *expecting* it to be harder to score in the centre, and that actually there is no difference in ease of perception—top, centre or bottom. But she herself does not realize any difference or think anything about it. Naturally, since we think she can

---

[1] This work has been performed and inserted here since the first writing of this chapter. Cooper has only recently undertaken D.T. seriously.

achieve better abstraction without a close introspective analysis, we let it go at that for the time. The problem is a real one, however, and is still entirely unsolved, except that her results have eliminated any possible hypothesis, physical or psychological, that assumes greater difficulty in the centre than in the other regions of the pack. The explanation of such features may well take us back into complex personality factors not yet understood.

Among the other curves that I cannot explain, yet which show the working of some principle of order, are two operation curves of decline. The curves represent a decline in scoring rate during the run. The effect is probably due in part to the length of run, which Prof. Richet said many years ago would lower scoring in 'cryptaesthesia'. These two groups of data, too, are the only long-run data we have. We commonly stop at 25 trials per run, sometimes after each 5 and occasionally check after each one. But in one of these series the runs were of 100 trials each, and in the other of 50, in the latter case with a check-up only after 300 trials. It was certainly among the most monotonous and tedious work we have yet inflicted on our subjects. Both curves are obtained by plotting number of successes divided by chance expectation against cross-sections of the number of trials. The first work, by Frick, described in Chapter IV, consists of 900 trials, run 100 per day at a single sitting. The scores are totalled for the ordinal 20's, making 5 subdivisions of the total, each representing the 20's in the run of 100. Graph No. 5, A, shows that Frick's scoring fell off by steps of 20's and actually went below chance expectation on the last two 20's. The total gain above chance was very slight but the extremes of the curve are significantly far apart, as they are also in Linzmayer's curve, to follow in Graph No. 5, B. Linzmayer's data are taken from B.T. work on 50 sealed envelopes which were called under conditions described in Chapter V. The 300 calls made in 6 runs over these envelopes yielded no positive deviation, and yet the curve is internally significant in its striking decline by 10's to a point below chance, suggesting, as with Frick and as with Linzmayer himself in his low-score test described in Chapter v, that there may be an internal factor conflicting with the effort to score. It is a curious fact that these two men, Frick and Linzmayer, are the only two subjects who have ever scored below chance to any noticeable extent, and they have both done so rather significantly, Linzmayer more definitely so than Frick. Now both these men have, in my judgment, rather definite negativistic tendencies of

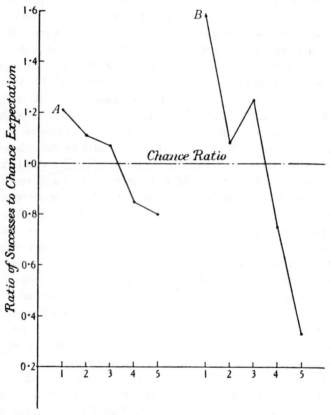

Graph No. 5. Decline of scoring rate in long runs. These curves show distribution of success in scoring over the average run. Curve A represents 900 trials at B.T.-100 by Frick, plotted in 5 units of 20 calls each. Curve B, 300 trials at B.T.-50 by Linzmayer, plotted for 5 units of 10 calls each.

which they are unconscious (although in neither is there to my knowledge any slightest socially evident defect as a result). With Linzmayer this has been demonstrated in hypnotic experiments; with Frick it is a judgment based on acquaintance covering 4 or 5 years. He is non-hypnotizable, too, which fact is in agreement. I venture the suggestion, then, that there is a connection here between a negativistic tendency, operative especially with relaxation, which, after the strain of long, tedious runs, sets up a rebellion that leads to purposively thwarting the scoring impulse, producing an effect of negative hallucination in E.S.P. This is the view I have in mind as a possible explanation of Linzmayer's drop below chance to 4·5 in 25 for 600 trials in June, 1931, immediately following 600 trials at more than twice that rate, 9·9. It is an hypothesis that can later be tested. There is already one logical test that gives it a favourable decision: if this unconscious-negativism hypothesis is correct, we might expect, then, that the longer the subject is urged thereafter to work, the more conflict would develop—the more internal opposition there would be and the more de-line. Both Frick and Linzmayer went on declining thereafter in their later work.

We have mentioned the 'fatigue curve' theory of Miss Jephson[1] from time to time as evidence arose touching on the problem. Our long series of 900, 950 and 1,300 trials (700 for high, 600 for low) in one day render the fatigue view inapplicable, especially since it was proposed on the basis of data of only 5 calls each. If three of our subjects get through 900 or more trials in one day without fatigue, it is not likely that 5 calls would induce it. Rather is it likely that Miss Jephson's interesting results represent an operation curve revealing a decline of the requisite 'concentration' condition; either the strain is cumulative, rational factors come in, self-conscious attention develops and disturbs, or the like. The first call is usually made more naïvely; but 2 or 3 calls make it harder to keep the intellect

[1] Jephson, Miss Ina, 'Evidence for Clairvoyance in Card Guessing', *Proc.* S.P.R. xxxviii, pp. 223-271, 1928.

at rest, since one is given commonly to reasoning in such matters. The imagination, too, may become too active. Or the curve may simply be a curve of decline with rising excitement over the experiment's possible outcome. Any of these several possibilities—but certainly not fatigue.

We have had decline curves of several kinds, in the run, in the series, for a season, and for years—but no ascending curves. We have been interested in learning and development curves too, but E.S.P. does not appear to be a developmental matter, as our data reveal it. It is true there are obstacles and inhibitions that have to be removed, such as initial doubts, self-consciousness, strangeness, distracting environmental conditions. But these might well inhibit the composition of poetry, too, and we should not say that their removal would constitute learning to write poetry. There is in E.S.P. no adequate evidence of primary improvement of the ability itself. Rather does it seem that we have here a basic function that can easily be inhibited but not developed. It is probably as innately given as is sensory perceptual capacity. This is, however, a point for further inquiry!

The general psychological setting of E.S.P. is still very vague. The experiments into this phase have scarcely begun as yet and the subjective exploration has not been pushed; first, because it is difficult to evaluate and, second, we must not, I think, start subjects thinking too much about how they do it, lest we unfit them for successfully doing it by inducing self-consciousness, over-curiosity or some other undesirable attitude. This has not been regarded as a first step, anyhow. With this as a preface, I will draw up a brief summary of the mental outlines of E.S.P.

First, no one—not even a psychologist—can reasonably doubt that E.S.P. *is* a mental process; and that there seems to be good ground for regarding it as a natural part of the endowment of mind. It is a more delicate mental process than most, suffering easily from dissociation or distraction, and returning again with reintegration of effort and improved attention. It is inhibited too by conflict, as in self-doubt (Linzmayer), doubt as to the possibility or wisdom of a procedure (Cooper and Pearce), or in conflict of desires (Linzmayer). It requires with most subjects rather good abstraction and close attention to the task in hand. It is less resistant to dissociation than sensory perception or even than simple reasoning. On the points so far mentioned, it is more like creative intellectual or artistic synthesis; yet it is not so fatiguing as these; and, unlike these, can be speeded up rapidly (faster than I can record); and it is not learned or developed, as far as we know yet, as are these; it is unanalysable introspectively, as are these mostly. But it substitutes for other forms of cognition, for visual or auditory perception, rational judgment or recall. It interoperates with them, combines in any way and works from a wide range of motivation, for money or for kindness, for play or for display, for science or for courtesy. It is like the sensory functions rather than rational cognition in its lack of development (if this is actually a fact, as it seems). But it is not like them in localization, feeling of real contact experienced, need of bodily orientation to function, resistance to distraction and dissociation. It is simple cognition, so far as subjective analysis goes as yet; but it uses memory, visual or other imagination —in fact, all of the mind that is needed—in its functioning. It is normal, not related to mental weakness or disease. In fact, physical disease, of some kinds, hinders it, and weakening, dissociating mental disease would probably do so likewise. There is no suggestion of incorporeal agencies in connection with experiments. As to personality traits and E.S.P., there are some suggestions or general impressions, as yet undeveloped; for example, possible correlations between E.S.P. and a tendency to day-dreaming and high imaginativeness. Stuart suggested a correlation between E.S.P. and artistic interest and ability that seems promising. Hypnotizability, too, is about on a par with these, in correlation with E.S.P. Sociability has a chance, too, of being correlated. But our data are yet too limited on this line of comparison. Relations of E.S.P. to age, race, and other stages and conditions, too, are yet for the future. This, then, is the tentative psychological sketch we have so far achieved.

There is much indeed to be paid about the bearing such facts as these of E.S.P. may have on psychological theory. It is most obvious that some very fundamental revolution is required in this field by this evidence for E.S.P., quite as it is in Physics. Since there is no end to what might be developed here, in a speculative way, the space must be limited to only a few hypotheses that seem to be more clearly suggested by the facts.

One of these is the hypothesis of the relatively independent agency of mind under certain conditions of the material world. This is an hypothesis, not a claim or conclusion; and I, for one, do not regard the facts given here as compelling. The facts that suggest this hypothesis are: first, the fact that distance, that basic feature of the material universe, seems to mean nothing to E.S.P. Nothing else we know operates in our material world and eludes the space limitations as does this principle. Space clearly does not limit it; it does not, therefore, function in it and we have, then, non-spatial processes of mind. Not that mind is absolutely space-free or necessarily predominantly so. Its processes are brought into space relationship by the motor nerve phenomena of response, if not several steps before. The point of importance for the hypothesis is that the mental system may elude the space-giving properties of the material medium, escape from 'inverse square' laws by an energy (or causal principle) we do not yet know, and mentally telescope the material universe into an extensionless immediacy, as naturally, perhaps, as a slow-swimming bird may smoothly escape on the wing through a medium that has (for it) less limiting laws. (A similar problem with the time dimension lies just ahead in our experimental future.)

A second fact that suggested this hypothesis is the relative indifference to the percipient's success, on the whole, as to whether it is a card or a thought image that is to be perceived. (The data for this conclusion will be summarized in the next chapter and not repeated here.) The diversity of the 'stimulus objects' here is so great as to suggest that the agency responsible is the percipient's mind—that his mind, in effect, 'goes out to' the object. Such different objects could not be expected to give such similar stimulation. It is much more reasonable to suppose that the percipient's mind can perceive in E.S.P. fashion a wide enough range of 'objects' to include thoughts and cards. It is this 'going out to perceive that points in our present picture of mind-body limitations to a relative independence of the material laws, as known. A 'going out' to great distances in defiance of 'inverse square' laws that all known matter-bound energies obey, as well as a 'going out' to a solid pack of cards and the selection of the right ones in the right order; and, again, a 'going-out' first to the right mind in a heavily populated region 250 miles away and selecting its thoughts, while evading doubtlessly similar thoughts originating nearer the percipient (circle, star, plus, etc.), selecting from the chosen agent's mind not the thoughts arising from her reading the book before her, but the very images intended for the very moment when the call is made; and, finally, a 'going out' of mind that selects one card on a table 250 yards away, when there are hundreds of similar cards in adjoining rooms that are nearer the percipient, many others in his own room and in the observer's room—such facts and conditions come close to persuasion of the necessity for the active and selective agency of the percipient's own mind, in escaping the limitations of its material nerves and sense organs, penetrating stone walls and evading distance, and accurately apprehending the desired 'object' on a level or scale or condition that is non-material and non-spatial.

The third fact suggesting this hypothesis of relative independence of mind from material properties is rather a whole set of facts; namely, those given in Chapter VIII, showing that, in P.T. work with good E.S.P. subjects for agents, better results were obtained than when poor ones functioned, with the same percipients for both. This suggests, along with the fact that even with poor E.S.P. subjects for agents a good percipient could score in a mediocre way, that the 'double agency' of two good E.S.P. subjects means a capacity in both to 'go out' to meet each other beyond the material and sensory range. That is, the demonstration of the greater advantage of having an agent who is gifted with E.S.P. ability showed that there was a 'going out' on her part, a 'meeting halfway', or joint agency.

It would seem to me, therefore, that this Capacity-to-Escape-Material-Conditions Hypothesis might be regarded as having at least a good beginning in plausibility, with no strong competition; but, nevertheless, as resting on relative fragments of fact and constituting only a 'working direction' at present.

This general hypothesis embraces at least two more special ones, which, I think, may be better stated independently. First, the agency[1] of the percipient's mind is 'going out' to the perceived object or image source, instead of merely receiving incoming energy patterns emanating from the card or the distant agent. The facts suggesting this view have been given above. The second hypothesis involved in the larger one is that of the relative or partial freedom of mind from the limitations of material and its property, space, as shown in the E.S.P. phenomena. Both these (the agency of the percipient's mind in E.S.P. and the spatial freedom of mind) have been involved as phases in the discussion above, and need here only be mentioned as separable units that need to be criticized and tested, each on its own merit. Together they harmoniously fit the facts in their present incomplete state and give us the rational picture of the purposive mind of the percipient operating between two energetic orders, one related to the spatial world and another not directly related. There is thus a perceptual interweaving between these realms of reality, somewhat as the clever play of the switch on a radio-victrola set can interweave from two widely different energetic sources two musical themes into one. So may (still hypothetically speaking) the E.S.P. subject look at his watch (contact with the spatial world) and call the card 250 yards away or get an image

---

[1] Dr Osty's frequent insistence that the percipient is 'not passive' is a supporting judgment of great weight, coming from an observer of the many years' experience which he has had. *Op. cit.* p. 161.

250 miles away (through a hypothetical non-spatial world). I mention this speculation merely as the play of the mind about and upon these interesting facts. It seems to be the only rational line of treatment that fits the facts we have.

In much less important, though more practical, ways these results bear upon the techniques and theories of psychology. We have pretty good ground in these results to suppose it possible that in hypnotic suggestion there may well be an extra-sensory component of *rapport* that satisfies, in some respects, the old 'mesmeric fluid' theory. It would not, however, be correct to imply, even hypothetically, that some extra-sensory perception from hypnotic agent to subject is required—merely that it is a possible factor that may hasten and aid good trance and good response. As such it may play a minor but effective role. It has already the support of Alrutz and Richet in the more modern period of the history of hypnotism.

E.S.P. might well figure effectively, also, in the realm of psychotherapy in general, as one may readily see. Though here, too, the role may always be a minor one. Only in the establishment of splendid *rapport* and in the development of delicate and difficult mental attitudes, where every aid is needed and every shade of thought needs to be caught, where mere words are often felt to be inadequate, can we see a responsible part left for extra-sensory perception in the psychotherapeutic field. What the actual facts are we, of course, do not yet know.[1]

Again, we have the problem of E.S.P. as a possible spurious factor in the experimental laboratory. If we can get such good responses to mere thought stimuli as 26 straight hits between Miss Ownbey and Zirkle, or 23 and 22 with two walls between them, what degree of safety is there in most of the conclusions of much of the experimental evidence obtained in situations where the observer, screened as he may

---

[1] A case of the practical use of telepathy as a method in psychotherapeutic exploration already on record is related briefly by Dr Prince in B.S.P.R. Bulletin xx, p. 66. The consulting psychologist was Dr Thos. P. Bailey of Rollins College.

be, is thinking of how he would like the subject to respond? And, in view of the work of Bechterew on dogs and of Rhine on the horse already referred to, what shall we say even about animal studies?

Again we are asking questions in an hypothetical spirit. I am not myself disposed to question on this ground any great amount of psychological experiment, but it is nevertheless a matter that we can not afford to ignore.

CHAPTER XIII

E.S.P. from the Viewpoint of General Parapsychology

No branch of science can have a central and stable body of knowledge until it has established inner relationships between its own phenomena. There have been frequent and persistent attempts among scientific students of parapsychology to do this, yet, so far as I know the literature, never experimentally.[1] Telepathy (or telepathy and clairvoyance) has been offered by students of the subject in England as an hypothetical explanation for phenomena representing themselves as of incorporeal origin; clairvoyance, expanded to include telepathy and named metagnomy, cryptasthesia, etc., has been offered among the French in a similar way for the same purpose. There have been those (notably Prof. Hyslop) who reverse the matter and suggest the 'spirit' hypothesis as a possible explanatory principle for telepathic and clairvoyant phenomena. The principal French students of parapsychology (métapsychique) have

---

[1] Prof. Hans Driesch, in a recent book, *Psychical Research,* transl. by Th. Besterman (Bell, London, 1933), in which he gives a very interesting discussion of methods, problems and theories in the field, comes to the conclusion that clairvoyance and telepathy are fundamental phenomena; that is, fundamentally different phenomena. Not only are these fundamentally different, but prophecy and psychometry also are added to the list of fundamentals. These questions, however, of what is ultimate and fundamental must surely be settled rather by the results of experimental exploration, just as the questions of what are the fundamentals in physics can be settled only in the light of experimental evidence.

favoured clairvoyance (lucidity, etc.), although they recognize telepathy and make a branch of it. The English students of the subject, while recognizing clairvoyance (telaesthesia), have given emphasis and attention almost entirely to telepathy, with comparatively little work on clairvoyance. And on neither side of the Channel has work been done with a view to finding out the relations assumed to exist between the two. In fact, as we saw in Chapter II, most of the work done on the subject has been under conditions that would allow both telepathy and clairvoyance. This was pardonable, perhaps, at a stage where proof of a new mode of perception was the major point.

The plan of this research undertaking is, first, to interrelate the simpler phenomena (simple from the point of view of production) of telepathy and clairvoyance, and to relate these, as far as may be, with physiological conditions and with other mental processes. Along with the interrelating of telepathy and clairvoyance will go an attempt to relate these to dowsing, parapsychic cognition of remote past events and the prevision of future events. Next it is hoped to invade the incorporeal parapsychic branch; *i.e.,* into the so-called 'mediumistic' phenomena. The plan will be to try to work with the same subjects, in part; subjects, that is, who are capable in the simpler capacities. The objective is to discover the basic laws underlying the whole; and to go on to find, by similarities and differences, to what the general character of the greater phenomena of the parapsychological field can be analysed and reduced.

It may be said now, I think, on good experimental evidence, that in clairvoyance and telepathy we are dealing with the same basic process. They have been carefully separated under the conditions of these experiments and found to exist in clearly demonstrable capacity in seven of eight major subjects, as well as in some of the minor ones. Both capacities have been independently demonstrated in these seven and, since less than two months have elapsed since the discovery of the only subject (Zirkle) who cannot do both

P.T. and P.C., we are not sure that he will not yet discover that he can do P.C. work also.[1]

Not only do the subjects possess both clairvoyant and telepathic capacity, but, what is more meaningful still, they score in both conditions at about the same rate. Our use of the figures from the cards as the basis for thought images in P.T. work makes comparison easy. The averages per 25 for all subjects are remarkably close when we compare the P.C. and P.T. from the same periods of time (when that is possible).

These score averages are assembled for comparison in Table XLI. In all cases where we have the data on both P.T. and P.C. for the same period, these alone are given. P.C. is made up of B.T. in these data; no D.T. results are used.

TABLE XLI

Comparison of P.T. and P.C.

Subject	P. Clairvoyance		P. Telepathy		Remarks
	Trials	Av. per 25	Trials	Av. per 25	
Linzmayer	1,000	5·8	1,000	6·0	Same period only
Pearce	1,700	7·2	1,225	7·2	Same period only
Stuart	950	5·7	500	5·8	Same period only
Bailey	1,550	8·0	1,250	9·4	Totals
Turner	3,900	9·0	675	9·1	Totals
Ownbey	700	11·2	375	8·8	Totals
Cooper	1,900	8·5	2,950	8·1	Same period
Totals	11,700	8·1	7·975	7·9	

The results summarized in this table are most impressive; all the more so, when we remember that the subjects were not themselves aware of the averages they were making. To produce such regularity as this in such large numbers is indeed to reveal what can hardly seem other than a funda-

[1] Two months later Zirkle was encouraged to try B.T. again and with a somewhat different approach. He succeeded very definitely in the 1,150 trials made during this later period. These yielded 368 successes or an average of 8·0 per 25. There was a positive deviation 15·2 times the p.e. It is most important to add, too, that Zirkle's P.T. for this period was 8·8, which is very close to the B.T. average.

mental law—that P.C. and P.T. are similar phenomena and that, like the blind brothers who went to 'see' the elephant, we have long had in these different 'limbs' a hold on the same 'body'. E.S.P., then, can work as well under P.T. or P.C. conditions; *i.e.*, telepathically or clairvoyantly. But, as referring to distinct processes, there is probably no clairvoyance and no telepathy. There is just this mode of perceiving extrasensorially. The averages per 25 for the large totals in Table XLI should especially be noted. Back in Table XXIX, where the P.C. and P.T. comparisons were given for four major subjects, the averages per 25 for the four were 8·9 and 8·6 respectively. As the totals expand here to large figures and include all seven subjects, the difference is cut still smaller, 8·1 and 7·9.

The results cited under P.C. for the first three subjects, Linzmayer, Pearce and Stuart, are low for them. It just so happened that we had them begin their P.T. work during their low period, and of course, the P.C. offered as a basis of comparison must be taken under the same conditions as nearly as possible. The P.C. and P.T. work here given was done on the same days.

Not only do individuals score at roughly similar rates under both P.C. and P.T. conditions, but, in the fluctuations occurring from day to day, success under the two conditions, P.T. and P.C., go up and down together (so far as we have data for these conditions), with only a few exceptions—and these are clearly understandable as due to special discriminating factors in three out of the four instances. In the 8 days in which we have comparisons of P.C. and P.T. with Pearce (see Table XXIII in Chapter VII), and in the 8 days of the same sort with Cooper (Table XXIX, Chapter VIII), there are altogether 14 such fluctuations, and of these only four are exceptions to the rule that P.T. and P.C. go up and down together. This is all the better in view of the fact the P.C. and P.T. were often hours apart on the same day. In one of these, the 4th day for Pearce, we have only one run of 25 and it went unusually high, upsetting the balance. There were also only two runs of P.C. This day's work could well be omitted as not being represented by enough trials. On the 3rd day for Cooper, there was an important difference in conditions between P.T. and P.C. The P.C. was run in a comfortably cool room, the P.T. in our warm laboratory where we almost always use an electric fan in summer and on this one day the fan could not be found. It was, too, one of the hottest days of the season. Cooper dropped flatly to chance, the only time he ever did this in P.T. work at close range. Obviously, this too should be ruled out of this special consideration. On one other day, the 5th, he could not, for some reason, get started for the first 75 trials. The last 75 of the 150 were therefore taken as his level for the day, since the merely 'chance' scores of the first 75 simply meant nothing to the particular comparison value sought here. On one occasion, the last day for Pearce, he, too, dropped to chance (5·2), but for no known adequate reason. It was his only day of this sort on the series and, so far as can be recalled, in the whole of his experience. With these exceptions, explained so that the reader may use his own judgment in excluding or retaining them, the 14 daily fluctuations stand as a fairly clear picture of similar changes in both P.T. and P.C. scoring under roughly similar conditions. These joint fluctuations of both types of E.S.P. under the influence of the factors affecting the work from day to day add further weight to the evidence of Table XL, all urging that we have here but two applications of the same perceptual function; that 'telepathy' and 'clairvoyance' are not merely separate processes changing together; that seven of our eight subjects did not just happen to score alike in P.T. and in P.C., and have almost exactly similar averages (P.C. and P.T.), all together. Rather, it is likely that the extra-sensory mode of perception fluctuates daily and its results under both conditions must be similarly affected.

There are other special experiments and observations that have given similar results in both P.T. and P.C. For instance, the sodium amytal tests reduced alike the P.C. capacity and the P.T. It will be recalled that a large dose completely reduced Linzmayer to chance scoring in P.C., while a dose of 6 grains lowered Pearce from 10·0 to 6·1 in 25. Now, a similar dose reduced Zirkle on P.T. work from 14·7 to 7·0 (in all 600 trials combined). On the other hand, caffeine affected Pearce on P.C. and Zirkle on P.T. in the same way, raising the scoring in the direction of the normal in both cases but not above it. Illness (tonsilitis) lowered P.T. with Zirkle and P.C. with Pearce. Fatigue affects both adversely and alertness helps both. All the dissociative and reintegrative factors affect both sets of results in the same direction.

What, then, about the effect of screens and other possible obstructions? Both P.C. and P.T. can be done with a heavy cardboard screen concealing the cards or agent. Both P.T. and P.C. work through walls of construction blocks made of tiling. Both are disturbed by new changes with certain subjects; *e.g.,* Pearce on P.C. and P.T. Both can be done at the same rates of speed in general, if the agent is not a limiting factor. Both show about the same range of fluctuation from day to day. Both require about the same mental conditions, of 'concentration', effort, interest, absence of conflict, integration, etc., so far as the data go to show. In a word, there has not been found a single difference, as yet, in any phase of the experiments; everything pointed to a single general process of E.S.P., divided here merely by the class of 'objects' perceived; *i.e.,* figures in ink or in the thought process.

The most crucial point in the examination of the two conditions, P.C. and P.T., was on the question of effect of distance on the two. On several different hypotheses of the nature of P.C. and P.T., distance might distinguish between the two. Distance data eventually came in strikingly with P.T., which was taken up first. The evidence was highly satisfactory, when there was scoring above chance at all. (See Table XXXVII, Chapter VIII, especially Miss Turner's brilliant long-distance scores.) For some time then the P.C. at a distance was an unsettled point. But as I write this chapter the data are rolling in magnificently from the dependable work of Pearce on B.T.-25 at 100 yards distance from the cards. He began low, as is his wont in new conditions.

Then he rose above his old level and held it until we changed him to a longer distance, where he is now beginning. His results at 100 yards, from one building to another, were, in hits per 25 trials, 3, 8, 5, 9, 10, 12, 11, 12, 11, 13, 13, 12, which is an average of about ten; but, after the adjustment period, the average is 11·4, which is higher than Pearce's B.T. average at close range (which is 9·4). (In fact, his average for 300 trials made at close range with the observer handling the cards, as in the distance P.C., which is really the comparable condition, is rather low—approximately 7.) Here again is a similarity which is peculiarly significant, I think. Not only do both P.T. and P.C. succeed at a distance, but they both seem to succeed, when the conditions are favourable, definitely better than at close range. It will be recalled that Miss Turner, Zirkle and Miss Bailey all improved their P.T. with distance; Pearce improved his P.C. with distance, after the initial adjustment period, in a brilliant series that gives a deviation of 12·6 times the probable error.

The cumulative effect of these uniformly favourable comparisons of P.T. and P.C. results under various conditions has been to convince me of their being a single function, simply with two conditions of application—to two types of perceptual 'object', card figures and thought images. It will be of interest for the future to explore and measure the extent of this E.S.P., carrying the search into all branches of the field. It seems plausible to hope to be able to follow the E.S.P. thread throughout the more typical parapsychical phenomena, since it would appear to be necessarily basic to them, if not indeed to all parapsychological phenomena.

If the percipient's mind is, as hypothetically suggested in Chapter XII, a relatively free agent that can, under certain conditions, go out space free, escaping material limitations, it might well be expected to be able to find in this spaceless order of reality whatever (if any) strange forces or entities there may be. If there are incorporeal personalities, it could 'contact' them. If there are reservoirs of knowledge, it might tap them, by a more transcendent clairvoyance. The active agency of the percipient's mind and the non-spatiality of the E.S.P. phase of mental life would, if established, make much more plausible the complex mental phenomena of this field, as they are reported and accepted by many. At least, the track of E.S.P. research leads us straight towards all the higher phenomena, not regarding it as a necessarily all-explanatory hypothesis but as a basic fact of the natural capacity of mind that may serve as a guiding principle in the necessary stages of hypothesizing and reorganizing in the general parapsychological field.

By way of a minor suggestion, I have said earlier that the fact that alertness and integration seem to favour E.S.P., while dissociation hinders it, seems to me to make a point of difference between the spontaneous parapsychic phenomena (often explained as telepathic, such as premonitory dreams), on the one hand, and E.S.P. on the other. Such spontaneous instances seem to be largely either dreams or experiences occurring in a sleepy or relaxed condition, when E.S.P., as measured by our tests, would be at a low ebb. It would appear, then, that there must be a different process involved in these spontaneous cases—perhaps an agency from without, that may, as in our P.T. work in which two good E.S.P. subjects co-operate as agent and percipient, augment the percipient's E.S.P. capacity by its own. In other words, it may intrude largely in its own capacity. This possibility needs to be tested by ascertaining by careful experiment whether a good E.S.P. subject can intrude or force his thoughts upon a sleep-dissociated or relaxed individual who is not attending or expecting this to happen. Cases are reported of such occurrences, but we need repetition under good conditions, with 'chance' expectation clearly measurable. The difference here suggested between the majority of the spontaneous cases that are called 'spontaneous telepathy' or 'spontaneous clairvoyance' instances and our E.S.P. phenomena may be a very fundamental one, I think, in our future parapsychological theory; on the other hand, it may be entirely superficial and misleading.

Two great sub-headings of parapsychology, then, have been clearly separated experimentally, independently established, each in its own conditions, and then, by experimental evidence, pretty closely identified as the same fundamental principle, merely with two different applications. This has something of the synthetic value that the discovery of the basic interrelationship of sound and wave mechanics, for example, had in the early history of physics, constituting much more elaborate experimentation but, no doubt, much more modest reflection. It was just such progress in the unification of its branches that gave to physics its great central system of laws. I think we may hope for the same ultimate effect in parapsychology, if the work of synthetic reorganization can be pursued with vigour and persistence.

There is a basis of encouragement for the hope of the last paragraph, which is little more, perhaps, than a 'clinical impression' and which I mention in that spirit. I have come to think it a very reasonable hypothesis that all the truly parapsychological phenomena for which there is fairly general acceptance among the more critical investigators may well be but various manifestations of the *same* function we have here in E.S.P., most probably *in combination with other special factors,* in the more peculiar types. That is, E.S.P. may be the general fundamental capacity, possibly an essential one for any parapsychological occurrence. The ground for this 'clinical impression' is this: among these 8 major subjects and their very close blood relatives (I omit names here by request of some and out of consideration for all) there have occurred almost all the usual run of psychic phenomena that are at all commonly accepted by the critical. I might mention the general clairvoyant 'hunches' or impressions, monitory dreams, premonitory 'intuitions' and visions, several varieties of phantasms of the dead, two haunted house cases with several hallucinated witnesses, a number of mediumistic phenomena, including violent physical manifestations with the table and other furniture, and the like. None of the individuals involved has been a professional clairvoyant or medium. None of the subjects has taken the phenomena reported over-seriously; *e.g.,* they have not fully accepted the common spiritualistic beliefs regarding them. Without at all judging the reality of these instances reported, except that I know of no reason to question the veracity of any of the subjects who reported them—indeed, I even feel certain of their utter honesty—I wish to say that, should such phenomena actually occur, it would appear somewhat probable, then, that our own subjects might be led to go on to produce them 'in the laboratory'. That is, if they or their close relatives have done these things (or something, even less spectacularly, like them), and the subjects are known to be parapsychic by their 'telepathic' and 'clairvoyant' capacity, may we not with some justice hope to go on to a development of other parapsychological phenomena and to a laboratory study of them through known subjects of known powers? Of course, it is as yet an hypothesis but not, I am sure, a wholly irrational one. And I repeat, first, that this is not to assume that the reported occurrences are proved to be genuine but merely that they are justly regarded as problems worthy of serious study; and, second, that this is not an attempt to make E.S.P. a simple explanation for everything parapsychological. It is an attempt to follow it as far as it goes, and to recognize, by methods of difference, other factors, *if* and when they come in, and to establish the facts we work with, as we proceed.

CHAPTER XIV

Some General Biological Considerations

There are a few general points of interest that do not belong to the more special departments of the preceding chapters and they justify, I think, a brief one of their own.

One of the questions of some importance not yet considered is that of family strains and E.S.P. Does the ability 'run in the family'—is it heritable? This is a difficult matter to answer, but an impression may be of interest. This impression cannot yet be clearly supported by adequate evidence, though we have some data in its favour. It is also in line with the popular notion, so far as there is one. My impression is that there is some heritable basis for marked E.S.P. ability. When I learned that the mother of a certain individual had possessed mediumistic ability, I rather expected to find a good subject in him and this judgment proved to be correct. All my major subjects, except one, have a parent or aunt, and often both, who are reported to have had at least one indefinitely parapsychological experience. And the one exception states that his mother is 'very intuitional', which, as she used it, means 'clairvoyant' in small daily things. In five of the other seven cases, there is more than one relative that has been parapsychic. These are all (with one exception) on the same side of the family, too (that is, always blood relations), but are of both sexes. The reader may better judge in how far these are applicable to the general rank and file of humanity if some of the details are given. Since some of these details are confidential, I shall give the subjects arbitrary numbers and refer to them as masculine. No. 1 states that his mother and her uncle were both parapsychic. The phenomena consisted of premonitions, mind reading and character reading. Instances have been related to me. No. 2 had a parapsychological family on the father's side, with only a minor experience by the mother, and this was coincident with the father's experience. The joint case was of a prophetic dream, experienced on *two* successive nights by *both* father and mother, of an unexpected event. The other experiences, by the father's side only, consisted of detailed prophetic dreams and monitional experiences connected with death. The father's father, too, was reported to have been parapsychic. No. 3 has a very parapsychic mother, who had strong clairvoyant power, believed she was in touch with spirit agencies and that through them she could give parapsycho-physical manifestations. The subject testifies to having witnessed these himself, under good full light conditions, and remains convinced that they occurred, although doubtful about the explanation given. Brothers of the sensitive also possessed some ability of the sort; on these, however, there are no further details given. No. 4 states that his uncle has experienced different parapsychical occurrences, chiefly of clairvoyant and previsionary character, and has had, in general, much the same sort of experience as he, himself. His own have included hearing a decreased relative's familiar footsteps, hauntings of hallucinatory sounds that did not disturb others, previsionary clairvoyance, etc. He and his uncle are said to be much alike in personality. At least four members of the family have been awakened by apparent 'haunting' phenomena. No. 5 says his mother has had many premonitional dreams and monitions of the death of friends. She occasionally warns the children of a coming danger and often knows of their unexpected danger when they are at a distance. She is generally clairvoyant but it is a casual sort of thing with her. No. 6 informs us that his mother had one veridical spontaneous psychic experience, a visual hallucination of a brother being wounded in France and carried off the field, with close time and fact coincidence. Her sister was given, in life, to veridical dreams concerning relatives particularly. Although No. 7 himself has had an hallucinatory experience of his deceased grandfather's voice, he can credit his mother only with being unusually 'intuitional'; the mother says playfully that she is clairvoyant. No striking experiences can be related, however. No. 8 has an aunt and grandparent on the mother's side who have had parapsychic experiences in connection with religious experiences. The mother herself is very intuitive, especially on character judgment. It must be emphasized strongly that these subjects are all normal, healthy, intelligent young men and women, not peculiar in any way and without pathological heredity, so far as they know.

More of the subjects have parapsychic relatives, apparently, than do people in general, but a general questionnaire and statistical study would be needed to evaluate these cases. It will be better, however, to do this when the number of subjects becomes larger, since an extensive study would be required for final decision. There is, then, only the general impression that there is perhaps some inheritance of a general parapsychological sensitivity which is represented by the E.S.P. we are measuring. Casual inquiry among friends who may or may not have marked E.S.P. ability does not reveal the high percentage of psychic family connections given in these eight subjects. The four of the poor E.S.P. subjects who have been asked have not been able to claim any parapsychic relatives; of course, this number is not regarded as large enough for a basis of judgment.

The very biological question of the comparative range of the E.S.P. capacity among the species does not enter into the work here reported, directly. This interesting question has, however, already its own literature. Our own work with the filly, reported in 1929,[1] has convinced us of the E.S.P. capacity in at least one horse and the work of Bechterew on telepathy in dogs seems quite satisfactory as reported. Further than this, I feel disinclined to venture. There are claims for telepathy in the more social animal species but there is not the rigid experimental proof required for so important a conclusion. The point was made in Chapter XI that the drug and fatigue data seemed to indicate that E.S.P.

[1] See Chapter II.

may be a higher, more complex development than sensory perception and, the suggestion follows logically, is probably a later development in mental and cerebral evolution. This is unfavourable to the view held by some without even this amount of facts to support it, that E.S.P., in man, is an atavism.

The extent and level of E.S.P. in our own species constitute points of importance. We cannot say how large a percentage of people are capable of E.S.P. until we have tried larger numbers under good conditions. There is no ground for a decision, as we now can see, in a few tests given in a classroom, or under any other conditions preventing abstraction. Even our best subjects cannot succeed under such conditions after months of experience at the work. Negative results are never final. It is impossible, with our present knowledge, to know if the conditions are adequate for judgment. But some small notion of the number of good E.S.P. subjects existing[1] may be gained from the facts about our own departmental students. Of the 14 graduate students in psychology present in the last two years, six have shown E.S.P. ability that is statistically significant. One other has been reported to have done work appreciably significant but I have not got his results. There are seven others remaining. These have never been tested, to my knowledge. But even allowing for no ability in the remaining half, we have 50%. Will someone say that psychology students are a select lot? Estabrooks said he found them singularly poor as subjects; they were too introspective.

Very few subjects have run very long without scoring above chance, to some extent. Of course, initial failure soon discourages many. And about them we never really know. With persistence, they might succeed! My impression is, on this, that most people can run at least a little above chance, with patient persistence and interest, under favourable conditions of quiet, isolation and abstraction. Stuart's work,

[1] I now have more subjects than I can myself work with; the experimentation needs institutionalizing, *i.e.* needs special endowment and special assistants. No one individual can manage it adequately.

and that of Dr Lundholm and myself, carried out with all the subjects who came (a total of 77 subjects), all back this up. Then, too, whether the poorer are really weak in E.S.P. or whether there are merely obstacles in its way, we cannot yet determine. The better subjects may simply be better able to abstract or they may be better able to retain patient interest. For aught that may be said to the contrary, E.S.P. may be as widely disturbed a natural capacity in the species as is that highest mode of cognition, reasoning. Even this requires conditions for success—purpose, degree of integration of effort, not too much distraction to permit attention. Very possibly the delicate nature of E.S.P. and the complex conditions required may conceal it from our tests —even without preventing its functioning in the freer circumstances of daily life.

Among the better subjects there is what may well be a kind of 'species level'. They mostly score on an average of between 8 and 11 per 25, both P.T. and P.C., if conditions are good. See column 3 of Table XLII. All eight subjects do this, except when a disturbing factor enters, as illness, drugs or a decline of E.S.P. capacity (as with Linzmayer and Stuart). If we take the total normal scores of the eight major subjects (before they began to decline in the cases of Linzmayer and Stuart) and leave out drug, illness, D.T. and other special data that do not represent the regular function of E.S.P., we get only one exception. This is Zirkle, who is unusually high on P.T. and not significantly above chance on P.C. If we include the P.T. work done during his long,

TABLE XLII

Normal E.S.P. averages of major subjects

Name	Trials	Av. per 25	Remarks
Linzmayer	600	9·9	1st 600 trials before decline
Stuart	500	9·0	1st 500 trials before decline
Pearce	7,800	9·4	All B.T. trials up to iv. 1. 33
	11,250	8·9	All E.S.P. trials to iv. 1. 33; no decline
Miss Ownbey	1,075	10·3	B.T. and P.T. trials; no decline
Zirkle	1,300	14·8	P.T. only; health good; no decline
	5,000	10·7	Includes his illness data
Miss Bailey	2,800	8·6	B.T. and P.T.; no decline
Cooper	4,850	8·2	B.T. and P.T.; no decline
Miss Turner	4,575	9·0	B.T. and P.T.; no decline

mild illness (2,700 trials), his score average drops within the range indicated, 10·7, but this would, of course, not be justifiable.

The averages shown in Table XLII run remarkably close together, in view of the wide range of differences to be expected in such a group or any other delicate or complex mental endowment. Any complicated task we could propose might be expected to show greater differences, I think. These eight subjects represent, by the very fact that we have worked with them so much, the more successful subjects. But in most mental tasks the more one selects the better subjects, the greater the diversity and peculiarity between them. It is not common to find a 'species wall' as a limitation. Yet here such a limit is suggested. And this makes E.S.P. capacity appear more like native species endowment perhaps, since we should not expect acquired abilities to stop thus in their development, at a common level; that is, this appears somewhat more like an innately given perceptual range, like the species range of sound or light perception. This is, of course, speculative analogy, representing a beginning of inquiry rather than a conclusion. The subjects can all 'jump' this 'species wall' for short periods, as in the occasional very high scores, even ascending to 25 consecutive successes, but for the averages and the long runs, the 'species range' of from 8 to 11 seems to be (excepting Zirkle) the natural level. Of the two conditions, the P.C. remains the more stable. P.T. varies more widely; it has two human variables and two E.S.P. elements probably at work.

We have yet to explain the curious decline of Linzmayer and Stuart, or, as more experienced parapsychology students would put it, the curious failure to decline on the part of the others. It has been the great misfortune of so many workers to find that their telepathic subjects have lost their ability after a period of very good results. From the Creery sisters, on down to Van Dam (in Brugmanns' laboratory) and Lady, the filly, in our own experience, this disappointment has been an all too common one. (It may explain the tendencies of some subjects in the past to have recourse to deception in their later work, when they have achieved a reputation that has to be maintained—as they see it—at all costs. Or it may well be that they have 'rationalized' the earlier telepathic results from a later viewpoint of incapacity and have decided they must have been cleverly deceiving, without realizing it perhaps; this would make it 'reasonable', at least, and might be the only way for them to make it so.)

The decision of Linzmayer began in June, 1931, with my urging him to work against his obvious wish to leave. He ran below chance then, as I had expected and hoped he would do. This was, however, a great strain for him, and

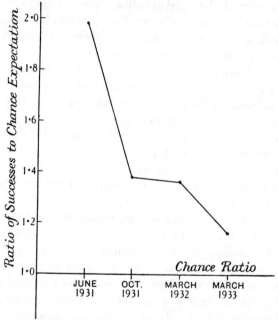

Graph No. 6. Decline of E.S.P. ability in Linzmayer. The curve represents scoring rate for 4 major periods of work.

perhaps the ruthlessness of the method permanently injured his capacity for E.S.P. by inducing strained or unwholesome memories and attitudes. He is still interested, but I think that possibly he can never really feel the same towards the experimenter and his plans; he has also a strong negativism of which he is hardly conscious (but which is apparent in hypnotic tests), which may be activated to cause a certain conflict, and oppose the abstraction necessary for high scoring. Failure is very discouraging to Linzmayer, and he has become more and more chagrined by his inability to return to his original level. This makes it still harder for him to 'concentrate' and so the 'vicious circle' of decline goes on. His 'decline curve' is given in Graph No. 6, representing the four periods of work he has gone through, omitting the purposively planned low-scoring period mentioned. For the fuller data see Table XII in Chapter v. The averages per 25 trials dropped as follows: 9·9, 6·9, 6·8, 5·8.

· Stuart declined slowly over a long period of about a year, rose again and, a few months later then, he declined once more—this time much more promptly, in less than two months. The first 500 trials were within the 8-to-11 range, which I have come to think may be typical of most normal E.S.P. subjects at their best over long periods. But, while this first 500 gave an average per 25 of 9·0, the next 500 dropped to 6·6 and the next still lower. The decline, as shown by dividing the 7,500 into 5 groups of 1,500 runs each, is as follows, in averages per 25 trials: 7·1, 6·1, 5·7, 5·9, 5·4. See Graph No. 7, A. On the return to scoring, while the graph shows the B curve starting higher than the A, Stuart really did not rise in the second period to the level of the original 500. 7·3 was the highest he made for as many as 400 trials. For about the same number of trials he held up above 7·0, both times, and then dropped to around 6·0.

The explanation of these declines is not easy and at most a hypothetical suggestion is offered. Stuart worked alone and thus would be likely to get the full monotony of the procedure—certainly so in the course of many thousand trials. He was working without any other motivation than his own interest; at least, without pay, and without any urging or suggestion on my part. What wonder if the motivation of his own interest should weaken somewhat after so much work that is so exhaustive of time and patience! This is my preferred hypothesis—he lost interest, became a little tired of the business and needed a rest from it. Let the reader try 7,500 trials, if he doubts the need for a rest and change of scene. This view may not be correct, but it is both an adequate hypothesis and a probable situation. At the end of the 7,500, when he complained of low scoring and I suggested he might be bored with the business, he admitted that he might need a change. Only a few months later he returned to a level of 7·3 but has not yet come back to 9·0 in 25.

While, then, there may be a 'species level' at the top—at least, it is favoured by the facts so far—there is none at the bottom. Subjects can be made to decline, either indefinitely,

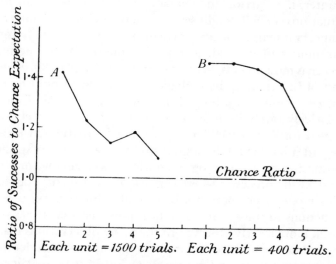

Graph No. 7. Decline of E.S.P. ability in Stuart. A, first period, 1931–2. B, second period, Summer 1932. Average scoring rate is shown for each period, in each case subdivided into five parts, by number of trials.

as if by a fixed limitation, or perhaps just until a rest is had, or a new interest aroused, as illustrated by Linzmayer and Stuart, respectively. Several of our minor subjects, too (Miss Weckesser and Pratt, for example), have declined to a 'chance level', how permanently we do not yet know. But most of the major subjects are holding up very well, with no serious signs of decline. (Just at the moment of writing this I am informed that Pearce, who has worked more than any other subject, has scored 11 and 9 in two runs of P.C. with the cards in one building and himself in another, 250 yards away. A few days ago he finished a series at 100 yards with 13, 13, 12. He is evidently not in danger of running down.) This is important not only in its experimental convenience nor merely as a further fact in the psychology of the E.S.P. processes, but in the general biology of E.S.P., with which we are at the moment most concerned.

For E.S.P. is a biological phenomenon and one that might obviously be of tremendous value to the species. To the hunter, the warrior, the seaman—in fact, to nearly all life situations—E.S.P. might serve in many ways to give man an important margin of advantage over his enemies and his environment in general, so that the question of its permanence is most serious. Were it characteristically to flit in and out of functioning, its biological significance would be reduced almost to nothing. But if it does, as we find, only relatively rarely decline (if, indeed, it has not merely declined for our particular experimental situation), we can regard it has having biological survival value to any species possessing it. In homing, migration, food-seeking, mating and all the processes where cognition is a primary essential this mode of perception might be of value if it exists and functions in the species. The fact, however, that it has not been more clearly observed in the many observations made on animals would seem to exclude it from any considerable importance to animal existence. Or could it be that it has not been seen because it has not been looked for?

In our own species, however, extra-sensory perception occurs and may be demonstrated in many normal people in undeniable fashion. In the light of the foregoing observations, it seems to be a fairly dependable and persistent capacity, when it is given proper conditions for its functioning. These are facts which any comprehensive biology must face and study, if it is to treat faithfully of the natural history of our species.

CHAPTER XV

Summary and Concluding Remarks

I t seems likely that a table summarizing the general totals of those chapters giving the main figures would be of some convenience to the reader here. There are two columns showing X values[1] (anti-chance) for the results, the last column giving that obtained by formula; and the next to the last the X value given by the pooled results. The formula method is, I believe, the more proper, but figures of both are so high as to leave dispute pointless. Also there are included in these totals all the results of all experiments, even those made with a view to reducing the score-level (drug experiments, etc.). However, in the low-score work of Stuart and Pearce in which they purposely reversed the calling, I change the negative sign of deviation to positive in pooling these results with the others. There were altogether 1,575 of these. The average successes per 25 trials are given in column 4.

TABLE XLIII

General summary of the results of E.S.P. tests to August 1, 1933

Reported in Chap.	Subjects, Conditions, etc.	No. of trials	No. of hits	Av. no. of hits per 25 np 5	Dev.	p.e.	X $(D/\text{p.e.})$ pooled results	X $(D/\text{p.e.})$ by formula
IV	$p = 1/2$, $1/4$, $1/10$, $1/26$, etc. misc. subjects	5,450	—	—	—	—	—	7
IV	$p = 1/5$ misc. subjects	18,100	4,200	5.8	+580	±36.2	16	23
V	$p = 1/5$ Linzmayer	8,724	2,077	6.0	332	25.2	13	22
VI	$p = 1/5$ Stuart	14,700	3,575	6.1	635	32.7	19	24
VII	$p = 1/5$ Pearce	17,250	5,486	8.0	2,036	35.4	57	65
VIII	$p = 1/5$ five major subjects	26,950	9,026	8.4	3,636	44.3	82	82
Total	$p = 1/5$	85,724	24,364	7.1	7,219	78.9	91	111
Total	All values of p	91,174	—	—	—	—	—	111

[1] See Appendix to Chapter II, page 39.

Several thousands of test data have accumulated as I have worked at this manuscript, but these cannot be included in the totals here without some description of conditions; furthermore, it seems very doubtful if anyone can have the appetite for more of these figures. I need only say that these data are in general in line with those already presented and would alter no conclusion offered here, if fully incorporated.

MAJOR CONCLUSIONS AND SUGGESTIONS

1. It is independently established on the basis of this work alone that Extra-Sensory Perception is an actual and demonstrable occurrence.

2. E.S.P. is demonstrated to occur under P.C. or pure-clairvoyance conditions, with not only the sensory and rational functions, but telepathic ability as well, excluded by the conditions.

3. E.S.P. is also demonstrated to occur equally well under P.T. or pure telepathy conditions, with clairvoyance excluded along with the sensory and rational cognition.

4. E.S.P. occurs equally well and at similar levels of scoring in both P.C. and P.T., as shown by actual measurement, using equal probabilities and similar general conditions. The reasons are many for believing that in P.C. and P.T. the same general mental function is at work.

   (a) All major subjects, except one,[1] have ability in both P.T. and P.C.

   (b) Their results, individually and totally, are of nearly the same scoring level in both P.T. and P.C.

   (c) Daily fluctuations in both take the same direction, preponderantly.

   (d) Both are affected in the same way and in approximately the same degree by sodium amytal.

   (e) Caffeine affects both in the same direction.

   (f) Both function with considerable distances between percipient and perceived (agent or object).

   (g) Both show with distance, when the subject can work

[1] Later this exception was eliminated when Zirkle became successful in B.T. as well as in P.T., and at roughly the same rate.

at all above np, a rise in scoring rate over that achieved in the same room.

These and other similarities all strongly favour the hypothesis (though I do not say they establish it) that in P.C. and P.T. we have to do with a common underlying process, capable of functioning in the cognition of two different perceptual units, mental activities (images in these tests) and material objects (card figures). No differentiating circumstance whatever has been discovered contrary to this hypothesis.

5. The wave theory seems to be inapplicable to these results, in view of the distance experiments and the absence of any decline of results with distance. The asumption that the wave theorist must make—namely, that the ink figure would radiate the same kind of waves as the active mind of the agent—is fantastic. A further difficulty for wave theories is found in the D.T. work, which ought, on that theory, to give a hopeless jumble of waves. These and other difficulties compel the rejection of the wave theory—which is the only type that modern physics has yet to offer.

6. Likewise it is shown that E.S.P. is not a sensory phenomenon. The absence of any need of orientation, of any sensory localization, of any recognized stimulating energy such as the senses receive and of any awareness of reception all lead to the rejection of the sixth-sense hypothesis as well. E.S.P. shows also much greater need for integration than does the sensory level of mental processes.

7. At the same time, the definite volitional control over E.S.P. shown by all the percipients, the large role of effort and voluntary attention apparent in all, the retarding effect of dissociative drugs and other factors all tend (first) to exclude the hypothesis that the percipient is a mere passive receptor of an incorporeal agent's intruding action, and (second) to make E.S.P. a part of the natural organization of the species. E.S.P. is directed by the conation of the percipient, and interoperates naturally with the other cognitive and with the effective processes of the percipient's mind.

SUMMARY AND CONCLUDING REMARKS

SOME MINOR POINTS AND IMPRESSIONS

1. Good abstraction is required for success in most percipients, along with effort and attention to the task; in a word, 'concentration'.

(a) New changes in procedure may disturb. this for a time.

(b) New visitors as witnesses are likely to do so for a time.

(c) Conflict of purposes (and similarly, of course, of emotions) spoils concentration.

(d) Dissociation lowers, along with other functions, the capacity to concentrate.

2. Since E.S.P. harmonizes with the other mental processes and adds its function as a less restricted mode of perception, it can conceivably have great practical personal value.

3. E.S.P. would seem to possess, potentially, a considerable biological (species survival) value. It may be inferable from the drug data that it is a later evolutionary acquisition, as evidenced by its higher organization, which is in turn indicated by its easier disturbance by amytal and fatigue. This chain of inference is none too strong and may be put down, not as a 'point' but as an 'impression'.

4. It seems favourably suggested, at least, that E.S.P. may be heritable or perhaps its more common inhibiting factors may be.

5. The loss of E.S.P. ability with long use is the exception rather than the rule. The ability may decline and return. It may also decline with the daily run.

6. E.S.P. may run consistently below chance expectation if there be unconscious (and, of course, if there be conscious) negative tendency of sufficient strength.

7. The 'curves of operation' found are probably motivational in origin. There is evidence that interest, effort and attention vary, and cause results to vary; there is no clear evidence yet that E.S.P. ability *per se* varies.

8. Improvement in E.S.P. is limited, usually to a short initial period; and this may be purely a matter of learning

to abstract and achieve good concentration. There is no good evidence of improvement of the ability. A level seems to be reached and not far exceeded. When it is exceeded for particular runs, it seems to be through special effort.

9. Variation of the procedure, without introducing new changes, helps to keep up the scoring level. Encouragement is usually helpful. Light humours and moods are the best in which to work at E.S.P.

10. There are many facts supporting a view that E.S.P. is easily encroached upon by rational and sensory processes, and that the delicate balance required for good E.S.P. may be concerned chiefly with the maintenance of the field of attention free from these encroachments. Perhaps this is why improvement is shown so uniformly with distance (*i.e.* when complete failure does not attend it). Distance discourages sensory attention and would aid abstraction.

11. The following laws or relations seem to hold between agent and percipient, but the evidential support is as yet not fully adequate, particularly so for No. 3:

(1) Good E.S.P. ability in both agent and percipient seems to give highest results.

(2) Good E.S.P. ability in the percipient with poor ability in the agent gives mediocre results.

(3) Poor E.S.P. ability in the percipient, regardless of what the agent may be like, does not give results above chance.

12. E.S.P. is not easily fatigued. In P.T. the agent tends to suffer from fatigue, but the percipient does not.

13. Loss of E.S.P. ability by an occasional subject may be due to incapacitation for the necessary abstraction under the conditions, rather than a loss of the E.S.P. function itself.

SOME HYPOTHESES OFFERED

1. The general impression is given by the life histories of these major subjects that there may be a general connection between E.S.P. and many other parapsychological phenomena. This may at least be offered as a working hypothesis.

2. The distance data, along with the general facts, suggest the freedom of mind in E.S.P. from the common material relations of extension or distance. It would argue for the nonphysical nature of mind if it can operate under these conditions. This is psychologically important, as bearing upon the question of the body-mind relation, upon personality-survival and some of the other questions in the natural philosophy of mind.

3. The large role of conation evidenced in E.S.P., the failure of the radiation laws to apply to its phenomena and the fact that P.C. scoring is as good as P.T., along with the accuracy attained in D.T. at short distances and in B.T. at longer ones, all suggest the view that the percipient's mind acts upon the object or mental act that is to be perceived, and that this projection of mind is a peculiarly non-mechanistic procedure, since on a physical theory there would be no projection—simply radiation on a spherical front, with intensity declining with the square of the distance.

4. E.S.P. influences other processes that direct overt behaviour and hence it affects, however indirectly, the recognized doing of work. This is itself doing work, however little it may be. It is thus inescapably 'energetic' (even as the physicist means the word—'capable of doing work'). We have, then, for physical science, a challenging need for the discovery of the energy mode involved. Some type of energy is inferable and none is known to be acceptable, since wave mechanics are inapplicable to the case.

5. Likewise, the challenge may be given to physiology that a new mode of energy reception is required—reception of an unknown energy form by an unknown mode of reception. It involves the nervous system quite as much as does any other cognitive process, as judged by drug effects and other physiological evidence.

6. In psychology E.S.P. is a possible uncontrolled factor in the experimental laboratory, a possibly helpful one in hypnosis and in therapy, a challenge to the adequacy of our concepts of the place of mind in nature and a lead to understanding the energetic principles of general mental life. It

may, too, be an innate ability, since certainly there is no evidence of its being acquired; *i.e.* no evidence of real development.

7. There seems to be in this work thus far a 'species level' of E.S.P. ability reached by most subjects and not much exceeded, on the average, over large numbers of trials. The evolutionary origin and the biological survival value of E.S.P. are problems at which we have only hinted possible answers.

8. One is tempted to point, as a final suggestion, to the analogies of E.S.P. found in religions and mystic lore, and to refer to the apparent applicability of the principles of E.S.P. to some religious 'experiences' and claims. Might we not find good E.S.P. subjects in the medicine-man, the mystic and the prophet?

FIRST APPENDIX TO CHAPTER XV

Suggestions to those who may care to repeat these Experiments[1]

It is hoped that others will repeat these experiments or, better still, perform more advanced ones. Much depends upon the conditions of the tests as to whether success or failure will follow. The following suggestions, along with the discussion in Chapter XII, may help to avoid failures:

1. The subject should have an active interest in the tests and be fairly free from strong bias or doubt. These would, of course, hinder effort and limit attention. An open-minded, experimental attitude is all that is required. Positive belief is naturally favourable but not necessary.

2. The preliminary tests should be entered into very in-

[1] The views of Mrs Sinclair given in *Mental Radio* and already mentioned should be read by those interested in this phase. See also the abstract and discussion of Mrs. Sinclair's report by Dr. Prince, in B.S.P.R. Bulletin XVI.

formally, without much serious discussion as to techniques, or explanations or precautions. The more ado over techniques, the more inhibition is likely; and the more there is of explanation, the more likely is introspection to interfere. Playful informality is most favourable.

3. If possible to do so honestly, it is helpful to give encouragement for any little success but no extravagant praise is desirable, even over striking results. The point is that encouragement is helpful, apparently, but only if it does not lead to self-consciousness. If it does, it is quite ruinous. Many subjects begin well, become excited or self-conscious, and then do poorly.

4. Some begin more easily with P.T. and some with P.C. It depends upon personality, I think, but I cannot explain it except to link sociability with P.T. preference. However, both conditions should be tried, following the subject's preference in the beginning.

5. It is highly important to let the subject have his own way, without restraint, at first. Later he can be persuaded to allow changes, after he has gained confidence and discovered his way to E.S.P. functioning. Even then, it is better for him to have his way as far as experimental conditions can allow. It is a poor science that dictates conditions to Nature. It is a better one that follows up with its well-adapted controls and conditions.

6. It is wise not to express doubts or regrets. Discouragement seems to damage the delicate function of E.S.P. Here again no doubt personalities differ. One subject I know has worked in the face of doubt expressed; but she is exceptional in this.

7. Above all, one must not, like several investigators, stop with only 25 or 50 or even 100 trials per subject. Most of my good subjects did not do very well in the first 100. With few exceptions, the first 50 to 100 trials give the worst scores. With all my major subjects this is true. Several different occasions or sittings, too, should be allowed, for there is with most subjects an adjustment phase at first that may take some time.

8. It is best at first to have the subject alone with the agent in P.T. and in P.C. to leave him alone entirely. If not, he may be inhibited from the start; but, once he has a start, he can gradually work back to other conditions. When he has observers present, the experimenter should do all he can to put the subject at ease.

9. Simple cards with five suits seem best as a compromise of several features of concern: easy calculation, easy recall, easy discrimination of images, etc.

10. Short runs are desirable, say five at a time, with a check-up after each five. Then it is best to go casually and quietly on without too much discussion of results.

11. It is advisable not to bore or tire the subject. When he wants to stop, or even before he expressly wishes to, it is better to stop work.

12. It is best to try good friends for P.T. at first—or couples, single or married, who feel certain they have thought transference; and, above all, to try those people who say they have had 'psychic' experiences or whose ancestors conspicuously have had.

These are suggestions, not rules, for we do not yet know enough of the subject to lay down rules. They will help toward success, without endangering conclusions. One can always tighten up on conditions before drawing conclusions later. But any investigator must first of all get his phenomena to occur—or exhaust the reasonable possibilities in trying to.

SECOND APPENDIX TO CHAPTER XV[1]

Higher Anti-Chance Values, with Table of Probability

Throughout this report the values of groups of data have been presented in the form $X = D/\text{p.e.}$ In the beginning of

[1] I am indebted to Mr Charles E. Stuart, Graduate Assistant in Psychology, for this Appendix, as well as for much assistance in the earlier mathematics of the production. He has been, as mathematician, assistant, and subject, an extraordinarily useful and competent man.

the experiment this ratio was important as a proof of the inadequacy of the chance hypothesis. When the values grew far beyond the limits of any available tables the X ratio was useful mainly as an arbitrary quantitative measure of differences between blocks of data and between the work of individuals. These X ratios may serve their original purpose as anti-chance ratios, however, if any reader still clings to the chance hypothesis.

The following table (Table XLIV) gives an approximation to the meaning in terms of chance probability of the X values listed in Table XLIII (10^{-14} means 1 fourteen places to the right of the decimal point (0·000 000 000 00001). This gives odds of 100 thousand billions to one against mere chance as an explanation. It is left to the reader to write out the figure corresponding to 10^{-1220}].

TABLE XLIV

X	P	X	P	X	P	X	P
13	10^{-14}	22	10^{-51}	57	10^{-330}	91	10^{-820}
16	10^{-22}	23	10^{-56}	65	10^{-435}	111	10^{-1220}
19	10^{-34}	24	10^{-61}	82	10^{-666}		

The figures given are rough approximations computed by using only the coefficient of the series expansion for the probability integral.[1] As the error of such an approximation is less than the last term used in the series, and as we have used only the first term, 1, the error in P is equal to the figure given; that is, an error of 100%. This would be a serious error in a pay envelope or cost estimate, but with these tiny ratios it is negligible. For example: if $X = 20$ the approximation would give $P = 10^{-40.744}$, but with an error of 100% the actual value of P may lie anywhere between $10^{-44.443}$ and $10^{-\infty}$. As we are here concerned with only the upper limit of the error the difference between 0· (40 zeros) 18 and 0· (40 zeros) 36 is considerably less than the errors

[1] The formula is given in Rietz, H. L., *Handbook of Mathematical Statistics*, p. 15.

introduced by our using only two and three significant figures in the tabulation of the exponents.[2]

And a final word of warning to the mathematical enthusiast. Mathematically the difference between $X = 20$ and, let us say, $X = 40$, is enormous beyond our capacity to experience. For the purpose of evidence against a chance hypothesis the difference is simply superfluous, because unappreciable. The higher values do give the experimenter a quantitative measure of comparison and a feeling of comfortable certainty, but the sceptic who refuses to be convinced by a value of 15 or 20 will scarcely be moved by any mathematical treatment of the data whatever.

[2] This paragraph may be regarded as primarily for mathematicians since it would require much space to make it clear to the layman. It simply justifies the approximation method used in measuring the odds against chance implied by a given X value. Since few men have ever required such odds for establishing belief in a principle, the tables are not available; and the computation by more exact methods would be a burdensome—and a uselessly burdensome—task.

APPENDIX TO THE ENGLISH EDITION

I take this opportunity to make brief comment on the main criticisms that have been made on the report.

One of the criticisms offered on the report is that the methods of shuffling the cards were not adequately described. This is a matter that may seem more important to the reader, since he is probably thinking of playing cards, than it actually is. In the first place, the cards used in the tests for E.S.P. have no individual numbering. There are 5 of each suit, and even if, by some sensory cue, the subject could locate, let us say, a circle, in order for this to indicate the cards following, he would need to know which of the five circles he had located. If a single card is displaced and the pack is merely cut once, at a point unknown, then no one can know the order of the cards in the pack, even though he had memorized them all just before the cut. Then, if we consider the work done at a distance, behind screens, with cards left in the unbroken pack until it is called down through, etc., we can see that with such conditions eliminating all possible cues, even one shuffle of the simplest variety is quite enough to destroy knowledge of order in the pack.

As state in the text, the pack of cards was always shuffled and cut. The pack being constituted as it is, it matters little how it is shuffled or how much. Our shuffling varies with the shuffler as to method and amount. It consists of several 'shuffles' at least, ending with the invariable and safeguarding cut. An empirical shuffling check, made by correlating consecutive card sequences in the pack, with intervening shuffling reduced to one 'middle spread' shuffle (a batch from the centre divided loosely between the top and bottom of the pack), and one cut, showed only a chance result. The average was even slightly below the most likely number expected from chance.[1]

The corresponding criticism for the telepathic work is that the question of possible accidental similarity of order of symbols chosen by the agent to that called by the per-

[1] *Character and Personality*, Dec. 1934, p. 98 (Allen and Unwin).

cipient was not adequately dealt with. I will therefore add here the following information on the point. As is pointed out in the text (*e.g.* page 158), the agents were instructed to vary systematically but irregularly in their selection of symbols. It is stated also that checks showed this to have been done. But figures on the success of this variation may be desirable. The correlation of consecutive runs of the agents' choices give the figure in question. For the best series of distance telepathy (pages 141–3) this is only 3·9, showing that the deliberate avoidance of routine order in the run of 25 is so effective as even to run below chance average. These runs were made at the rate of one per day, and this figures is evidence also against the suggestion that there may be a daily habit of special sequences. This question of normal similarities is more fully dealt with in the study of the medium, Mrs Garrett, where six different agents were used.[1] For example, in this study a good series was made using code cards to determine the agents' choice. But perhaps the best answer to the question of 'normal similarities' is the fact that, in most of our telepathy work, good results are obtained with an agent without any 'habituation period', and since many agents were used, as well as many subjects, the coincidence hypothesis loses all applicability. The other common hypotheses are dealt with in the text.

Rarely—in fact only twice—has there been to my knowledge any question raised of the adequacy of conditions excluding deception. But it may be that there have been others who have been prevented from expressing this view only by considerations of delicacy. I have to assume that these have not read Chapter IX, sections (*b*) and (*d*). Few reasonable beings will suppose, to take up one point, that twenty college people, all in good standing, some of them on the instruction staff of the University, would all be guilty of planned deception. Since first publication this number has increased, and has included persons still more difficult to suspect.

[1] *Character and Personality,* Dec. 1934, p. 101 (Allen and Unwin).

The witnessing of performances too has gone on, with added confirmation. But no critic has ever suggested *how* the witnessing reported, say on pages 103–4 of this book, was lacking. No one has explained *how* fraud could have entered into the 1,675 New Card results (page 102), or the D.T. work (same page), or the Screen work, or, as a climax, the Distance work (*e.g.*, pages 115–16). Since the first writing, I have myself been a secondary observer of the first observer, Mr Pratt, in this work, with good results under double observation.

I can see no profit to going on with merely trying to be more convincing on this point. If 30 of our people at present writing are frauds, 300 may be, of course. Apparently no one can see how fraud can account for all of the best experiments as they stand; yet some few will probably still suspect it does, and will these not persist, even if we double our number of witnesses and multiple details of precaution until they become a bore to the reader?

There are two other points of importance to the fraud (conscious or unconscious) theory. The first is that those to whom this may be a stumbling block need to remember that no piece of scientific work can rightly claim finality on all frontiers. Certainly I would not claim it for this. I hope to *interest* readers, to *stimulate* them, to *challenge* them— all with a view to their *doing something about these claims.* This does not pressuppose conviction; it may represent merely an urge to investigate them or help someone else to do it. The comfortable, satisfied, stagnant conviction that 'everything is settled now' is not to be desired.

The other point is that, in work done during the eighteen months since the report was written, a special condition has been introduced (with success) that completely eliminates all chance for deception, except through the joint collusion of all of us involved in the work.[1] This condition cannot here be described and is mentioned merely to encourage

[1] This reference was to the tests of *precognition* (or E.S.P. of the future order of the cards in the pack) begun at the time but not yet published. See *The Reach of the Mind.*

the possible few who may be seeking something still more reassuring on this score, not to give up hope.

It has been lamented that more introspective observation of Extra-Sensory Perception is not given. I share this feeling, but the subjects can give almost nothing to enlighten us on its inner nature. It sems to be a truly unconscious mode of perception. Variations of the experimental material may help in this, and should be introduced in the course of time. We have been pursuing a programme of exploration for special capacities that has required our *adherence to a routine* affording a comparable basis from one phase of the research to another, and this has' postponed variation.

No one has raised with me a serious question as to the soundness and applicability of the mathematics used—no one except an American who clearly does not understand it. Such a question requires for its answer more than a paragraph; it is an education that is needed. Since I cannot give that, a blast of heavy authority is my only available reply. I refer the reader to a letter kindly given me by the great English statistician, Prof. R. A. Fisher, of the Galton Laboratory, University of London (see footnote at the end of Appendix to Chapter II.

I think I may say that the criticisms that have come to my attention arise more from inadequacies in my reporting than from deficiencies in the research, and I shall not attempt to excuse these.

Since my greatest interest is in stimulating others to repeat some of these experiments, I should like to mention here what has seemed to me to be the most important condition for E.S.P. This a *spontaneity of interest in doing it.* The fresh interest in the act itself, like that of a child in playing a new game, seems to me the most favourable circumstance. Add now the conditions referred to in the Appendix, page 277, the freedom from distraction, the absence of disturbing scepticism, the feeling of confidence or, at least, of some hope, and I think many good subjects can be found in any community or circle.

INDEX